D1328544

THE GROWTH OF PUBLIC EXPENDITURE
IN THE UNITED KINGDOM

NATIONAL BUREAU OF ECONOMIC RESEARCH

NUMBER 72, GENERAL SERIES

The Growth
of Public Expenditure
in the United Kingdom

BY

ALAN T. PEACOCK

AND

JACK WISEMAN

ASSISTED BY JINDRICH VEVERKA

A STUDY BY THE

NATIONAL BUREAU OF ECONOMIC RESEARCH

1961

PUBLISHED BY

PRINCETON UNIVERSITY PRESS, PRINCETON

The study on which this volume is based was financed in part by a grant to the National Bureau of Economic Research by the Ford Foundation, to which grateful acknowledgment is made. The Ford Foundation is not, however, responsible for any of the statements made or views expressed in the report.

RELATION OF THE DIRECTORS
TO THE WORK AND PUBLICATIONS
OF THE NATIONAL BUREAU OF ECONOMIC RESEARCH

1. The object of the National Bureau of Economic Research is to ascertain and to present to the public important economic facts and their interpretation in a scientific and impartial manner. The Board of Directors is charged with the responsibility of ensuring that the work of the National Bureau is carried on in strict conformity with this object.

2. To this end the Board of Directors shall appoint one or more Directors of Research.

3. The Director or Directors of Research shall submit to the members of the Board, or to its Executive Committee, for their formal adoption, all specific proposals concerning researches to be instituted.

4. No report shall be published until the Director or Directors of Research shall have submitted to the Board a summary drawing attention to the character of the data and their utilization in the report, the nature and treatment of the problems involved, the main conclusions, and such other information as in their opinion would serve to determine the suitability of the report for publication in accordance with the principles of the National Bureau.

5. A copy of any manuscript proposed for publication shall also be submitted to each member of the Board. For each manuscript to be so submitted a special committee shall be appointed by the President, or at his designation by the Executive Director, consisting of three Directors selected as nearly as may be one from each general division of the Board. The names of the special manuscript committee shall be stated to each Director when the summary and report described in paragraph (4) are sent to him. It shall be the duty of each member of the committee to read the manuscript. If each member of the special committee signifies his approval within thirty days, the manuscript may be published. If each member of the special committee has not signified his approval within thirty days of the transmittal of the report and manuscript, the Director of Research shall then notify each member of the Board, requesting approval or disapproval of publication, and thirty additional days shall be granted for this purpose. The manuscript shall then not be published unless at least a majority of the entire Board and a two-thirds majority of those members of the Board who shall have voted on the proposal within the time fixed for the receipt of votes on the publication proposed shall have approved.

6. No manuscript may be published, though approved by each member of the special committee, until forty-five days have elapsed from the transmittal of the summary and report. The interval is allowed for the receipt of any memorandum of dissent or reservation, together with a brief statement of his reasons, that any member may wish to express; and such memorandum of dissent or reservation shall be published with the manuscript if he so desires. Publication does not, however, imply that each member of the Board has read the manuscript, or that either members of the Board in general, or of the special committee, have passed upon its validity in every detail.

7. A copy of this resolution shall, unless otherwise determined by the Board, be printed in each copy of every National Bureau book.

(Resolution adopted October 25, 1926 and revised February 6, 1933 and February 24, 1941)

CONTENTS

CONTENTS

CONTENTS

xi

TABLES

TABLES

xiii

Charts

Preface

THIS study was begun in 1953 at the invitation of the National Bureau of Economic Research. At that time, its primary purpose was seen as the filling of a gap in the existing economic statistics of public expenditures in the United Kingdom during the last sixty years.

In the process of compiling these statistics, we have become increasingly aware of the lack of any satisfactory explanation of the changing characteristics and importance of the public economy. We have, therefore, ventured to widen the scope of our study in order to offer our own explanation and to test it against other statistical and historical evidence.

It is a pleasure to acknowledge the debt we owe to fellow economists. In the compilation of the statistics, we have been given invaluable help by J. E. G. Utting and Dorothy Cole of the Department of Applied Economics, Cambridge, and by Philip Redfern of the Central Statistical Office. Utting and Cole generously allowed us to use their estimates for central government expenditures for the period 1920–1938 which were extracted from their as yet unpublished study, "The Income and Expenditure of U.K. Public Authorities, 1920–38", while Redfern helped us reclassify local government financial statistics for years before 1938. The companion study, *The Growth of Public Employment in Great Britain*, by Moses Abramovitz and Vera F. Eliasberg has eased our task of historical presentation, especially of local government financial development. These authors kindly offered helpful comments on the first draft of the manuscript.

The compilation of central government expenditure by economic and functional categories for the period 1890 to 1920 was a difficult and tedious business, and we must pay tribute to the industry and good nature of Leroy Dunn, who spent many months on the task. Latterly, we have relied on assistance from the Economics Research Division of the London School of Economics and Political Science. We must thank the Division for allowing us to call upon the services of Winston Chambers. We reserve a special word of thanks for Jindrich Veverka, who so far exceeded his duties as research assistant that we are delighted to couple his name with ours as authors of this study.

A first draft of the manuscript was fairly widely circulated to specialists in the field of public finance. We thank those who spared the time to plow through it and send comments and criticisms. We acknowledge more especially those received from James Buchanan, M. Slade Kendrick, and Lawrence H. Seltzer of the United States; Anthony Scott of the

University of British Columbia; F. W. Paish of the London School of Economics and Political Science; Douglas Grant, Scottish Statistical Office, of Great Britain; and Fritz Neumark and Paul Senf of Germany.

Finally, we must thank the patient officials of the National Bureau of Economic Research, particularly William J. Carson, Solomon Fabricant, and Geoffrey H. Moore, for their help and guidance especially during the anxious period which covers the conversion of manuscript into print; H. W. Laidler, Harold M. Groves, and V. W. Bladen of the Board of Directors, who read and commented on the study; the editors, Margaret T. Edgar and James F. McRee, Jr.; and H. Irving Forman, who drew the charts.

ALAN T. PEACOCK,
University of Edinburgh

JACK WISEMAN,
*London School of Economics
and Political Science*

Introduction and Summary

THE purpose of this study is to present the facts about the behavior of British government expenditures since 1890, and to explain that behavior by reference to basic propositions about the character of government and the facts of British history. Here we shall outline our methods and findings, and comment upon the possibilities for further research.

Statistical Evolution

The period saw considerable economic growth and technical and social change in Britain, accompanied by a striking increase in government spending. Electricity, the automobile, the airplane, the telephone and radio, the oil-burning ship, and cellulosic fibers caused the growth of great new industries and industrial regions, and contributed to the decline of older ones. These changes are reflected in the statistics of community output. In 1890, the gross national product of the United Kingdom (at factor cost) was £1,472 million; in 1955 it was £16,784 million, a money increase of more than eleven times. If we allow for price changes it increased two and a quarter times. Over the same period, the population rose 50 per cent (from 37.5 million to nearly 51 million), and there was considerable change in its age distribution. Real product per head of population thus rose about one and three-quarter times.

A growing proportion of the working population of Britain is now engaged in public services. In 1891, 3.6 per cent of the working population was employed by central and local government, compared with 13.9 per cent (24.3 per cent if we include nationalized industries) in 1950.[1] This growth of government activity is even more strikingly brought out by the statistics of government spending.

Total United Kingdom government expenditure increased forty-seven times in money terms and tenfold in real terms between 1890 and 1955. This is a sevenfold rise in real expenditures per head of population, and it implies a growth in the share of government expenditures in gross national product from 9 per cent in 1890 to 37 per cent in 1955. The growth of expenditures has not been regular; the change has come about through periodic jumps in the volume of public spending. Thus, the curve of government expenditures outlines a series of plateaus separated by expenditure peaks which coincide with the periods of war or preparation for war (1900, 1918, 1943, 1952). At the same time, the period has been marked by considerable changes in the relative importance and broad responsibilities of central and local authorities, with the latter failing to share fully in the general growth of government functions.

[1] For details, see Moses Abramovitz and Vera F. Eliasberg, *The Growth of Public Employment in Great Britain*, Princeton University Press for National Bureau of Economic Research, 1957, p. 25.

Approaches to Interpretation of Expenditure Growth

At present, there are few fields of applied economic study which lack some useful general, albeit frequently incomplete, frame of reference; for example, there are plenty of business cycle theories to test against the facts. But it is difficult to find theories of public expenditure that explain rather than justify or condemn the facts of expenditure growth.

It is obvious why attempts to provide a satisfactory general theory of government economic behavior, or of collective behavior in the provision of public goods, should run into difficulties. To be general, such a theory must inevitably become highly abstract. Consider the attempt by Pigou to reduce the problem to manageable proportions by assuming that the government was a "unitary being," capable of determining the "correct level" of government expenditure by reference to the marginal principle.[2] In reality, governments are complex organisms whose functions and objectives may change greatly even over short periods of time. If any general theory is to be useful, it must somehow take these things into account.

In other contexts, where economic analysis requires that some recognition be given to the role of the public sector, government is usually treated as an exogenous factor outside the particular model's area of mutual interdependence, or is incorporated into it by postulating simple relationships between such magnitudes as government expenditure and the other variables in the model. In the latter case, the relationship assumed appears usually to be determined by analytical convenience rather than by the facts. From our present point of view, such a procedure has little or no value.

A somewhat different approach—at one time much discussed, but now referred to only in textbooks on public finance—is Adolph Wagner's attempt at the turn of the century to relate government expenditure growth to economic development. Briefly, Wagner's "law" asserts that government expenditures in any society will grow at a faster rate than community output. It was not expected necessarily to be valid for all time, but was certainly believed relevant both to the periods that Wagner studied and to the near future, which includes a large part of our own period. Wagner adduced a number of reasons for the existence of his "law," concerned not only with the nature of the state but also with such things as the essential complementarity of demand for and supply of private and public goods. In our view, Wagner's general approach seems more productive than those discussed above. Since, however, we

[2] Dalton's famous attempt to apply the Pigovian approach in formulating his principle of maximum social advantage ends with the significant words: "Those who are oppressed by a sense of difficulty of this calculus should console themselves with the saying of the Ancient Greeks that 'it is not the easy things, but the difficult things, which are beautiful'." See his *Principles of Public Finance*, 4th ed., London, 1954, p. 11.

do not accept it entirely, a brief summary of his argument may be a useful preliminary to the explanation of our own position.

Starting from observable facts in a number of countries, Wagner asks what general causes there might be for a rising trend in public expenditures. He divides expenditures into four broad groups and, considering each in turn, produces reasons why the rate of growth of expenditures in the group should be faster than the rate of growth of community output. The arguments are held to be valid irrespective of the political and social nature of the society concerned; the more rapid rate of growth of public spending is inherent in the nature of the public economy.

On the positive side, Wagner's approach starts from the facts and tries to explain them. This appeals to us more than other analyses which, while logically more satisfying, have no relevance to the facts. Further, Wagner draws attention to the importance of the permanent influences upon public spending and to the effect of the increasing complexity of economic life upon the necessary functions of government.

Against this, Wagner's argument suffers from two serious defects. First, he adopts an organic theory of the state which we do not believe to be superior to other explanations of the character of the state, or to be equally applicable to different societies. Second, Wagner's interest is in the secular trend of public expenditures. There are other aspects of the development of public expenditures, such as the time pattern of expenditure growth, which seem to us equally significant.

Our own approach acknowledges the influences to which Wagner directs attention, but does not regard them as inevitably causing expenditures to grow faster than GNP in all societies or at all times. Indeed, if there are generalizations to be made about the relation between public expenditures and GNP, they should be concerned with the characteristics of social and economic change that require examination, and not with the "inevitable" results of such change. Also, we do not confine our attention to secular change, as Wagner did, but also consider (and attempt to explain) the time pattern of expenditure growth to be observed in the British statistics. We believe that the hypothesis we offer about this time pattern may be of some value for the explanation of the behavior of public expenditures. Finally, we do not base our discussion upon any all-embracing theory of the state; our sole "political" propositions are that governments like to spend more money, that citizens do not like to pay more taxes, and that governments need to pay some attention to the wishes of their citizens.

Working Hypotheses Developed in This Study

It is fundamental to our thesis that decisions about public expenditure are taken politically, and so can be influenced through the ballot box or by whatever media citizens use to bring pressure to bear upon the government. Political choices about the use of resources differ from choices made through the market system. In particular, citizens can have ideas about desirable public expenditure which are quite different from, and perhaps incompatible with, their ideas about reasonable burdens of taxation.

When societies are not being subjected to unusual pressures, people's ideas about tolerable burdens of taxation, translated into ideas of reasonable tax rates, tend also to be fairly stable. Fixed, if low, rates of taxation are obviously compatible with growing public expenditure if real output is growing, so that there may be some connection between the rate of growth of real output and the rate of growth of public expenditure. Much more rapid rates of expenditure growth are unlikely; in settled times, notions about taxation are likely to be more influential than ideas about desirable increases in expenditure in deciding the size and rate of growth of the public sector. There may thus be a persistent divergence between ideas about desirable public spending and ideas about the limits of taxation. This divergence may be narrowed by large-scale social disturbances, such as major wars. Such disturbances may create a displacement effect, shifting public revenues and expenditures to new levels. After the disturbance is over new ideas of tolerable tax levels emerge, and a new plateau of expenditure may be reached, with public expenditures again taking a broadly constant share of gross national product, though a different share from the former one.

This displacement effect has two aspects. People will accept, in times of crisis, methods of raising revenue formerly thought intolerable, and the acceptance of new tax levels remains when the disturbance has disappeared. It is harder to get the saddle on the horse than to keep it there. Expenditures which the government may have thought desirable before the disturbance, but which it did not then dare to implement, consequently become possible. At the same time, social upheavals impose new and continuing obligations on governments both as the aftermath of functions assumed in wartime (e.g., payments of war pensions, debt interest, reparation payments) and as the result of changes in social ideas. Wars often force the attention of governments and peoples to problems of which they were formerly less conscious—there is an "inspection effect," which should not be underestimated.

Alongside the displacement effect, there is another influence, called here the concentration process. It is concerned not so much with changes in the total volume of public expenditures as with changes in the responsibility for such expenditures. In many societies, the functions of government are shared between a central authority and other (state and local) authorities whose powers may be protected by statute (as in legal federations) or conferred by the central government. In such countries local autonomy usually has many defenders, and its preservation is frequently a matter of political importance. At the same time, economic development produces changes in the technically efficient level of government, and also produces demands for equality of treatment (e.g., in services such as education) over wider geographical areas. These opposing pressures are reflected in the relative evolution of the expenditures undertaken at different levels of government. Clearly, this evolution is distinct from the displacement effect, since the forces just described operate in normal as well as in disturbed times. Nevertheless, given the political importance of local autonomy and the barrier it may create to change, periods of displacement are also going to be periods of interest from the viewpoint of the concentration process.

There are subsidiary aspects of this analysis not considered in detail here. For example, we do not assert that social disturbances inevitably produce lasting upward changes in government expenditure, nor do we suggest that the more permanent influences on the behavior of government (such as population change) can be ignored. We do suggest that, given a period when increasing state activity has been the rule rather than the exception and in which social disturbances have occurred, the concept of a displacement effect helps to explain the time pattern by which the expenditure growth takes place, and that no explanation that ignores it can be very satisfactory.

We believe these concepts provide a means of profitable organization of study of the statistics of the evolution of public expenditures, by use of which we can obtain some understanding of the processes of change. As a corollary, we believe it to provide a useful approach to that neglected aspect of economic history concerned with the evolution of fiscal systems. An explanation follows of our use of these ideas in the examination of the British statistics, and of our results.

Use of Conceptual Framework for Examination of British Statistics

Our approach must incorporate examination of the time pattern of expenditure growth as well as consideration of the secular trend of public expenditures. At the same time, it must take into account both the displacement effect upon expenditures of periods of social disturbance (here the periods of the two world wars) and other more "permanent" influences (such as those suggested by Wagner) that may have affected the development of public expenditures.

We have tried to meet these requirements, first, by examining the other factors that might have affected public spending during the period, and then by eliminating these from the total expenditure series and considering how far the displacement idea is capable of explaining the data so adjusted. We then deal with the behavior of expenditures classified

xxv

by responsible authority (the concentration effect) and with the expenditures of nationalized industries. The final chapter considers methods of projecting future British government expenditure.

We have already pointed out that the curve of total government expenditures (in current money terms) shows a peak and rising plateau pattern, which suggests that the growth in expenditures has come about through upward displacements in the periods of war. Our first task is to see whether this inference is destroyed when we take account of the more permanent influences. Two such influences, population and price changes, can be disposed of easily. The growth in population from the turn of the century until the present day has been about 22 per cent, which is certainly slower than the absolute rate of growth in government expenditure in money terms. Moreover, the irregular time pattern associated with the incidence of wars still remains in the statistics of government expenditure per head. Further, although there are many difficulties associated with the elimination of price changes, the peaks and plateaus still occur when the influence of price changes has also been removed. This elimination of population and price changes, however, reveals the real rate of growth of public expenditures per head of population to be much slower than the rate of growth of total money spending.

Another possible influence might be the business cycle as manifested in changes in the level of employment. But we show that, while there may be short-term increases in the ratio of government expenditure to GNP when there is a considerable rise in the unemployment index (particularly in the 1930's), no permanent upward shift in government expenditure can plausibly be attributed to the cycle. This is not to say that the Great Depression may not have had a profound influence upon attitudes toward public intervention, but rather that any such influence is not manifested in a permanent shift in public spending related to the periods of unemployment. It is possible to conclude, then, that the "permanent" factors influencing the level of government spending cannot satisfactorily explain the pattern of growth in public expenditures. We must look elsewhere.

Upward displacement of government expenditure has come during and after two major wars. The next possibility to consider, therefore, is how far the growth in expenditure can be explained simply as the direct and inevitable consequence of war for the continuing level of government spending in the postwar periods. Wars clearly affect public expenditures outside the immediate period of hostilities. We also need to consider the influence of peacetime spending on defense, which shares some common characteristics with the last group, but is sufficiently different to require separate examination.

We cannot know what government expenditures would have been in some hypothetical situation in which no wars had occurred. Nevertheless, if we find that "war-related" expenditures cannot account entirely for the displacement effect, we shall know that war itself cannot provide a complete explanation of the growing size of public expenditures. In fact, we find that as the influence of different types of war-related expenditure is cumulatively removed (even including peacetime defense expenditures, not specifically war related), the residual expenditures of government continue to show the peak and plateau sequence.

We can now examine the displacement effect over the period of the two wars in more detail. We begin by breaking down the national statistics; a classification by functional and economic categories gives insight into the changes that occurred at these times, and directs our attention, among other things, to the growing importance of social welfare spending. But the statistics cannot tell the whole story. Their value in the form just described is to guide us toward the facts of history that have been significant in encouraging the growth of public expenditures. The short survey which follows picks out some of those facts.

About the changed possibilities of government spending that have resulted from the two wars there can be little doubt. The exigencies of war produced significant improvements in tax administration, under the compulsion to increase government revenues. These changes, which would have been politically impossible earlier, were borne without protest. More to the point, the new burdens and methods became a lasting feature of British society.[3]

The government came out of the two wars, then, with the possibility of undertaking public expenditures on a much wider scale than before. But why should it wish to do so? There are two reasons, of the general kind earlier elaborated, and to which our statistical classifications direct attention.

In the first place, there is reason to believe that ideas about "desirable" expenditures and about "tolerable" taxation did begin to diverge over the period. From at least the time of the election of the Liberal Government of 1906, there was growing agreement about the desirability of increased public expenditure, particularly for purposes of social welfare. At the same time, the extension of the franchise began to increase the political power of those with most to gain from increased spending on

---

[3] Parliamentary discussion of the first Conservative Government budget after World War II, for example, was concerned, not so much about the continuance of a tax burden so much larger than that of 1937, but rather with the right distribution of the marginal gains and losses that would result from the budget changes. Such facts support the concept of a notion of taxable capacity that is "customary" in character, i.e., broadly unchanging in time of stability, but liable to violent adjustment in periods of upheaval. Further backing is provided by the contemporary observations of other economists (Bastable, Giffen, Clark) concerning the "limits" of taxable capacity.

social services. Also, there were important changes in the character of Treasury control of expenditure; we count it to the credit of our approach that it has forced this neglected aspect of British fiscal history before our attention.

As we should expect, however, these developments give a less than complete picture. They provide a part of the explanation of the secular growth in public spending, but tell us little about the time pattern of growth, and particularly about the effect of wars in changing social ideas. The second group of reasons for the growth of British Government expenditure, then, concerns those developments that relate to periods of war; all we can do here is to illustrate how the concept of displacement provides a useful guide to the relevant and important facts of history.

As major wars have come more and more to affect all sections of the community, both through demands of the military services and through such things as air raids on the homeland, the lasting social effects of war have become more profound. In the first place, wars generate an "inspection process"; the emergency brings the government and the citizens new knowledge about the nature of society. This phenomenon has roots in the past; it was the Napoleonic Wars which first laid bare the deficiencies in education of the "lower orders." More recent wars have been the means of directing attention to deficiencies not only in education but also in health services and housing conditions. At the same time, war produces a feeling of community, encouraging support for extensions of the public sector increasingly as its effects come to be more directly felt by the whole community. Indeed, as Titmuss has shown, provision of social services in World War II became an integral part of the British war effort and war aims.[4] The development of the National Health Service was thus the immediate outcome of wartime bombing which made the replacement of voluntary hospital services a necessity, and also the response to a community desire for continuing provision of state health services on a larger scale. Such illustrations could be multiplied, as will be seen in Chapter 5.

The characteristics of the concentration process during our period are dealt with in Chapter 6. The statistics do show such a process, manifested as a failure of the expenditures and direct revenues of local authorities to share fully in the growth of total public expenditures. Moreover, the process is an outgrowth of displacement within those periods, especially of World War II, since it is the growth of central government functions over those periods that has brought about the relative decline in importance of local authorities as spending agents of the central government. The changes have come about in a variety of ways—concentration of new

[4] See, R. M. Titmuss, "Problems of Social Policy," *History of the Second World War,* Civil Series, London, 1950, Chapter XV.

governmental functions at the center, shifting of local responsibilities to newly created authorities such as nationalized industries, and so on— which cumulatively have changed the nature and relative importance of local authority functions.

Nationalized industries are included in Chapter 7 for the sake of formal completeness. The available data on net expenditures of these enterprises cover only part of our period and are left outside the general statistics. But they are presented both because of the current importance of nationalized enterprise, and because many of the activities concerned (such as electricity supply) were controlled earlier by some other public body, and hence affect our statistics for the period before the present organization was established. Besides, we believe even the restricted material presented can be used to demonstrate the utility of the displacement concept, which is fundamental to our general approach to the interpretation of government expenditure statistics.

In the final chapter, we have made use of our suggested approach, albeit in a very general way, to offer a projection (but not a forecast) of British government expenditure in the immediate future. We do not subscribe, despite the influence of prevailing fashion, to the view that the sole purpose of economics is to formulate hypotheses that enable prediction. We are not bold (or foolish) enough to attempt such prediction, but we do believe that a discussion of methods of projection based on the assumption that social disturbances will be absent, and formulated in a fashion similar to that found useful in the interpretation of the historical data, can be valuable as a guide to policy. Too often, policy issues involving changes in the size and character of public expenditure are discussed in terms of some vaguely specified and inadequately quantified future "burden." We believe our approach to be more informative in defining the range of possibilities.

Our aim is simply to introduce clarity by making quite specific assumptions about particular groups of expenditures and other relevant magnitudes and by translating them into money values. Our assumptions are not the only ones possible; further enlightenment can be obtained by computing the results of changing them. It is our view that such a procedure can provide a more realistic basis for policy argument than is common in this field. Support for that view appears in the outcome of our projection, showing a much larger scope for the peacetime growth of British public expenditures (or for the reduction of taxes without reducing public services) than is generally believed possible.

Bearing on Future Research

It is appropriate to conclude with a consideration of the possible bearing of our study on future research. To reiterate our general position: We are not trying to formulate some general "law" which governs the growth of public expenditure in all circumstances. Nor do we believe that our concepts of displacement and concentration will be equally significant, in all countries and at all times, and relative to the "permanent" influences on expenditure growth, as guides to the evolution of public spending. Not all countries have been equally affected by social disturbances, and not all countries have the same political system. Nevertheless, we feel that the general approach, using these concepts alongside the facts about absolute expenditure growth and its historical time pattern, provides a useful technique for imposing order upon the study of government expenditure generally. Indeed, we feel sufficiently confident of the value of our approach to have embarked on a comparative analysis of a number of other countries, using the same general technique.[5] It is perhaps of particular interest to compare our conclusions with those reached in recent studies of government expenditure growth in the United States.

We can draw upon four recent studies.[6] Most of the authors rely upon the *Historical Statistics of the United States, 1789–1945, 1949*,[7] and the Department of Commerce national income series, which show only selected years for the period before 1929. The exception is Kendrick, who is concerned solely with the federal government, which played a much smaller role than the British central government did in the overall development of public expenditures in the same period. All these studies point to the importance of the two World Wars as influences upon the growth and structure of government expenditures. Kendrick notes the same plateau effect with reference to federal expenditures, and Musgrave and Culbertson show that war-related expenditures cannot account entirely for the trend increase in expenditure.

Most interesting from our point of view is the study of Colm and Helzner. These writers demonstrate the importance of war in the evolution of United States expenditure patterns. They note that if defense expenditure and social insurance are excluded from consideration, the relative

[5] A comparative study of twenty to twenty-five countries is now under way, sponsored jointly by the University of Edinburgh and the London School of Economics and Political Science and financed out of a Ford Foundation grant. Findings so far confirm the value of the general approach, though of course the character and importance of displacement vary from country to country.

[6] Solomon Fabricant, assisted by Robert E. Lipsey, *The Trend in Government Activity in the United States since 1900*, New York, National Bureau of Economic Research, 1952; R. A. Musgrave and J. M. Culbertson, "The Growth of Public Expenditures in the United States, 1890–1948," *National Tax Journal*, June 1953; M. Slade Kendrick, *A Century and a Half of Federal Expenditures*, Occasional Paper 48, New York, NBER, 1955; G. Colm and M. Helzner, "The Structure of Government Revenue and Expenditure in Relation to the Economic Development of the United States," in *L'Importance et la Structure des Recettes et des Dépenses Publiques*, International Institute of Public Finance, Brussels, 1960.

[7] Supplement to *Statistical Abstract of the United States*, Bureau of the Census, Department of Commerce.

proportions of the remaining federal and state expenditures have not altered over the period, but as a result of war—and this is interesting in view of British experience—the distribution of tax receipts has shifted in favor of the federal government. Moreover, their explanation of government expenditure changes, while placing much more emphasis on the changing structure of the economy accompanied by spectacular urban development, is similar. They state that "the traditional resistance to central government control has weakened only in time of war or serious depression. Thus, government functions do not always respond gradually to the needs of an industrial and urban (suburban) society. An increase in government activity or responsibility often depends on events happening which dramatize the need for such measures and help to overcome traditional resistance."[8] Our views receive support from their emphasis on the increase in tax rates and the broadening of the income tax base during World War II.

There is one striking difference between the United States and the United Kingdom. The Great Depression had surprisingly little effect on the trend of government expenditures in the United Kingdom; there was no displacement effect. On first examination, the depression in the United States would seem clearly to come within our category of social disturbance of a major character; the upward displacement particularly in federal expenditures was most marked.

It would also be interesting to investigate and compare further the influence of the growth and the distribution of population on government expenditure in both countries. Probably the proper parallel for the influence of urbanization on public expenditure would be mid-nineteenth-century Britain with mid-twentieth-century United States.

However, these are questions for future examination. All we wish to suggest is that the technique developed in this study of Britain, if applied to other countries, gives promise of illuminating results.

---

[8] Colm and Helzner, *op. cit.*, pp. 60–61. They illustrate their point with reference to the growth in education expenditures.

THE GROWTH OF PUBLIC EXPENDITURE
IN THE UNITED KINGDOM

CHAPTER 1
Scope and Method

THIS book has three related but distinguishable aims. First, it is intended to fill a gap in the available statistical information about the British economy; the statistics of British government expenditure for the period since 1890 have not previously been made available in a single convenient source and in a form suitable for interpretation by economists. Second, it is an attempt to relate these statistics in a general way to the economic history of the period; we believe that our method of approach contributes to the understanding of the economic development of Britain during the first half of the century. Third, we have tried, by relating the time pattern of government expenditure statistics and the facts of British history, to evolve hypotheses that may help to explain the evolution of government expenditure in other countries and at other times. In this respect, we do not profess to have discovered "laws" of government expenditure, and we are not particularly impressed with the "laws" of this kind that have been suggested by other writers. We also present, in the final chapter, some conjectures about the trends of British government expenditure in the near future, but we intend this to be treated rather as an adventure in speculation than as the result of an impeccable analysis. We do not pretend that we can forecast wars or earthquakes, and (in our view at least) he who would forecast the future of government expenditure would have to face such tasks.

None of these aims can be satisfactorily pursued without some discussion of techniques and background. The compilation and presentation of the statistics give rise to important problems of technique and interpretation. A proper understanding of the economic history of Britain since 1890 requires some knowledge of previous periods. And the hypotheses tested call for some initial explanation and for comparison with existing theories and propositions about government expenditure. These distracting but essential preliminaries are the subject of this chapter, which is devoted to discussion of the statistical techniques and methods used. The following chapter is a discussion of some theories of government expenditure growth, including those tested in this study.

Conceptual Problems

A study of this kind inevitably encounters statistical problems set by the nonavailability or noncomparability of data. We regard the collection and presentation of a continuous series of government expenditure statistics since 1890 as an end in itself. Other difficulties arise in making use of the data for our wider purposes; while concerned with the use of statistics, they are conceptual and interpretative in character. They

3

would have to be solved even if all the requisite material were available in a suitable form. The conceptual problems are therefore considered at the outset.

These conceptual problems arise because no general statistical measures can be expected to give unambiguous answers to all the kinds of questions we wish to ask. In the main, our concern is with the relations between the size and character of government expenditure and of its components on the one hand and such magnitudes as the total community output and its composition on the other. But particular methods of demonstrating such relations statistically, which may be valuable in offering support for an individual argument, can be seriously misleading if taken outside the immediate context, and indeed often require careful interpretation even within that context.

The difficulties can be explained more concretely by considering a statistical comparison fundamental to our study—the relationship between the growth of total government expenditure over time and the growth of aggregate community output. At first glance, a comparison of this kind might be thought to give a clear general indication of changes in the influence of the government in the community's economic life. But a closer look suggests that great caution is required, not only in interpreting the results, but also in giving a precise meaning to such terms as government and output when compiling the actual statistics to be compared. Thus, the influence to be measured is not unambiguous. For example, a given aggregate level of government spending is compatible with a wide range of different effects on the free choices of individual citizens, the actual effects being determined by the composition of public expenditure, the distribution of control over spending between different levels and organs of government, and so on.[1] If our interest were in the effect of government expenditure on individual choice, therefore, we would need to interpret the results of such a general comparison with care and to supplement them with other information. To take another instance, it is of direct relevance to our study that total government expenditure includes both expenditure on goods and services and on transfers and subsidies. Transfers and subsidies are not components of national income, so that if we express total government expenditure (including such transfers) as a proportion of national income the result gives an exaggerated impression of the share of total community output

[1] To form a balanced view, we would also need to know what other government influences on choice were in operation, e.g., whether the armed forces were recruited by conscription and whether or not any rationing schemes were in existence. For a further discussion of this point in relation to the growth of government employment, see M. Abramovitz and V. Eliasberg, "The Trend of Public Employment in Great Britain and the United States," *American Economic Review, Papers and Proceedings*, May 1953, pp. 203–215; with comment by Ronald Coase, pp. 224–236.

4

taken by the government.[2] On the other hand, a similar ratio omitting transfers and subsidies would be without any general significance as a rough indicator of changes in the government's overall influence in the community over time, since transfers and subsidies also have to be financed and are clearly of importance in many economic contexts (e.g., in the use of government expenditure as an indicator of the tax burden implied by the activities of government).

We cannot do without a general comparison of this kind, then, but we need to be careful how we use it. No economist would deny that the relation between the size of total government expenditure and the size of an aggregate such as national product may tell us a great deal about the nature and consequences of government intervention or participation in the economic system. An increasing volume of government expenditure, arising from such causes as a growing demand for the employment of resources to satisfy collective needs, indicates important changes in the structure of the economy. The most satisfactory solution, therefore, and the one we have adopted, is to accept this relation as our fundamental indicator of the importance of the government in the community, but to do so in the knowledge of its shortcomings and to supplement the information it provides with other statistical series and indicators specifically directed to the elucidation of particular issues. It is our hope that the series of ancillary statistics built up in this way around the general indicator will provide an adequate justification for the method.[3]

It now becomes necessary to look more closely at the components of the general indicator itself. What, for example, is to be understood by the term "British Government" for our purposes? There are certain difficulties in defining the geographical region Britain in a fashion that enables compilation of comparable statistics for the whole period from 1890; these are explained in the Appendix. There is also a need to decide which of the community's economic activities should be treated as the activities of the government, once defined. For our purposes, it is most important, conceptually at least, to distinguish those activities of the government which arise out of a collective demand for goods and services

[2] For further discussion of this issue with particular reference to the neglect of the distinction in the British literature on public finance, see A. R. Prest, "Government Revenue and the National Income," *Public Finance*, VI, No. 3, 1951; and R. L. Marris, "A Note on Measuring the Share of the Public Sector" *Review of Economic Studies*, 1954–55, XXII, No. 3, p. 214.

[3] A potentially more precise (but also more cumbersome) procedure might be to eschew any general indicator, but to express expenditures on goods and services as a proportion of national income (though this does not avoid the problem of measurement of real income discussed below), transfer expenditures as a proportion of personal income before or after tax, subsidies as a proportion of (say) consumption expenditure at market prices, and other types of government expenditure as proportions of similar "ideal" economic magnitudes.

(e.g., health services) and those which are a part of the ordinary productive activities of the community (e.g., rail transport) although carried on or controlled by government agencies. Expenditures of the latter type must be much more affected by market criteria than other public expenditures are, and generalizations about the behavior of other government expenditure are therefore likely to be of dubious relevance to developments in the "public production" sector. The tendency in social accounting is to treat such government activity as part of the general productive activities of the community, or at least to separate it from the other functions of government. This has obvious advantages from our point of view; our general indicator would be less rather than more meaningful were total government expenditure defined to include expenditures by nationalized industries.

The most satisfactory procedure, then, would be to exclude production expenditure from our definition of government for purposes of general discussion, but to provide statistics of such activities, to be taken into account when the context makes them relevant. Unfortunately, this is quite impossible in practice, and a compromise has to be made. Statistics of government expenditure are not recorded with such conceptual distinctions in mind, and many activities of government are not easily allocated to the government or to the production sector, but appear to belong in different degrees to both. At the same time, the production activities of government have so changed in size and character over the period that comparable expenditure data simply cannot be obtained. In addition to the shifts from private to public control brought about by the post-1945 nationalizations, there have been important changes within the public production sector—notably, transfers of control over such activities from local authorities to other public bodies.

We have adopted the definitions used by the Central Statistical Office as the basis for our distinction between general government expenditure and the other (production) activities of the government and its agencies.[4] Quite apart from the practical difficulties of any alternative procedure, this method facilitates the preparation of the general statistical series on a comparable basis over time, which is one of our primary aims. But the definition that guides the official classification emphasizes the degree of autonomy enjoyed by the various public authorities, rather than the economic characteristics of their activities. As a result, the transactions of all agencies whose finances are administered through the general accounts of the public authorities are included in general government

---

[4] For complete details, see Central Statistical Office, *National Income Statistics, Sources and Methods*, London, H.M.S.O., 1956 (hereafter cited as C.S.O., *Sources and Methods*). A list of nationalized industries is given in Chapter 7 of this book, and details of statistical procedure in the Appendix.

expenditure, while the transactions of other public enterprises, not so financed, are excluded from the government sector and appear in the official statistics as a special section of the Companies' Account. In following this official convention we have had to depart to some extent from the conceptual distinction that we desire our data to reflect. History rather than logic has decreed that the financing of the General Post Office and local authority housing, for example, are treated with government, while other public enterprises whose functions are not markedly different in economic character are not. These other enterprises are the ones examined separately in Chapter 7. Such compromises are unavoidable, and this one is not seriously misleading for our present purposes, though it would need to be borne in mind if the figures were being used as a basis for international comparisons of government expenditure growth.

Having determined what is meant by government expenditure, it becomes necessary to decide what measure of community output (i.e., what national income concept) that magnitude might most usefully be related to. We have used gross national product at factor cost. Once again, this is to some extent a compromise. If our wish is to relate the total creation of economic wealth by the community and the consumption of that wealth by government, then *net* national product might be more suitable. The calculation of depreciation presents such problems, however, that even if broadly comparable series for net product were provided, they would be unlikely to give more reliable information than the gross product measure.[5] It might also be argued that gross national product at market prices would be a more suitable magnitude for purposes of general comparison; government purchases (and hence total government expenditure) may have an indirect tax content, and such taxes should, therefore, be reflected also in our measure of total product. This issue could be debated on technical grounds, but its practical significance is not large enough to make such a discussion worth while. In 1950, government current expenditure at market prices was £2,067 million, of which approximately £50 million represented taxes on expenditure. Since national product at factor cost is otherwise our most satisfactory measure of output, the "watering" of government expenditure by such a small amount will not invalidate its use for comparative purposes, particularly since the amount of watering is presumably fairly constant from one year to another.

Two final conceptual questions remain, those arising out of changes over time in the level of prices and in the size and composition of the population. It is clearly desirable that the general measure of the influence

---

[5] To illustrate the difficulties, how should the "depreciation" of government capital investment be defined, much less calculated?

7

of government discussed so far should reflect changes in the real share taken by government of the real product of the community. But only money measures are available. How does this affect the validity of comparisons over periods when prices are changing? At first sight, the money value of government expenditure as a proportion of the money value of national product might seem to be a satisfactory indication of real changes, despite price movements: changes in the value of money will be reflected both in the size of (money) national product and in the size of (money) expenditures by government on goods and services. But there are two reasons why we cannot be content with this. First, we are interested in the absolute changes (i.e., the rate and character of growth) in government expenditure, as well as in changes in its share in total output. Money expenditures are an unsatisfactory measure of this over periods of changing prices; we need to deflate the money figures by an appropriate price index. Second, the money comparison will in any case provide a true reflection of real changes only to the extent that the prices of the things consumed by government change in exactly the same way as prices as a whole. It is common practice, for example, to deflate government expenditure and resource use as well as the gross national product by a common index such as the wholesale price index. While this may be a justifiable method for some purposes (e.g., it may give a reasonable impression of growth), it can also be misleading. There is no reason to suppose that the composition of government purchases will be the same as that of the purchases of the community as a whole. Indeed, the great importance of some kinds of government expenditure (e.g., on public employment of particular types of labor) is enough to suggest that such a coincidence is unlikely. We have tried to meet this difficulty by presenting the major statistical facts in two forms: in current prices, and also in figures deflated by price indexes constructed particularly for the magnitudes concerned. The construction of these indexes follows standard procedures.[6] Use of the selected indexes had little effect on our conclusions, though we are aware that a different approach (e.g., one which distinguished the prices of goods and services and of transfers) might have produced a somewhat different result. This the reader must judge for himself; the construction of any separate price index for government expenditure presents difficult statistical problems (discussed in the next section), and the computation and use of more than one such index would in our judgment have added more to complexity than to enlightenment.

For certain purposes, the usefulness of our general indicator of the growing importance of the government may be enhanced by expressing

[6] The construction and interpretation of index numbers presents particular difficulties which are not discussed in detail here.

government expenditure or government resource use and gross national product as real or money amounts per head of population. A comparison between government resource use and GNP per head, for example, would illustrate changes in the average proportion of real income derived by individuals from public and private sources. However, a crude average derived by dividing total government expenditure, either in real or money terms by total population, may be misleading. Obviously, the extent to which different social or age groups benefit from government expenditure will differ over time or at any point in time, both with changes in public policies and in the composition of population. Further, the use of such an average implies that collective benefits can be assigned to individuals, which is doubtful when we consider such services as defense or the preservation of law and order. We have not found it possible to avoid these difficulties by more detailed statistical calculations, but have been content to draw attention to instances in which the relation between the composition of population and government expenditure may be import-ant.[7] The reason for this lies partly in the difficulty of assigning benefits, just discussed, and partly in the difficulties encountered in attempting to allocate benefits among social groups, such as age groups, even were such benefits assignable to individuals.[8]

Statistical Problems

The actual collection and collation of suitable statistics has been a matter of some difficulty. It will be appreciated from the earlier discussion that statistics following the classification conventions now generally accepted for the explanation of the place of government in the economic system were required. The first necessity, therefore, was to produce a consistent series of statistics of both government money expenditure and of gross national product. Official statistics classified in this way do not exist for years before 1938. For the period up to 1920, our source of statistical information about the central government has been the *Appropriation Accounts*, published annually. These adopt the conventional classification of expenditure by service, and also incorporate a good deal of double counting because of interdepartmental transfers. Consequently a detailed reclassification of the central government accounts for this period was carried out. A similar reclassification of the local government expenditure

---

[7] The statistical problems involved in breaking down the data to overcome the draw-backs of the crude per capita average are enormous if not insurmountable. Their general nature can be appreciated by a perusal of Chapter 8, since the projection we make there requires such a breakdown.

[8] For a short illustrative discussion of this point in relation to education expenditure, see Alan T. Peacock and Jack Wiseman, "The Finance of State Education in the United Kingdom," *Year Book of Education for 1956*, London, 1956.

statistics as given in the *Local Taxation Returns* and, after 1934, in *Local Government Financial Statistics* was also necessary. It was not possible to do this for more than a few years before 1920. For the period from 1920 to 1938 we were able to use the reclassification of central government expenditure undertaken by J. E. G. Utting and Dorothy Cole in their detailed study of government income and expenditure, 1920–38, which the authors kindly made available to us.[9] Although these writers have also compiled separate estimates of local government expenditure, we found it more convenient to compile our own classification.

Our second problem was to break down the total figures of government expenditure into suitable functional classifications. In this case official figures have been recorded only from 1950 onward. We have, however, been able to produce a classification that is consistent over time; the Central Statistical Office made available to us the official method of classification for both central and local government expenditure, and the same procedure was followed by J. E. G. Utting and Dorothy Cole in their statistics for the period 1920–38. We have departed from the official classification in some minor respects, and made adjustments in the official figures published since 1950 in order to make our classification consistent for the whole period. It must be pointed out, further, that the local government statistics for earlier years necessarily contain some guesswork. The years between 1939 and 1950, too, cannot be covered, although for 1946–49 the difficulty was lack of resources rather than lack of information. A full functional classification for those years would necessitate detailed examination of hundreds of pages of the *Appropriation Accounts*. We have preferred to direct our efforts to the improvement of the statistics for earlier years.

Finally, a major problem is presented by the need for separate price indexes for the deflation of government expenditure and of gross national product. The most illuminating indexes for this purpose would probably be one for government purchases of goods and services and another reflecting changes in the purchasing power of money for those who received government transfer payments. No price index of government purchases exists for the period covered by our study, and for good reasons. In the first place, the task of constructing such an index would be enormous.[10] In the second place, we know of no satisfactory means of constructing a suitable index by which to deflate expenditures on the services of

[9] To be published in the series of Studies in National Income and Expenditures, 1920–38, under the auspices of the National Institute of Economic and Social Research.

[10] Some idea of the labor involved can be obtained by consulting the detailed study of National Health Service purchases at constant prices made by R. M. Titmuss and Brian Abel-Smith. See their *Cost of the National Health Service in England and Wales*, National Institute of Economic and Social Research, Occasional Paper 18, Cambridge, Eng., 1956, especially pp. 62–66 and Appendix B.

10

government servants, whose output is not sold on the market.[11] To follow standard official procedure here would require the valuation of such services by analogy with the valuation placed on similar services by private enterprise.[12] This would call for some arbitrary assumptions (e.g., about what constitutes a "comparable" service), and would also entail enough statistical labor and discussion for another treatise. An alternative possibility considered was to construct a crude index of "real" services by assuming that the productivity of government servants was constant. This might be statistically feasible, but the initial assumption is so arbitrary as to be positively misleading. In effect, we should merely be calculating an index of government employment and inferring from it that a rise in government employment reflected a concomitant rise, not only in government expenditure in real terms, but also in total national output.

We have, therefore, fallen back on what must be admitted to be very much a second best—although we regard our method as less misleading than the common one of deflating both government expenditure and national product by a single retail or wholesale price index, in that it does attempt to bring out at least some of the consequences of changing relative prices in the public and private sectors. Separate price indexes for current goods and services and for capital goods were compiled from a number of sources,[13] and these indexes were used to deflate the current and capital components of both government expenditure and national product. Accordingly, the difficulty associated with the change in composition of government expenditure compared with the composition of national output is to some extent overcome. The deflation of transfers and subsidies presents the further difficulty of identifying the recipients of such payments and their consequent purchases. The best available procedure seemed to be deflation of these items by the general price index of current goods and services. A final problem is presented by changes in stocks and the value of work in progress. We adopted the arbitrary procedure of using the indexes of current goods and services as a deflator; fortunately, this item is not an important component of government gross capital formation for most of our period.

[11] We leave aside the broader question of whether all such services can be said to constitute a part of community output at all (cf. Simon Kuznets, "Government Product and National Income," *Income and Wealth*, Series I, Cambridge, 1951, pp. 193–194). For our purposes, such expenditures clearly cannot be ignored and they do constitute a loss of factor services to other uses.

[12] This is the method used by the Central Statistical Office. See C.S.O., *Sources and Methods*, p. 38.

[13] For full details of the method of construction, see Appendix, section on price indexes.

CHAPTER 2

Determinants of Government Expenditure

THE subject of government expenditures has not received much or satisfactory attention from economists or students of public finance. It can hardly be said that he who wishes to study the subject finds the tools of analysis necessary for the interpretation of public expenditure data lying ready to hand. "The tremendous growth of government expenditures here and abroad," says Lowell Harriss, "has been one of the striking economic developments of recent years. Economic analysis of these changes has dealt primarily with the probable effects on levels of employment and prices. . . . On the whole, however, the analytical results are generally unsatisfactory. Economists specializing in public finance have generally concentrated on taxation. Perhaps there is not much more that the economist can say about spending. The nature of the problems, especially the unavailability of bases for appraising results, make study difficult. Description, and the statement of rather obvious generalities, may about exhaust the possibilities."[1]

This position cannot be accepted without misgiving. Economists like to feel that their studies have a bearing upon issues of public policy, and commonly pass judgment on such issues. But what significance can such judgments have for a world in which government spending activities frequently account for 25 to 40 per cent of community output, and the characteristics of these activities go unexplained? We must surely seek further insight if progress in other fields is not to be nullified by our inadequacy in this one. Further, as explained previously, our purpose is to evolve and to test against our data for Britain tentative hypotheses that might be generally valuable for understanding the behavior of government expenditures over time. A first and essential step must be to establish hypotheses that seem worth the trouble of testing. With this in mind, we devote the next section to those earlier writings which presumably generated Harriss's pessimism.

The Study of Public Expenditures

THE WELFARE THEORIES

Historically, many economists have approached the study of public expenditures from a prescriptive point of view; it was perhaps this group more than any other that encouraged the comment quoted above. Such studies attempt to set up criteria for the size and nature of government

---

[1] C. Lowell Harriss, "Public Finance," *A Survey of Contemporary Economics*, B. F. Haley, ed., Homewood, Ill., 1958, II, 261–262. It should be pointed out that Harriss has done much to remedy the deficiency. See, e.g., his "Government Expenditures: Significant Issues of Definition," *Journal of Finance*, December 1954.

expenditures and income by utilizing techniques usual in the study of market economics.[2] Starting from some concept of economic welfare, defined in terms of individual choice, they attempt to specify the taxing and spending activities of government that would conduce to the ideal conditions of such welfare. At the extreme, this leads to proposals for systems of public finance in which the government provides only the services that individuals would pay for directly, if that were feasible, and levies only such taxes as individuals would voluntarily pay in return for the services they receive. This transference of the concepts of individual choice in markets to the activities of government can lead to such peculiar "liberal" suggestions as the proposition that those who are unwilling to pay taxes in such a situation are "pathological."[3]

Alternatively, the government may be regarded by such writers as a unitary being, with tastes and preferences like other beings. Its income and expenditure can then be examined as those of an individual, and the size and character of the public sector prescribed by the application of marginal criteria similar to those generally employed, for instance, in the study of individual consumers.[4] Further sophistication can be introduced by recognizing that people can "choose" to use the political process rather than the market to make decisions about the utilization of economic resources. The political voting system is in this context an alternative to the market voting system. This approach leads to consideration of alternative political voting systems, but with a view primarily to the discovery of what kind of system will best achieve the postulated objective: attainment of the "ideal" conditions of individual choice. The ideal political system is thus regarded as one that best promotes economic liberalism, and the ideal volume and type of government expenditure is that which such a system would generate.[4a]

These theories all derive from, and to varying degrees depend upon, the system of market analysis that is commonly known as welfare economics. There is considerable and growing skepticism among economists as to the value of welfare economics as a basis for economic policy and as a starting point for the study of actual economies. To the extent that such skepticism is well founded, the associated theories of public expendi-

---

[2] Such studies have a long and continuing history. See R. A. Musgrave and A. T. Peacock, eds., *Classics in the Theory of Public Finance*, London, 1958, Introduction. In recent years, there has been considerable discussion of the topic by P. A. Samuelson, S. Enke, and J. Margolis in the *Review of Economics and Statistics* (November 1954, May 1955, November 1955, November 1958).

[3] F. Benham, "Notes on the Pure Theory of Public Finance," *Economica*, November 1934, p. 453.

[4] A. C. Pigou, *A Study in Public Finance*, 3rd rev. ed., London, 1947, Part I, Chapter V.

[4a] A sophisticated discussion of political and market choices is to be found in J. M. Buchanan and G. Tullock, *The Calculus of Consent: A Preliminary Analysis of Individual Constitutional Choice* (forthcoming).

ture must become more dubious. But this need not concern us here, important though it may be in other contexts. What is more destructive, from our point of view, is the fact that although these theories of government income and expenditure purport to be prescriptive in nature, even the most sophisticated of them (which do at least admit consideration of voting systems) treat the problems of government and political behavior in a fashion that any political scientist must consider unrealistic. No government is concerned, as the theories imply, solely with interpreting the choices of the individual members of the community. All governments depend for their existence upon their power to coerce as well as upon the consent of the governed, though the importance of these two ingredients may vary from one country to another.

In short, governments have not in the past tried to achieve the aims that the welfare theories postulate for them, and, however much we may deplore the fact, they are unlikely to do so in the future. Consequently, these prescriptive theories are simply not operational.

GOVERNMENT EXPENDITURE AND ECONOMIC GROWTH

The development of Keynesian theories of economic stability has encouraged consideration of government expenditures as one element in a macrostatic model. The more recent and growing interest in the associated problems of economic dynamics and economic growth, a marked characteristic of economic studies since World War II, has stimulated further interest in public expenditures along similar lines.[5] The work of this second school is of particular interest from our point of view.

To be of value for our purposes, however, it is necessary that the models of the growth theorists should incorporate some plausible and realistic theory as to the relationship between the time evolution of public expenditures and of other magnitudes of economic interest. There is no point (even if there were a possibility) in trying to interpret the statistics of actual public expenditures by reference to a model incorporating assumptions about their evolution that have been dictated by analytical convenience rather than by inherent plausibility. This is, of course, a perennial problem, and its importance for this study is especially clear. We may be able to use a theory of economic growth which incorporates some explanation of the place of the public sector (and of public expenditures in particular) in the general explanation of the economic growth process, but we can do little with a theory which ignores the public sector altogether, or treats it as an unfortunate nuisance to be got rid of by global and unconvincing assumptions. In the words of Domar, ". . . gov-

---

[5] See, e.g., R. F. Harrod, *Towards a Dynamic Economics*, London, 1948; E. Lundberg, *Studies in the Theory of Economic Expansion*, Stockholm, 1937; and E. Domar, *Essays in the Theory of Economic Growth*, New York, 1957.

ernment is the most troublesome of the three [forms of expenditure] because we have no theory of government expenditure. In its absence we may dump government expenditure on top of the other two as an exogenous factor, merge it with consumer expenditure . . . or assume it away altogether. This last suggestion is certainly the most convenient of all and such treatment of a troublesome factor is richly supported by precedents in economic theory."[6] For Domar, as for those who have developed static Keynesian models, aggregate government expenditure is either to be left outside the system of mutual determination of the economic model or assumed to be zero. Neither treatment is particularly satisfactory. Government expenditure is clearly not usually nonexistent, and it is implausible to argue that it neither influences economic growth over time, nor is itself influenced by that growth.

More recently, some writers have tried to incorporate a more positive theory of the public sector (including an explicit or implicit theory of public expenditure) in long-period growth models.[7] While these models are certainly an improvement, from our point of view, on what went before, it cannot be said that either their formulation or their present degree of refinement makes them suitable for our immediate purpose. The models cannot be discussed in detail here; it must suffice to point out the general ways in which they continue to be unsuitable.[8]

It is possible to criticize such models, in the first place, on the ground that the number of variables that they take into account is much smaller than is necessary for their satisfactory utilization for purposes of economic policy or for the interpretation of history. There are, for example, awkward problems remaining to be tackled in relation to the treatment of transfer payments and the effective incidence of taxes and public expenditures. But other objections are of more significance in the present context. In particular, the models cannot easily take care of changes in the coefficients of the constituent variables, whether such changes are induced by the process of growth itself or whether they result from historical eventualities incapable of inclusion in a generalized economic growth model. This difficulty has particular importance in the sphere of government: Can we really expect either the character and determinants of government

[6] Domar, *op cit.*, p. 20.
[7] See J. G. Gurley, "Fiscal Policy in a Growing Economy," *Journal of the Political Economy*, December 1953, pp. 523–535, with reply by Warren L. Smith, *ibid.*, October 1954, pp. 440–441; also Smith, "Monetary-Fiscal Policy and Economic Growth," *Quarterly Journal of Economics*, February 1957, pp. 36–55, and A. Smithies, "The Control of Inflation," *Review of Economics and Statistics*, August 1957, pp. 282–283. For a model of a different order, see K. Kurihara, "Growth Models and Fiscal Policy Parameters," *Public Finance*, 1956, pp. 148–161.
[8] A fuller discussion of the problem is to be found in Alan T. Peacock, "The Public Sector and the Theory of Economic Growth," *Scottish Journal of Political Economy*, February 1959.

behavior, or the precise impact of that behavior upon the rest of the economy, to remain constant over any long period of time?

It is the third group of objections to these models, however, which is decisive from our point of view. Perhaps in order to cope with the difficulties already described, growth models have been developed in the direction, not of providing a more and more realistic picture of actual economies, but rather towards providing more and more prescriptions for the simplified societies described in the models themselves.[9] Thus, a typical procedure is to begin from some statement of objective (or simple set of objectives) such as the maintenance of a prescribed stable rate of economic growth. Then, using a model assuming, for example, the initial absence of government activity, and postulating defined relationships between a chosen group of variables, the necessary tax and expenditure policies required to attain the defined objective are discovered. In other words, the structure of the public sector is prescribed by the initial assumptions and characteristics of the defined model. The actual behavior of governments is not considered, and often the question of whether the objective is one which any government is likely to wish to pursue, or to pursue exclusively, is also left aside. The alternative would be to try to evolve a theory of the public sector from a study of the actual process of decision taking at different levels of government and at different periods of time and in different countries, and to incorporate the results in a generalized growth model. It seems unlikely that such a procedure would produce anything more than considerable distrust of models incorporating a government sector. Nevertheless, failing some such study, the growth models in their present form cannot be treated as anything more than exercises in a technique of arrangement.

WAGNER'S LAW

There is another school of thought about public expenditures, also with a long and continuing history, but explanatory rather than prescriptive in character. Its aim is to establish generalizations about government expenditures, not from postulates about the logic of choice, but rather by direct inference from historical evidence. The approach is perhaps better known on the continent of Europe than in Britain or the U.S., and therefore requires rather full explanation. It was encouraged by a growing awareness towards the end of the last century (i.e., at the beginning of our period) of the correlative growth of community output and public expenditure that was observed in a number of countries (e.g., Prussia, Bavaria, Britain, North America, Switzerland). These countries had in common a rising trend of output per head, but differed markedly in other

---

[9] In this respect, at least, the growth theories are similar in essential character to the welfare theories described earlier.

important respects. Attempts were made to explain the phenomenon by growing military and national debt commitments, but the increases in expenditure affected too many other services, and the military and debt commitments varied too much from one country to another for this to be plausible. Consequently it came to be argued that the data supported the existence of some kind of general "law" relating the growth of output per head and the growth of government spending. Clearly, the existence and character of any law of this kind, if it can be established, must be a matter of importance for our study.

In general, economists writing at the turn of the century inferred no more than that the available statistics suggested a "law" that government expenditure must grow in proportion to a community's output per head. This was the view of H. C. Adams, writing in America in 1898.[10] In the same period, however, Continental writers of the Younger Historical School, and particularly Adolph Wagner, went further than this, arguing that government expenditure must increase at an even faster rate than output. Wagner's influence continues to pervade Continental writing on problems of public expenditure. The core of his argument, in his own words, is that "The law [of increasing state activity] is the result of empirical observation in progressive countries, at least in Western European civilization; its explanation, justification and cause is the pressure of social progress and the resulting changes in the relative spheres of private and public economy, especially compulsory public economy. Financial stringency may hamper the expansion of state activities, causing their extent to be conditioned by revenue rather than the other way round, as is more usual. But in the long run the desire for development of a progressive people will always overcome these financial difficulties."[11]

The first point of importance about this argument is its implication that the growth in expenditure derives from the growth in state activity, which is in itself the consequence of social progress. In other words, Wagner's "law" is really a law of increasing state activity: to the extent that such increased activity is the inevitable accompaniment of social progress, and only to that extent, increased expenditures are inevitable also. It is also clear from the quotation that the law is concerned with the secular behavior of expenditure rather than with short-run change or the actual *process* of change. Further, Wagner does not suggest that the actual extent of state activity can be fixed *a priori*. His concern is with the rate of growth of expenditure; he cites as proof of his law the fact that for a number of countries it was empirically verifiable that as

---

[10] H. C. Adams, *The Science of Finance*, New York, 1898, Chapter 2.
[11] Adolph Wagner, *Finanzwissenschaft*, Leipzig, 1890, 3rd ed., Part I, p. 16.

output per head increased in the past, state activity and expenditure grew more than proportionately.

To explain the existence of the law, Wagner distinguished between three types of state activity. These were the maintenance and enforcement of law and order internally and externally (*Recht- und Machtzweck*: roughly, the provision of the necessary social preconditions for markets to function), participation in material production, and the provision of such economic or social services as postal, education and banking services. Separate reasons were adduced for expecting the law to hold for each type of activity.

For the first group of activities, he suggests, the need for increased participation by the state originates in the "inevitable" centralization of administration and in the "atomization" of social and economic life that result from economic development. At the same time, the state has to increase its activities in order to ensure the maintenance and improvement of the quality of the services it provides. Also, increasing division of labor multiplies the complexities of economic life and hence the possible causes of friction. Thus if the economy is to function efficiently, state activities of both a preventive and a repressive character have to increase. Growing state participation in material production (the second type of state activity) develops because new technical processes (Wagner was thinking particularly of steam power) make the public corporation the only alternative to the joint stock company. In his view, it is a necessary and a preferable alternative, because the joint stock companies might not be able to handle large amounts of capital as effectively as a public corporation, and because private enterprises mismanage and waste capital during business cycles and enhance such cycles by causing speculative disturbances. Finally, increased activity of the third type (provision of other economic and social services) must arise where technical developments produce favorable conditions for monopolies, where the social benefits of the service are not susceptible to economic evaluation (e.g., education), and, once again, where the state could become a source of stability by taking over large enterprises whose dominating influence encourages instability.

Wagner himself did not put forward his law as perpetual and ineluctable, like the law of gravitation. On the other hand, he did consider it to be something more than a simple historical accident; he expected the law to hold at least for the near future, that is, for at any rate some part of the period of our study. So interpreted, the law is still subject to important criticisms. It is based upon historical evidence, but its acceptance as anything more than a statistical observation requires acceptance also of Wagner's own very special view of the nature of the state as a political entity. True, he adduces reasons why government expenditure will increase in any developing state, and some of these reasons are technical in character and might be expected to operate whatever view is taken of the role of the state. But these are only a part of his argument, and would not alone justify the expectation that public expenditures must always rise at a faster rate than community output. Further, careful examination suggests that what appear to be simply technical reasons for expenditure growth in Wagner's exposition are often not independent of his views about the state. Thus, his most concrete proposition as to the nature of the increased expenditures of government is the argument from stabilization. At first sight, this has a surprisingly modern look, in that subsequent developments in macroeconomics have encouraged the view that a large public sector may be necessary for purposes of employment policy. This view is perhaps coming to be less widely held, at least without considerable qualification; economists are indeed beginning to treat the possible rigidities of public sector expenditures themselves as a source of price and employment fluctuation.[12] In any case, Wagner's argument is really very different from the more modern one. Certainly, he believed that the creation of public corporations could help to reduce instability. But he does not demonstrate why all countries must always treat economic stability as an important aim of policy, and his basic reason for expecting a growth in the importance of public corporations lies elsewhere—in his own conviction of their general superiority to private joint stock enterprise. Similarly, his assertion that other public services must expand both qualitatively and quantitatively as output rises stems not only from technical considerations, but also from Wagner's view that it is the duty of the state to behave in this way.

It cannot be accepted, then, that Wagner succeeded in demonstrating that a secular increase in community output must inevitably produce a more than proportionate secular growth in the importance of government services. Ultimately, the law of increasing government expenditure is a corollary of the political philosophy and interpretation of history that Wagner accepted. His "proof" of the existence of such a law, therefore, depends upon the validity of the organic theory of the state upon which he relies. But there are many other interpretations of the nature and duties of the state, not demonstrably less valid than the views held by Wagner. For example, J. Shield Nicholson was writing in Edinburgh in 1903: "In the progress of society, moreover, it is necessary to incur new modes of expenditure. No provision of machinery to meet old wants will suffice for the satisfaction of new demands. In many cases, however, the expense ought to be met not by increased taxation, but by substitution. With increase of wealth the increasing demands for education ought to

---

[12] See, for example, W. Drees, Jr., *On the Level of Government Expenditure in the Netherlands after the War*, Leiden, 1955.

19

be partially met, at any rate, by diminished demands from the poor; as the education rate rises, the poor rate ought to fall."[13] Why should Wagner's law operate in a country where such views might be accepted?

A Suggested Approach to the Study of Public Expenditures

We must now ask whether there is any alternative approach which might be potentially more fruitful than those so far discussed, and we can usefully broach this question by considering first of all what is worthy of retention in the existing approaches.

The preceding discussion suggests two general propositions from which we might start out. First, insofar as we attempt to establish generalizations that we might expect to have validity for more than one country (and which we can subsequently test against our sample of one), those generalizations must inevitably be concerned with procedure rather than prescription. Our aim should be to provide enlightenment as to how public expenditures can be expected to behave, of a kind that might be of value in the study of countries other than Britain, rather than to try to compare the facts of expenditure growth with some "idealized" model. That is, any general hypotheses should be concerned with the likely characteristics of expenditure growth in actual communities, taking all necessary account of the economic, political, and social differences between one community and another.

Second, and arising partly out of the above, our broad approach must follow that of Wagner rather than that more familiar to British and American economists, since, like Wagner, we are concerned with the actual facts of public expenditures. But we shall need to adapt and modify this approach. It is also of relevance to this decision that the available evidence for a number of European countries during the present century does show a public expenditure growth of the character that Wagner prophesied, and this has persuaded later writers (particularly Continental writers) that his law continues to be valid. Indeed, as one authority points out, the rate of growth of such expenditures in many countries has been faster than Wagner himself would have expected.[14] This, and the fact that Wagner's argument certainly directs attention to matters of real practical significance in the historical development of public expenditures, suggests that dissatisfaction with the law as Wagner argued it ought not to prejudice us against his general approach.

Further study along these lines, seeking the kind of hypotheses described, and using Wagner's general approach while rejecting the conclusions he reached by it, can take two directions. We can examine afresh the possibility that there are permanent influences affecting government

---

[13] J. Shield Nicholson, *Elements of Political Economy*, London, 1903, p. 510.
[14] See G. Schmölders, *Finanzpolitik*, Berlin, 1955, Chapter IV, pp. 125–140.

expenditure at all times and in all societies, and that these must generate expenditure growth in developing societies, irrespective of their political and social characteristics. This may help us to decide whether the search for general hypotheses about government expenditure growth is either plausible or useful, and should in any case indicate some influences on expenditure that we cannot afford to ignore. At the same time, there is no reason why we need confine our investigation to the relationship (between the secular growth in government expenditure and in community output) that interested Wagner. A second direction for study is suggested by the fact that even a superficial examination of the recent history of public expenditures indicates other questions, a consideration of which might possibly be productive of fruitful hypotheses. It is in these two directions that our own approach evolves.

PERMANENT INFLUENCES ON GOVERNMENT EXPENDITURES

In considering whether there are any permanent influences on the size of public expenditures (i.e., forces operating continuously to affect the size of such expenditures), we can suitably begin by some further examination of the consequences of the increasing complexity in economic life, to which Wagner directed attention. It is certainly true, as he pointed out, that as an economy develops the tasks of the organs and institutions of the government (e.g., in making and enforcing laws, providing a police force and an army, governing large towns) must both change in character and become more intricate and difficult. This may well make for some growth of government expenditure on those functions with economic progress, and it is also likely to stimulate changes in the nature of the responsibility for expenditure, as the efficient scale at which public activities of particular kinds can be carried on will change.[15] But the nature and extent of the growth in government expenditure due to such causes must depend upon the specific circumstances being considered. There is no reason to believe, for example, that the impact of the development of the internal-combustion engine and electric power has been of the same character and importance from this point of view as the results of the use of steam power of which Wagner wrote. Also, it must not be forgotten that technical change affects not only the problems of fulfilling particular tasks of government, but also the means available for the performance of those tasks. Thus, whether a government which tries to maintain a given level of services over a period of economic and technical change will absorb an increasing share of community output as a result depends on how the process of change affects the relative productivity of the resources (including labor) used in the public and private sectors. There is no reason to expect that relative productivities will change in the same

[15] See Chapter 6.

21

way in all societies at all times; this must be a matter for empirical verification in each case.[16] Consequently, there can also be no certainty about the consequences of growing complexity, or of economic development *per se*, for the behavior of government expenditure; there is no point in trying to adumbrate some general hypothesis that might be valid for all times and places.

Analogous to questions of the effects on the cost of providing public services of changes in the character of economic life, there are questions raised by economic development on the demand side. Such development makes available new forms of consumption, and it is possible and perhaps likely that countries will want to indulge these in part by increasing expenditure on government-financed communal consumption. For example, insofar as a rising GNP is associated with the devotion of an increasing proportion of consumption to services, there is some reason to expect the share of government to increase. Services constitute an area in which government provision may be efficient and in which private markets may function unsatisfactorily, whether because of difficulties in making charges, in assigning benefits to individuals, or in taking account of the "community" (as distinct from individual) benefits to be obtained from expenditures on such services as education. However, development also brings with it at least one similar influence to reduce government expenditure: the fact that as the general level of individual income rises, dependence upon the state for the relief of extreme poverty and distress ought to diminish in importance. On the other hand, it is plausible to argue that the criterion of poverty and distress which determines who is to be helped by the government, and how much, is not absolute but is, within broad limits, conventional. Attitudes may differ from society to society, but there is likely to be a broad general relation between the standard of life of a community and its views about a tolerable level of existence to be provided I y the government for those in need. Further, the causes of poverty and distress are likely to change radically as a society develops. The nature, incidence, and problems, e.g., of unemployment may become quite different. It appears to be even more difficult to make any positive and general assertion about these "demand" influences on the level of government spending than about the "cost" influences.

The influence of population change must also be considered. The total output of a community can increase without output per worker rising, as a result of population increases. Rising total output might well be associated with constant or falling output per head and thus with an increasing need for government expenditures on services concerned with

---

[16] For an empirical study of this kind, see Solomon Fabricant, assisted by Robert E. Lipsey, *The Trend of Government Activity in the United States since 1900*, New York, NBER, 1952, Chapter 5.

the relief of distress, and simultaneously with increasing difficulty in transferring resources from the private to the public sector.[17] In these circumstances the relation between government expenditure and population change is unlikely to be simple, predictable, or constant over time or between societies. If on the other hand we restrict ourselves to consideration of the effects of increasing output per head of population (the definition of a developing economy implicit in much of our earlier discussion), an increasing population becomes more likely to be associated with rising total government expenditure, though not necessarily with increasing expenditure per head. But the effects of population change are still not easy to forecast even in this case, since government expenditure is likely to be affected not only by changes in total numbers but also by changes in the composition of population (number of pensioners, children, and so on). Many types of expenditure are designed to meet the needs of particular groups and tend to be affected by the numbers in those groups rather than by the size of the population as a whole, and there is no reason why the numbers in any group should vary directly with total population.[18] The dangers of attempting to make any general proposition become even more apparent when it is recognized that changes in population almost inevitably follow an irregular time path, whether we consider total numbers or detailed composition. Any general expenditure "law", therefore, would either have to operate despite population change or be restricted in relevance to the periods (if there are any) in which trends in total numbers and in composition are broadly constant. As a further complication, there is one particular relation between population and government spending which requires special mention: where rising output per head and increasing population occur together, there is often a simultaneous growth in the size and importance of conurbations. This reinforces the argument that increased public expenditures may be required to deal with the growing complexity of economic activities. Also, the growth of urban populations may affect the methods used by governments to control their expenditures and the relationships between different types of public authority. Growing urbanization was in fact important during the period studied by Wagner, and is relevant for our own period. Nevertheless, it is no basis for a general law of expenditure, but rather a special influence that may or may not be significant in any country or time period.

Similar difficulties are found when we turn, finally, to the influence of

[17] This is very likely to be the position, e.g., in a less developed country with a population problem.

[18] For a practical illustration of this point, see F. W. Paish and A. T. Peacock, "The Economics of Dependence, 1952–82," *Economica*, November 1954, and *Report of the Committee of Enquiry into the Cost of the National Health Service*, Command Paper 9663, 1956, pp. 37–45; also Chapter 8 of this book.

changes in prices and in the level of employment. Such changes may indeed affect the volume and the pattern of public spending in some circumstances. But since prices and the volume of unemployment can either rise or fall, it is not easy to see how these factors could operate in a secular fashion to create changes in the importance of government expenditure; once again, a general law would have to operate despite changes in these magnitudes, or be restricted to periods in which they followed one simple trend.

The diversity and complexity of these possible general influences upon public expenditures is apparent, and we do not believe that the factors just discussed exhaust the possibilities. But there certainly do not seem to be any permanent influences upon government spending capable of supporting the assertion contained in Wagner's law, or of suggesting some general hypothesis that might be expected to explain the behavior of government expenditures through time. The most definite general statement that it might be possible to make on the basis of our examination of these permanent influences is that government expenditures are perhaps more likely than not to increase in absolute real volume as a country develops economically. Also, it is quite possible that the rise of expenditures will be at least as fast as the secular rate of increase of national product. But there is nothing inevitable about this; not all the consequences of development encourage such a rate of growth of public spending. In fact, the behavior of public expenditures over any period depends on factors that can differ in influence and importance from one time to another and between one country and another. Further, we must add an additional (and fundamental) argument, so obvious as to need no discussion: changes in the size of the government sector and hence of public expenditures are bound to be affected by the political nature of the society concerned and by current views about the role of government. We have discovered no reason why the general influences arising out of economic and other change should be expected to reduce these political factors to unimportance.

In sum, we must clearly not ignore the permanent influences on expenditures which were so important to Wagner, but neither must we expect them to give rise to general hypotheses about public expenditures in general, or even to provide a complete explanation of the facts in any country over any particular period.

THE DISPLACEMENT EFFECT AND THE CONCENTRATION PROCESS

Both the secular character and the "historical inevitability" of Wagner's law make difficulties for the development of ideas about government expenditure that will be useful in considering shorter-term questions. Having abandoned the law, though without denying the importance of many of the characteristics of government expenditure to which it draws attention, we can pursue these other ideas more freely. In doing so, we shall be attempting less than Wagner but may achieve more, at least of a practical nature. We must seek, not universal secular laws, but a way of looking at the year-to-year changes in government spending that will not only illuminate the British statistics which are our direct concern, but also give us an approach to the subject that might be equally fruitful in studying other countries or periods, in interpreting the facts of history or in introducing realism into the discussion of present and future expenditure policies.

As a first step, let us consider some broad facts about the expenditures of Western governments during this century, concerning ourselves not with secular trends but rather with the precise fashion in which the actual changes have taken place. One immediately evident fact is that while government expenditure has clearly grown (at least in money terms) over the period as a whole for all countries for which adequate statistics are available, the time pattern of growth is less regular than, and quite different from, the corresponding pattern of growth in the size of community output. An inspection of Chart 1 (Chapter 3) makes this clear for Britain, and evidence is available of a similar pattern of change in other countries.[19]

The previous quotation from Wagner indicates that he was aware of at least one possible reason for these divergent time patterns—the dependence of governments upon revenues raised by taxation.[20] But it was not a question that he was interested in pursuing, as his concern was with the secular trend of expenditures and he did not believe these to be affected by the short-run problems of raising revenue. If we are to concern ourselves also with short-run phenomena, however, we must consider the reasons for the time pattern of expenditure growth with more care. Typically, the time chart of government money expenditures describes a series of mountain ranges, with peaks of increasing height separated by plateaus. In the British case, the major peaks occur in the periods covered by the two world wars. There is, of course, obvious reason to expect the share of community output taken by the government to rise in wartime; the divergence in the time patterns of the two series under discussion would be of little interest if it could be attributed simply to this. In fact, it cannot. Although British government expenditure declines after the wars, it does not return to the prewar level, and a

[19] See Schmölders, *op cit.*; and for information on the U.S., see M. Slade Kendrick, *A Century and a Half of Federal Expenditures*, Occasional Paper 48, New York, NBER, 1955.

[20] To repeat part of that quotation (in the section of this chapter on Wagner's law): "Financial stringency may hamper the extension of state activities, causing their extent to be conditioned by revenue rather than the other way round...."

25

similar pattern is to be observed in other countries similarly affected. In Britain, the plateaus of expenditure establish themselves at successively higher levels, and the share of government expenditure in national product remains much greater after the wars than it was immediately before them.

To provide a satisfactory explanation of this time pattern of government expenditures, we must begin with some kind of concept of the nature and behavior of governments. We should then be able to interpret the relevant historical phenomena of any period in the light of this conception, and so obtain an understanding of the changing magnitude of public expenditures. It is one thing, however, to criticize a political philosophy such as that used by Wagner, and quite another to provide a coherent statement that will stand in its place. In this respect, fortunately, we can profit from the more limited nature of the task we have set ourselves; we do not need a theory of government that will describe the character of public expenditures fifty years from now, but require only a sufficient understanding of the governmental process to provide insight into the year-to-year behavior of public spending. For this more limited purpose, we believe that some fairly simple propositions, certainly not sophisticated enough to be called a philosophy, will suffice.

We start from the trite but important observation to which Wagner himself has directed attention: that government expenditure depends broadly on revenues raised by taxation. That is, decisions about such expenditure are influenced or controlled through the ballot box, or by the use of whatever other media exist for citizens to bring pressure to bear upon their government. Now, these political choices differ from choices made through markets. It is inherent in the nature of choices made through the political process that the ideas of citizens as to what is desirable public expenditure can be separated from the ideas of those same citizens as to the reasonable burden of taxation. Clearly, both the views that citizens hold and their influence on government policy will be affected by the political organization of the society concerned. But while, for example, a dictatorship and a democracy with regular free elections may differ in this respect, no government is likely to act without any consideration at all of the views of its citizens. Thus, the divergence of the "revenue" and "expenditure" ideas of citizens is of potential relevance as a means of explaining the time pattern of government expenditure growth in a large number of societies.

When societies are not being subjected to unusually violent pressures or disturbances, people's ideas about the "tolerable" burden of government taxation tend to be fairly stable. Governments may of course have plans that would increase their expenditures, and the plans may be thought desirable by many of the citizens. Nevertheless, their implementation, and thus the rate of growth of government expenditure, will depend upon the view taken by the government as to the revenues that it is (politically) able to raise as well as upon its own views as to the desirability of increasing government expenditures in any direction.[21] Consequently, government expenditure may rise in such periods, but if so it will do so at a steady and relatively unspectacular rate, curbed by such economic factors as the disincentive effects of high marginal rates of tax and also by popular notions of tolerable tax burdens and by the degree of political control exercised by the citizens over their government, but encouraged by a rising output per head.[22] Also, both citizens and government may, throughout such periods, hold divergent views about the desirable size of public expenditures and the possible level of government taxation.

This divergence can be adjusted by social disturbances that destroy established conceptions and produce a displacement effect. People will accept, in a period of crisis, tax levels and methods of raising revenue that in quieter times they would have thought intolerable, and this acceptance remains when the disturbance itself has disappeared.[23] As a result, the revenue and expenditure statistics of the government show a displacement after periods of social disturbance. Expenditures may fall when the disturbance is over, but they are less likely to return to the old level. The state may begin doing some of the things it might formerly have wanted to, but for which it had hitherto felt politically unable to raise the necessary revenues. At the same time, social disturbances may themselves impose new and continuing obligations upon a government, as the aftermath of the disturbance (for example, the provision by a government of war pensions), as the result of the government being obliged by the disturbance to assume functions that it cannot easily return to others (for example, the wartime provision by government of services formerly financed by private charity), and as a consequence of changed ideas induced or encouraged by the disturbance itself.

We do not suggest that there is some absolute sense in which social disturbances "cause" changes in the economic activities of government. This would patently be too simple a view. It should be clear from the

[21] We do not of course suggest that the idea of a "customary" concept of taxable capacity is a completely novel one. See, for example, the interesting discussion in J. C. Stamp, *Wealth and Taxable Capacity*, London, 1922, Chapter IV.

[22] A rising real GNP per head brings increasing tax yields with constant tax rates, so that if people's ideas of tolerable burdens are concerned with tax *rates* rather than total payments, this provides a reason why the peacetime plateau described by public expenditures may have an upward slope. Clearly, a progressive tax system may further encourage this possibility.

[23] The 1950 British budget, for example, involved a tax burden that would have been unthinkable to a prewar government or electorate. Yet there was no serious argument for a return to the prewar situation: the social disturbances of World War II had created a new set of norms, broadly accepted by both citizens and political parties.

27

discussion so far that we recognize other permanent influences that may be of importance (though these seem unlikely to operate in a constant direction over time), and also the possible importance of changing social ideas for the growth (or decline) in the functions of government. Thus, it is possible to find peacetime periods (for example, just before World War I) when the rate of growth of British government expenditures was such that if it had continued steadily until 1955 the share of government in community output would not have been markedly different from what it was in fact. But this is the world of "might have been"; we do not know what would have happened to British public expenditures had the wars not happened, nor do we know how one can usefully speculate about such a matter. We must concern ourselves with the facts. In Britain during the period under study, those facts cannot be explained without consideration of social disturbances, and there are persuasive politico-economic reasons why this should be generally so.

Interpretation of our expenditure data, then, must take both kinds of influence into account. Changes in social and political ideas and institutions, as such, may condition the evolution of the functions of government, and may also affect the nature and significance for public expenditures of such social upheavals as wars. Conversely, the displacement effect may be the origin of lasting changes in ideas and institutions; periods of war are, for example, a fruitful source both of new ideas about society and of new administrative procedures. Interpretation is consequently complex; we wish neither to argue that the displacement effect alone explains the evolution of the public sector nor to ignore its significance. Instead we attempt an interpretation of what happens in periods of displacement against a background of history that takes the other influences continuously into account. It is only in this way that we can hope to turn the Wagnerian thesis into an approach offering greater insight into the time process and socioeconomic characteristics of expenditure growth.

It must also be made clear that we do not suggest that the displacement effect must inevitably be upward, though we shall find that it has in fact always been so in Britain in our period. Other things apart, such a proposition would imply the inevitability of eventual complete state control of economic activity. This possibility might itself produce social upheavals intended to produce a reduction in the power of government and hence a downward displacement in government expenditure. All we suggest, therefore, is that in communities and over periods in which the economic activities of the state are in fact increasing in importance and in which social disturbances occur, the nature of political power will usually produce a time pattern of growth characterized by a displacement effect of the kind described.

Loosely associated with the displacement effect, but distinct from it, is a subsidiary characteristic of government expenditure to which some indirect reference has already been made. The process of economic growth carries with it certain influences tending to change the size of the government unit upon which responsibility for public economic activities rests. This change in the division of responsibilities we call here the concentration process (see Chapter 6).

The economic factors making for change in the effective responsibility for particular public sector activities can be fairly easily stated, although their consequences may be less easy to trace. It is characteristic of economic development that it carries with it, and indeed depends upon, improvements in the ease of transport and communication, and that this is very likely to be associated also with a growth in the technically efficient size of economic and administrative units. Thus, the process of growth may generate two kinds of pressure for the movement of responsibility for public expenditures toward higher (larger) organs of government. First, the very fact of improved transport and communications, by increasing the knowledge of particular groups about the mode of life and standards of public service enjoyed elsewhere in the community, is likely to generate pressures for improved and uniform standards of public services, and these pressures may only be capable of satisfaction by greater centralization of control over the size and character of public spending. Second, the improvements in transport and communications may not only make such larger areas of control possible, but may also make them economically efficient. There can be scale economies in public as well as private economic activities, and such economies may be generated for both by the process of economic growth.

On the other hand, while economic growth may produce social pressures for uniformity of standards, there are other social pressures tending in the opposite direction. The lower levels of government (whether the creation of the central government as in Britain or units in a federal structure as in the United States and Canada) are themselves political units, with a history and a tradition. They cannot be expected to surrender their authority easily, and in many countries, both federal and unitary, the pressure to preserve local autonomy is important politically at both the central and local government levels. At the same time, the historical development of local governments usually leaves them with wide responsibilities of varying character. Changes in these different activities cannot be expected to be uniform, so that any concentration process that does occur must affect different local functions in very different fashions. It may do so in a variety of ways: by the higher levels of government taking the greater share of responsibility for the expanding types of government expenditure, by the shift of responsibility for particular services from lower to higher authorities, by lower authorities losing

29

effective autonomy because they become more dependent upon the higher authority as a source of revenue, and by the creation of new authorities under the broad control of central government to deal with such problems as urban conurbations or the provision of particular services such as water supply.

This concentration process can occur independently of any displacement effect, but we should expect to find some relation (though not a precise or straightforward one) between the two. In the first place, we have seen that the concentration process (or its absence) in any period must be regarded as the outcome of socioeconomic and political forces which may be pulling in opposite directions. During periods of social upheaval such as wars the political opposition to change is weakened, and the pressures for concentration can break through. At the same time, an event such as war has different impacts at the central and the subordinate levels of government. The central authority assumes responsibility for the prosecution of the war, and it is consequently at the central level that new tax revenues (which are the basis for the later permanent growth of the public sector) are concentrated. This must imply a relatively faster growth in central functions, in the absence of a deliberate decision to hand over new responsibilities for expenditures to local governments after the disturbance is over. Further, the needs of war become more important than such issues as local autonomy, and abrogations of local independence are tolerated that would have been unacceptable at other times. Once the change has been made, it is easier to make it permanent, and such a step may indeed become unavoidable.[24] Finally, the periods of disturbance may (though they need not) be characterized by a social cohesion that reinforces, among other things, the demand for uniform standards of public services. The result of this will of course depend upon the country concerned and upon its state of economic development; it must always encourage a concentration of responsibilities at higher levels, but whether the concentration will be at the center or at some intermediate level must depend upon particular conditions.

ANALYTICAL PROCEDURE

The concept of a displacement effect can be used as the basis for a general and systematic approach to the analysis and interpretation of government expenditure statistics. It provides a focus of attention that is lacking in other treatments of the problem, in that we can explain changes in the importance of government expenditure through time by examining what happens to government spending over periods of displacement. This is not to say that general or secular factors in expenditure growth

---

[24] In Britain, the transfer of local government responsibility for hospital services to an independent authority after World War II illustrates this point.

must be ignored; our earlier discussion was intended to demonstrate not that these factors were unimportant, but that their influence was not constant or predictable through time in a fashion that would enable them to be used as the basis for a general law of public expenditure. Indeed, it is clear that the approach now being suggested must begin with a systematic examination of the influences affecting government expenditure more or less permanently. Until we have discovered how such influences affect the expenditure pattern during our period, we cannot be sure either that a displacement effect exists independently of them or that we know which social disturbances appear to have been productive of expenditure displacements sufficiently important for detailed study.

We must begin, then, by considering government expenditure as a whole, from both a secular and a shorter-run point of view, and in relation to the behavior of those influences upon expenditure that must operate in a more or less permanent (but not constant) fashion. In the preceding section, we indicated three such influences that are always likely to be both relevant and capable of statistical interpretation: population, prices, and the level of employment.

It has already been pointed out that the secular relation between population changes and government expenditure is complex and uncertain. But we can be fairly sure that the rate of population change is unlikely to account for large short-period displacements in the general level of government spending.[25] In the case of Britain, we should not expect population movements to be responsible for the peak-and-plateau pattern of government expenditure statistics, or to provide the reason why the peaks should occur in wartime. Nevertheless, it is necessary to assess the influence of population on expenditure over our period by computing government expenditure per head. In this way, we can not only confirm the irrelevance of population as a factor in displacement, but also obtain a supplementary measure of the changing significance of government expenditure of a kind that is especially relevant to consideration of the importance of such expenditure to the individual citizen.

The relation between price changes and displacement is less easy to assess. True, we can deflate our current expenditure statistics by price indexes and so discover whether displacements occur in the "real" expenditure data so derived. But we cannot rule out the possibility that changing prices may themselves have affected the government's problems in raising revenues or deciding upon expenditures, and so have influenced expenditure statistics over time. As one example, a consequence of inflation is to increase money incomes. If a country's tax system is progres-

---

[25] There are exceptions—for example, when large-scale migrations and frontier adjustments, or both, result in rapid and radical population changes such as those characteristic of Western Germany since the Second World War.

sive, then even if tax rates remain unchanged during inflation, the real burden of direct taxes on individuals must increase, and this may increase the share of community product absorbed by government. The extent to which inflation in this way releases a government from the "bonds of the revenue" will depend upon the extent to which citizens think in terms of real sacrifices, tax rates, or actual money tax payments. If there is any "money illusion" in the tax attitudes (as is likely), inflation will enable the rate of increase of the share of government in total output to be faster than it could otherwise be, so making expenditure plateaus steeper. Indeed, it is not difficult to conceive of inflation being responsible for a very rapid change in the share of output going to government—that is, for a displacement effect. First, inflation provides an emergency reason for increasing tax burdens, as a means of curbing the price rise, and so may facilitate subsequent acceptance of a higher permanent level of government income and expenditure. Second, a runaway inflation, involving complete loss of confidence in the existing currency and its eventual withdrawal, clearly constitutes a break in the social pattern as distinct as that made by war. This second phenomenon has not affected Britain during our period, although we cannot leave the first entirely out of account when considering developments since 1945. But it is perhaps an indication of the utility of our approach that it would at once direct attention to the importance of a possible displacement influence of inflation in the study of, for instance, German or French government expenditures during the same period.

The influence of changes in the level of unemployment is also not obvious. At first glance, it might seem that we could treat the level of employment as being reflected in the level of prices, in which case it might not merit separate consideration. But the relation between price changes and changes in unemployment is not simple, and in any case the influence of unemployment on government expenditure is quite distinct from the influence of price changes. In contrast to the latter, the major influence of unemployment on spending is a direct one; the unemployed receive money benefits from the government, either because unemployment qualifies them for benefits or because it reduces them to poverty and so entitles them to relief, or for both these reasons. There is thus likely to be a direct relation between the volume of unemployment and the size of expenditures for these special purposes, although it may be difficult to verify the extent to which payments are made for relief of poverty rather than for unemployment *per se*. Of course, the extent to which unemployment generates public expenditure will depend upon policies that vary between countries and over time. Also, an increase in this part of expenditure does not necessarily imply a similar increase in total spending. A government may increase its expenditures, both on

32

the unemployed and for other purposes, as a deliberate policy for the reduction of unemployment. On the other hand, it may be more interested in avoiding an increase in the tax burden, and look for ways of cutting other spending when expenditure on unemployment increases. Both attitudes (there are of course others) have been important in Britain during our period.

As with inflation, it is also conceivable for unemployment to generate a displacement effect, if it is sufficiently calamitous to cause radical changes in accepted ideas about the role of government. The unemployment of the early 1930's in the United States may well have had such an effect. We shall have to consider whether this was so in Britain or whether the effects of unemployment on government expenditure were more temporary, disappearing when the unemployment disappeared.

When these secular influences have been studied, it will be sufficiently clear whether or not any displacement pattern in the statistics of government money expenditures can plausibly be accounted for by them, or whether there remain periods of displacement that demand explanation in other terms. If the latter is the case, we must turn for further understanding to a consideration of more transient influences and to our propositions about the political characteristics of the expenditure behavior of governments. We should expect if our approach has any validity to find that the periods in which we are now interested are periods in which the continuity of community life suffered serious disruption. Such disruptions should not be difficult to identify, and we can begin this part of our analysis by considering whether the disruption itself had any direct effect on government spending and, if so, whether that effect could have continued outside the immediate period of disturbance, so helping to explain the displacement in the expenditure plateaus.

This involves examination of the effects on British government expenditure of the two world wars, which is a less straightforward task than might at first appear. Direct expenditures on the prosecution of war can be identified within broad limits, and they are of course limited to the period of war. We may by study of these expenditures account for the wartime expenditure peaks. But we must recognize that this is not the only consequence of war for government expenditure. Wars generate commitments that continue into peace: debt commitments, war pensions, and so on. The idea that increasing government expenditure derives from increasing national debt, and hence from war, is by no means new; Wagner, for example, considered this possibility but rejected it. We must discover whether the continuing peacetime expenditures that resulted directly from the wars will entirely account for the "displacement" of postwar expenditures to plateaus higher than the prewar ones. If so, we need look no further for an explanation of the nature of the displacement effect during our period. Also, it will be useful to consider the influence of peacetime defense expenditures; these are clearly not the direct consequence of war, but they are hardly a normal peacetime expenditure.

This brings us to our final possibility. Any part of the displacement effect that still remains to be explained must be the result of the influence of the social disturbance on government behavior, either in making it possible for the government to implement existing plans or in changing the views of the government and the citizens, or both, about desirable levels of public spending. Assessment of what things were important to this process must be in some part a qualitative matter and dependent upon description. But we can facilitate interpretation by analyzing government expenditure statistics by groups, and particularly by economic and functional categories. At the same time, if we are to keep the displacement effect in perspective in relation to other relevant influences, we must also form a view of the extent to which the public sector has been changing from a "participating system" to a "control system"[26] and whether there have been changes in the character of government making control of public expenditure less easy and the effects of displacement consequently more striking. We can also examine expenditures at different levels of government (using the concentration concept to interpret the statistics) and review the spending activities of important public bodies falling outside the official public sector (in the case of Britain, the nationalized industries).

[26] These terms are explained in Chapter 5.

CHAPTER 3

The Growth in Government Expenditure and National Income

OUR case-study of British government expenditure since 1890 begins with presentation of the actual statistics of total annual expenditures and comparison of the changes indicated by these statistics with the changes in national income. We then examine the effects of the permanent influences (population, price, and level of employment changes) on government expenditure. First, however, we present a brief history of government expenditures in the earlier part of the nineteenth century, intended to serve as a useful general background for the later argument.

British Government Expenditure Before 1890

In his famous chapter on "The Limits of the Province of Government," John Stuart Mill stated the maxim that "the business of life is better performed when those who have an immediate interest in it are left to take their own course, uncontrolled either by the mandate of the law or by the meddling of any public functionary."[1] This maxim, shorn of Mill's own detailed qualifications of it, dominated the actions of the statesmen who followed the "old" liberalism. Translated into practical financial policy, it meant that the level of government expenditure was to be kept at the minimum consistent with the provision of adequate protection against the Crown's enemies and of the maintenance of law and order; a wide interpretation of the latter included, to the Victorian mind, the relief of certain forms of social distress.

So universal was the acceptance of this attitude that it is difficult to detect in the history of British public finance in the nineteenth century any pronounced disagreement. The main sources of disagreement were about methods rather than aims and were concerned with how best to hold expenditure in check or reduce it. On the expenditure side of the budget, the debate was thus for the most part about the ways in which the payments of national debt interest might be reduced and about how to provide the accepted government services as economically as possible, in order—in Gladstone's graphic phrase—to bring about "the saving of candle ends." The real struggle in Parliament was concerned not with expenditure but with methods of raising revenue, with the relative merits of direct and indirect taxation, the object of minimizing the level of government expenditure being taken for granted.[2]

---

[1] *Principles of Political Economy* (Ashley edition), London, 1909, Book V, Chapter XI, p. 952.

[2] The question of attitudes toward public spending and their effects is discussed in greater detail in Chapter 5.

Accurate and relevant statistics of government expenditure and its relation to national income for the period before 1890 are difficult to come by. Table 1 derives from provisional statistics collected for a study of this period by Jindrich Veverka, now in preparation (see Appendix, "Notes on Tables Not Derived from Appendix Tables"). The figures are not fully comparable with the data for the later period, but are sufficiently so for us to draw some general conclusions about how relatively narrowly the functions of government were conceived in the nineteenth century, and about the way the position of the government in the economy has changed since 1800.

The table shows that, after declining from a peak of £123 million during the Napoleonic Wars (1814), government expenditure at current prices remained fairly constant in size until the period of the Crimean War (1854–56). Current money expenditures were one-third higher in 1860 than in 1850, and then continued to rise slowly through the 1870's. In 1880 (the period of the Zulu Wars) expenditures were about 25 per cent greater than in 1860. Thereafter, there was a new period of gradual increase, until the rough expenditure plateau was broken by the expenditure peak in 1900—the period of the South African War, the end of the period under survey, and ten years after the beginning of our period proper.

These statistics of total expenditures at current prices may be thought to provide a misleading and unrealistic picture of the growth in importance of government, and from some points of view this is certainly true. Such statistics are given special interest for the period being considered, however, by the fact that the absolute level of government expenditure at current prices was uppermost in the minds of the nineteenth century Chancellors of the Exchequer. Writing just after the turn of the century, the statistician Robert Giffen justifiably complained that in this period there was "no real discussion of what the expenditure of the state should be and for what purposes, and of what could really be borne by the community, any more than there is now or ever has been at any time in my recollection."[3] Taken together with the attitude to expenditures just described, such thinking in money terms meant that the share of government in community output was perhaps more likely to be a passive consequence of changes in the level of prices than has been the case in later generations.

However, for us as for Giffen, changes in real government expenditures and in the share of such expenditures in real GNP are also matters of great interest, whatever their causes.[4] As Table 1 also shows, the pro-

[3] See Sir Robert Giffen, *Economic Inquiries and Studies*, London, 1904, II, 310–311, 325.
[4] But see our discussion of the problems of interpretation of these indicators of expenditure growth in Chapter 1.

TABLE 1

Total Government Expenditure and Gross National Product,
at Current and 1900 Prices, Selected Years, 1792–1900

(index, 1900 = 100)

	1792	1800	1814	1822	1831	1841	1850	1860	1870	1880	1890	1900
1. Government expenditure												
Total (£ mn.)												
At current prices	22.0	71.0	123.0	69.0	63.0	63.0	66.0	88.0	93.0	117.0	130.0	268.0
Index	8	26	46	26	23	23	25	33	35	44	48	100
At 1900 prices	17.0	39.0	60.0	49.0	48.0	48.0	62.0	72.0	74.0	103.0	132.0	268.0
Index	6	15	22	18	18	18	23	27	28	38	49	100
Per head (£)												
At current prices	1.6	4.5	6.5	3.3	2.6	2.4	2.4	3.0	3.0	3.4	3.5	6.5
Index	25	69	100	51	40	37	37	46	46	52	54	100
At 1900 prices	1.2	2.4	3.2	2.3	2.0	1.8	2.3	2.5	2.4	3.0	3.5	6.5
Index	18	37	49	35	31	28	35	38	37	46	54	100
2. GNP												
Total (£ mn.)												
At current prices	200.0	300.0	418.0	360.0	403.0	556.0	545.0	778.0	988.0	1,148.0	1,412.0	1,780.0
Index	11	17	24	20	23	31	31	44	56	65	79	100
At 1900 prices	154.0	162.0	203.0	255.0	310.0	418.0	514.0	643.0	790.0	1,016.0	1,441.0	1,780.0
Index	9	9	11	14	17	24	29	36	44	57	81	100
Per head (£)												
At current prices	14.4	18.9	22.2	17.2	16.8	20.8	20.0	27.1	31.7	33.2	37.7	43.2
Index	33	44	51	40	39	48	46	63	73	77	87	100
At 1900 prices	11.1	10.2	10.8	12.2	12.9	15.7	18.8	22.4	25.3	29.4	38.4	43.2
Index	26	24	25	28	30	36	44	52	59	68	89	100
(1) As percentages of (2)	11	24	29	19	16	11	12	11	9	10	9	15

portion of total government expenditure to GNP was around 11 per cent before the Napoleonic Wars. After those wars, a higher share persisted for some time, but the old proportion had become established again by the decade 1830–40. Such a return was not unexpected, given the prevailing attitude to public expenditures, and given the fact that the governments of the time were aware of the potential displacement effect of wars and were actively concerned to prevent a permanent upward shift in the share of government as a consequence of such wars. From 1841 until 1890 the share of government changes little, declining very slowly from 11 per cent of GNP in 1841 to 9 per cent in 1890. This compares with a share of 12 per cent in 1905, 24 per cent in 1923 and 37 per cent in 1955 (Appendix Table A-6). The gradual decline over the second half of the nineteenth century is the more interesting for being associated after 1875 with a declining price trend which (given the interest of the Chancellors of the day in money expenditures) might have been expected to encourage an opposite movement.

At the end of the Napoleonic Era the three largest items of expenditure were central government expenditure on debt interest, military expenditure, and local government expenditure on poor relief. The size of debt interest was being restricted, if not actively reduced, from that time until the beginning of the South African War, and was becoming a smaller proportion of national product in consequence. Thus, debt interest at current prices was £32 million in 1822, £26 million in 1860, and £20 million in 1900. Until the Crimean War, debt interest was almost a half of all government expenditure, in 1880 it was only a quarter and in 1890 a fifth. A hundred years after the Crimean War, as we shall see, debt expenditure represented as little as 11 per cent of total government expenditure, but it had been up to nearly 30 per cent between the two wars.[5] The costs of defense move in an opposite direction from that of debt interest payments. Drastically reduced after the Napoleonic Era, they gradually rose after the Crimean War until they overtook national debt interest in the 1880's. From that date onward, defense expenditure has always represented a major portion of central government expenditure.

If we remove these war-related and military expenditures from consideration, we find that the gradual decline in the share of total expenditures after 1840 is not reflected in the residual group. Thus, total expenditures less national debt were 6 per cent of GNP in 1841, and had risen to 7 per cent in 1890. If defense is also excluded, the residual grows in importance from 3 per cent of GNP in 1841 to 5 per cent in 1890. That is, nonmilitary expenditures shared in the displacement that appears to

[5] The 1800–1890 debt statistics include intragovernmental debt payments, and so slightly exaggerate the significance of the debt burden (see first section of Chapter 4).

have occurred over the period of the Napoleonic Wars, and also increased their share of GNP during the long period of relative stability thereafter.

Turning now to responsibility for expenditures, we find that perhaps the most striking development of the period was in the size and character of local government expenditure. At the beginning of the nineteenth century, the major function of local government was the organization and provision of poor relief. By 1890, expenditure had increased to five times the 1820 level, as more and more services were undertaken. Mrs. Dashwood in Jane Austen's *Sense and Sensibility* (published in 1797) sent her furniture by sea from Sussex to Exeter, road haulage being costly and dangerous. One hundred years later the position was quite different; the Turnpike Trusts had been wound up, a much improved road system had been created, and such a mode of transportation would have been thought must unusual. In the process, County Councils had become the main road builders. After the cholera epidemics in 1831 and 1848 much greater attention was paid to public health, and the Public Health Acts of the sixties and seventies fostered local authority enterprise in housing and sanitation. While comprehensive elementary education had to wait until the founding of the Board of Education in 1899, the local authorities had earlier begun to receive grants from the central government to encourage individual schools and were authorized to raise rates not exceeding one penny in the pound to finance technical education and manual instruction. In sum, poor relief, which had been by far the greatest single item of expenditure after the Napoleonic Era, was only about 12 per cent of local expenditure in 1890, and the change had taken place by way of a growth in the other functions of local government rather than by a decline in the importance of relief functions.

One final point needs to be made about these statistics, which we shall find of interest when we come to discuss the later period in Chapter 5. A remarkably large part of total government expenditure during this period represented transfers to private individuals (such as national debt interest, poor relief) and to private institutions (such as grants to private schools). National debt interest payments were much the most important of these. The direct share of government in the national product, therefore, was considerably smaller than government expenditure expressed as a percentage of national income. It is not possible to give very detailed or accurate statistics of government resource use, but we can say that in 1822 it was something like 8 per cent, in 1850 about 6 per cent, in 1870 about 5.5 per cent and in 1890 about 7 per cent of national product.

It is usually assumed that rapid industrialization must bring with it a considerable expansion in "social overhead capital." Certainly, capital expenditure by local government on roads and other economic services began to increase at a rate faster than the rate of growth of real national product in the second half of the nineteenth century, but the absolute size of such expenditure was still remarkably small, and (as we have already seen) real government expenditure as a whole did not constitute an increasing share of national income over the same period. Nevertheless, there is reason to believe that, before the period of this study, the seeds of increasing government economic activity had already been sown. The old liberalism was giving way to the new. In a public speech in September 1885, Joseph Chamberlain said, "The greater part of municipal work is Socialism, and every kindly act of legislation by which the community has sought to discharge its responsibilities and its obligations to the poor is Socialism, but it is none the worse for that."[6] A younger contemporary was to add to this the Wagnerian argument: "The whole tendency of civilization is, however, towards the multiplication of the collective functions of society. The ever-growing complications of civilization create for us new services which have to be undertaken by the state, and create for us an expansion of the existing services."[7] Fifty years later the self-same speaker presided over a government responsible directly or indirectly for spending a sum equal to no less than 37 per cent of the peacetime national income.

Government Expenditure and Gross National Product Since 1890

We now examine the annual statistics of total government expenditure since 1890, its secular growth, secular changes in the proportion of government expenditure to GNP, and the shorter-term changes in expenditure that make up the time pattern of growth and (perhaps) show a displacement effect in some periods that encourages further study. We also consider how these things are affected by changes in population, prices, and the level of employment. The analysis leads to the conclusions that there has been a considerable growth in government expenditure in real terms per head of population, that the rate of growth over the period as a whole was considerably faster than the rate of growth of gross national product in real terms per head of population, and (what is in some ways more important for our general thesis) that when we have taken account of population growth, price changes and changes in the level of employment, we are left with an important phenomenon to explain—the irregular time pattern of expenditure growth. The examination and explanation of this displacement effect provides the theme of later chapters.

[6] Cited in A. Bullock and N. Shock, eds., *The Liberal Tradition from Fox to Keynes*, London, 1956, p. 207.

[7] Extract from a speech delivered in Glasgow in 1906 by Winston S. Churchill, subsequently republished in his book *Liberalism and the Social Problem*, London, 1909. See Bullock and Shock, eds., *op cit.*, p. 210.

GOVERNMENT EXPENDITURE AND GROSS NATIONAL
PRODUCT AT CURRENT PRICES

Table 2 and Charts 1 and 2, derived from Appendix Tables A-2, A-5, and A-6, demonstrate both the growth in government money expenditures and the characteristic time pattern of that growth.

The great absolute increase in the size of money expenditures during the period is striking. From £130.6 million in 1890, spending rose to £1,592.1 million in 1920 and to more than £6,000 million in 1955. The index of total expenditure, taking 1900 as base year, was 47 in 1890, 567 in 1920, and 2,188 in 1955 (cf. Chart 2). The change in gross national product, however, was not nearly so rapid. GNP rose from £1,472 million in 1890 to £6,070 million in 1920 and then to over £16,700 million in 1955. Taking 1900 as base year, the index of GNP at current prices rose from 76 in 1890 to 312 in 1920 and to 863 in 1955. Expressed in another way, the proportion of total government expenditure to gross national product at current prices rose from around 9 per cent in 1890 to 26 per cent in 1920 and to 37 per cent in 1955. This increasing proportion appears in Chart 1 as a narrowing of the gap between the GNP and government expenditure curves.

The secular growth did not take place in a regular fashion through time; there is no growth trend of government money expenditure reflecting the year-by-year changes in national income. Instead, the curve of government expenditures has the outline earlier referred to—plateaus of ascending height separated by expenditure peaks. The pattern shows very clearly in the two charts. The expenditure peaks coincide with years of war (1900, 1918, 1943, 1952), and, as we should expect, the peaks themselves and the change in the height of the plateaus are less obtrusive in the case of the Boer War (1899–1902) and the Korean War (1951–52) than in the case of the two world wars (1914–19 and 1939–45). This obviously reflects the much greater disruption of the life of the community during the world wars. Also the years 1900 and 1952 are a little too near the beginning and the end of our period for satisfactory interpretation, and in any case the statistics for the Boer War period were collected at five-year intervals only.[8] There are consequently strong arguments for concentrating our subsequent analysis of the displacement effect of war upon the periods of the two world wars.

However, we have not yet demonstrated that there is a phenomenon of displacement of sufficient practical interest to merit detailed examination; we must first see how the pattern of money expenditures has been affected

[8] It appears from these five-yearly figures, however, that the South African War did produce some displacement of government expenditures, and other historical evidence tends to confirm this (see Chapter 5).

TABLE 2

TOTAL GOVERNMENT EXPENDITURE AND GROSS NATIONAL PRODUCT,
AT CURRENT AND 1900 PRICES, SELECTED YEARS, 1890–1955
(index, 1900 = 100)

	1890	1900	1910	1920	1928	1933	1938	1950	1952	1955
1. Government expenditure										
Total (£ mn.)										
At current prices	130.6	280.8	272.0	1,592.1	1,094.7	1,066.0	1,587.0	4,539.0	5,777.0	6,143.0
Index	47	100	97	567	390	380	565	1,616	2,057	2,188
At 1900 prices	133.3	280.8	263.6	565.3	554.8	615.9	851.2	1,195.0	1,311.0	1,309.0
Index	47	100	94	201	198	219	303	426	467	466
Per head (£)										
At current prices	3.5	6.8	6.1	36.4	24.0	22.9	33.4	90.5	114.5	120.5
Index	51	100	89	533	352	336	490	1,326	1,678	1,766
At 1900 prices	3.6	6.8	5.9	12.9	12.2	13.2	17.9	23.8	26.0	25.7
Index	53	100	86	189	179	193	262	349	381	377
2. GNP										
Total (£ mn.)										
At current prices	1,472.0	1,944.0	2,143.0	6,070.0	4,523.0	4,141.0	5,294.0	11,636.0	13,928.0	16,784.0
Index	76	100	110	312	233	213	272	599	716	863
At 1900 prices	1,508.0	1,944.0	2,057.0	2,168.0	2,289.0	2,377.0	2,829.0	3,024.0	3,131.0	3,505.0
Index	78	100	106	112	118	122	146	156	161	180
Per head (£)										
At current prices	39.3	47.2	47.7	138.8	99.2	89.0	111.5	231.9	276.1	329.3
Index	83	100	101	294	210	189	236	491	585	698
At 1900 prices	40.2	47.2	45.8	49.6	50.2	51.1	59.6	60.3	62.1	68.8
Index	85	100	97	105	106	108	126	128	132	146
(1) as percentage of (2) (1900 prices)	8.8	14.4	12.8	26.1	24.2	25.9	30.1	39.5	41.9	37.3

SOURCE: Appendix Tables A-2, A-5, and A-6.

CHART I
Total Government Expenditure and Gross National Product,
at Current Prices, 1890–1955

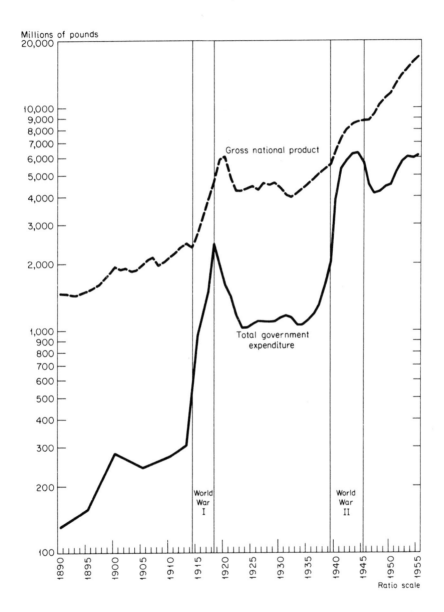

by other permanent influences, and whether the wartime displacement in the expenditure pattern remains as a "real" phenomenon when these influences have been removed.

GOVERNMENT EXPENDITURE, GROSS NATIONAL PRODUCT,
AND POPULATION CHANGES

The period of our study was marked by a very considerable change in the rate of growth of population as compared with the nineteenth century.

CHART 2

Indexes of Total Government Expenditure and Gross National Product, at Current Prices, 1890–1955

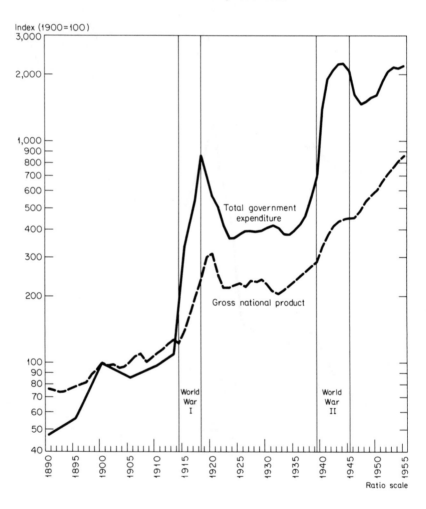

CHART 3
Indexes of Government Expenditure and Gross National Product, per Head of Population, at Current Prices, 1890–1955

As in other European countries, the fall in birth rates and the decline in the rate of change in mortality rates led to a marked slowing down in the rate of population growth. Between 1850 and 1900, the population of the United Kingdom rose by 51 per cent, while between 1900 and 1950 it only rose 22 per cent.[9]

How is this change reflected in the trends in government expenditure per head? Since population has increased, the rate of increase of money expenditure per capita must be less rapid than the rate of increase in

[9] See Table A-1. The break in the index in 1920 reflects the granting of independence to the Irish Free State (Eire).

total expenditure. Nevertheless, the per capita statistics are in some ways even more striking, since they provide a rather better index than total spending of the changing impact of government fiscal activities upon the individual. Money expenditure per head rose from £3.5 in 1890 to £6.8 in 1900, £36.4 in 1920, and to £120.5 per head in 1955. In index terms, with 1900 as base year, 1890 stands at 51, 1900 at 100, 1920 at 533, and 1955 at 1,766 (see Chart 3). In comparison, GNP per head rose from £39.3 per head in 1890 to £329.3 per head in 1955, with a rise in the index (1900 = 100) from 83 to 698.

Again, the irregularity of the time pattern of growth relative to the growth of GNP remains; taking account of population changes in the way we have done leaves us with peaks and plateaus in the same places as before. This is also demonstrated in Chart 3. The result is to be expected, since the adjustment of both GNP and government spending to take account of population changes must leave the time relationships of the two magnitudes unaltered.

GOVERNMENT EXPENDITURE AND GROSS NATIONAL
PRODUCT AT 1900 PRICES

Even a very slight acquaintance with the economic history of Britain would lead one to suspect that the absolute increase in government money expenditure is at least partly attributable to the rise in prices since 1890. The procedure we have adopted to eliminate the effects of price change consists in essence of the deflation of the money data by indexes derived from the capital and current components respectively in government expenditures and GNP.[10] The result can be seen in Table 2 and in Charts 4 and 5. If we accept the deflated figures as an indication of expenditure in real terms, we find that the thirtyfold growth in money spending since 1890 now represents a smaller (tenfold) real increase. The index of government expenditure at constant (1900) prices rose from 47 in 1890 to 100 in 1900, to 201 in 1920, and to 468 in 1954 (see also Chart 5). Correspondingly, there was a slower rate of increase in GNP at constant prices, which, in terms of our index, rose from 78 in 1890 to 100 in 1900, to 109 in 1924, and to 177 in 1954.[11] That is, unless our indexes are grossly misleading about the relative importance of price changes in the public sector and in the economy as a whole (which we think unlikely), the secular growth in money expenditures reflects a considerable growth in the proportion of real government expenditure to community output. Indeed, the disparity between the price indexes (of government expenditure and GNP) is not important enough to make

[10] The procedure is described in detail in the Appendix under "Price Indexes."
[11] The available data being unsatisfactory for the period 1914–23 (see Appendix, "Gross National Product at Factor Cost").

CHART 4
Total Government Expenditure and Gross National Product, at 1900 Prices, 1890–1955

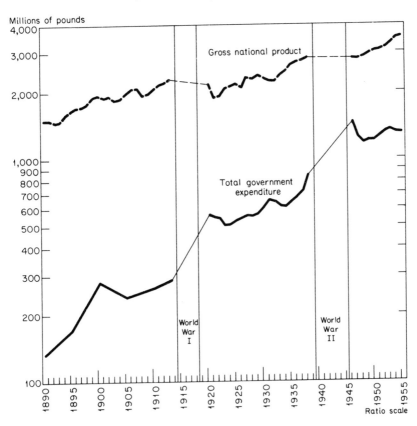

the "real" share of total government expenditure in GNP markedly different from the proportions we obtained earlier by using current money expenditures. In fact the proportions obtained by calculation in real and in money terms (which can best be seen from Table A-6) are close enough to suggest that we need not concern ourselves unduly with the influence of relative price changes in our subsequent discussion.

It also becomes clear from Charts 4 and 5 that the elimination of price changes, while it reduces the steepness of growth, has remarkably little effect on the shape of the curve of total government expenditure. The peaks and plateaus still remain, and at the same places and in the same relation to one another. In other words, price changes alone cannot account for the displacement effect.

47

CHART 5

Indexes of Total Government Expenditure and Gross National
Product, at 1900 Prices, 1890–1955

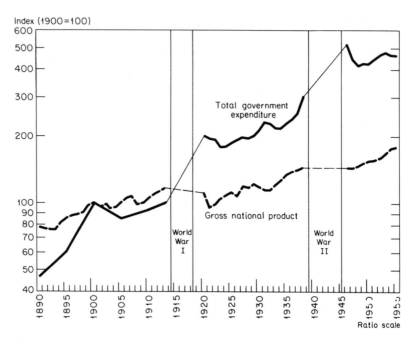

It remains to assess the combined effect of price and population changes.
It is apparent from the statistics already presented that growth in real
expenditure and real GNP per head must be slower over the period
than the growth in the corresponding per capita money expenditures.
But these same statistics also make it clear that the combination of the
two influences cannot destroy the characteristic time pattern of expenditure growth, since (as already explained) the per capita figures must
show the same increase in the proportion of real expenditures to GNP as
do the total statistics. Thus, Table 2 shows that while government expenditure in money terms rose from £6.8 per head in 1900 to £120.5 per head
in 1955, in real terms at 1900 prices it only rose to £25.7 per head. In
terms of our index, the money rise per head was, as we have seen, from
100 to 1,766 over this period, but the real rise was only from 100 to 377.
This is still a faster secular rate of growth than that of GNP, and the
time pattern previously observed is no less clear, as both Table 2 and Chart
6 demonstrate. The displacement effect is still present, that is, and remains
to be explained. Further, although there were considerable price movements during the period, as the price indexes show, the deflated statistics

and the charts provide no indication that these movements were ever large or rapid enough to produce an observable permanent influence upon the level of government real expenditures. In other words, there is no significant short-term displacement effect associated with periods of inflation or deflation.

CHART 6

Indexes of Government Expenditure and Gross National Product, per Head of Population, at 1900 Prices, 1890–1955

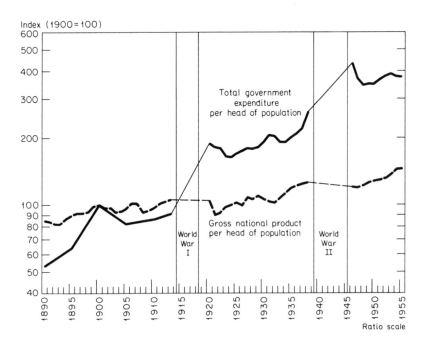

GOVERNMENT EXPENDITURE AND THE LEVEL OF EMPLOYMENT

While the level of employment must be treated as an influence of permanent relevance to the size of government expenditures, its effect, if any, on the secular growth of expenditures is not easy to assess. More interest attaches to its short-term influence, that is, to the possible role of rapid changes in the volume of unemployment as the origin of more permanent displacements in the level of government expenditures generally. This possibility was discussed in Chapter 2; we must now consider its importance for our particular case-study. The nature of the data and the question we wish to answer impose a rather different statistical treatment from that adopted so far. We wish to know two things: first, whether increases in unemployment during our period were associated with increases in government total spending; and second, where there was such an association, whether government expenditures were more permanently affected by the increase in spending generated during the unemployment period (in which case we could conclude that unemployment had stimulated a displacement) or whether they declined again with a decline in the amount of unemployment. Chart 7 presents the necessary information in the most convenient form possible; it plots indexes of the percentage of unemployed and indexes of the percentage of total government expenditure to GNP in three distinct periods on the same graph. This method is imposed by the fact that no series of unemployment statistics compiled on a comparable basis for the whole period can be obtained. We have therefore had to use three separate and noncomparable series, each for a distinct period of time. This is not likely to be seriously misleading, since our interest is in short-term changes and since when reduced to index form each set of statistics is generally believed to provide a reasonably accurate reflection of changes in the level of employment over the relevant period.[12]

The result shows that increases in the unemployment index often seem to be associated with short-term increases in the percentage of government expenditure to GNP, and the relationship becomes especially clear after World War I. The reason for this is obviously the introduction of unemployment insurance in the 1920's on top of the existing arrangements for the provision of poor relief. It is to be noted, however, that there was no permanent change in the level of expenditures following upon periods of high unemployment. Even in the case of the heavy unemployment in the early 1930's, the percentage of government expenditure to GNP fell again when the unemployment rate declined. There was no continuing displacement effect. This is not to argue, of course, that the conditions experienced during the Great Depression did not affect the attitude of governments and of the electorate to government intervention, but rather to stress the fact that the unemployment of itself produced no expenditure effects which outlasted its own duration; the timing of these more permanent changes is not closely associated with changes in the level of employment. However, the whole question of attitudes to state intervention and influences upon them must be reserved for later discussion.

[12] Full details of the nature and method of presentation of the unemployment statistics are given in the Appendix, under "Unemployment Series." The relevant statistics are in Table A-4.

CHART 7
Unemployment and the Growth of Government Expenditure, 1890–1955

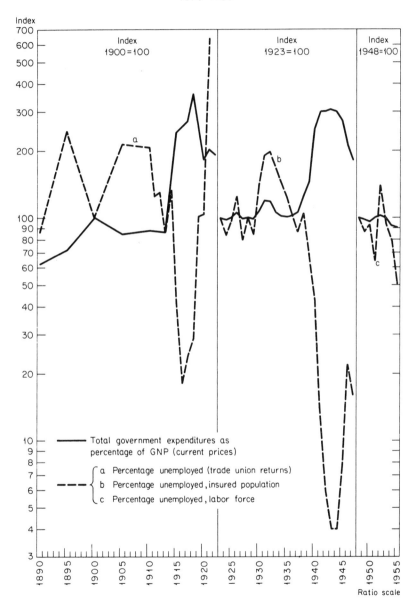

NOTE.—Percentage unemployment, in index terms, plotted against an index of the percentage of government expenditure to GNP.

CHAPTER 4
War-Related and Defense Expenditures

It is clear that the aggregate statistics of government expenditure change over time in a fashion that cannot be explained by the permanent influences affecting expenditures. When such factors have been removed, the relation between the growth of government expenditure and the growth of GNP is still not constant or regular. More particularly, a chart of real expenditures per head of population has peaks during the two major wars, separating plateaus at ascending levels. The association of this displacement in the level of expenditures (and in the proportion of national output devoted to government use) with war periods invites examination of the possibility that the rising plateaus are the direct consequence of the wars themselves. In this chapter, therefore, we shall examine the possibility that not only the time process of expenditure growth, but also the growth itself, is the direct result of war and not of the deliberate wishes of the citizens or the government. This means that we shall have to discuss war-related expenditures in two distinct contexts. In this chapter we are interested in the direct importance of the expenditures actually made for such reasons, as an explanation of the phenomenon of displacement. In the next chapter, where we break down total government expenditure into what we believe to be significant categories in order to examine the development of different kinds of government activity, we shall be concerned with the relative changes in expenditures for war-related purposes compared with changes in government expenditures of other kinds.

National Debt Interest and Other War-Related Expenditures

The notion that the growth in British government expenditure is the consequence of war is of course not new. Indeed, throughout British fiscal history writers have attributed rising government expenditures to war-related causes, and especially to the growth of interest payments on the national debt. The last chapter of *The Wealth of Nations* treats war as a major and direct cause of changes in the level of government expenditure,[1]

[1] See Adam Smith, *The Wealth of Nations*, Vol. II, Book V, Chapter 3, "Of Public Debts" (Cannan edition), London, 1904.

Smith says, for example (p. 418), "That the public revenue of Great Britain can ever be completely liberated, [i.e., from the burden of debt] or even that any considerable progress can ever be made towards that liberation, while the surplus of that revenue, or what is over and above defraying the annual expence of the peace establishment, is so very small, it seems altogether vain to expect." What Smith had in mind is that government expenditure must remain higher after wars because, given current views of the tolerable burden of taxation, sufficient revenues cannot be raised to repay the debt incurred in wartime, so that the debt interest charges become a permanent addition to government expenditure.

It will be recalled by the American reader that the peacetime burden of public debt interest was a major reason why Smith supported taxation of the American colonies—but taxation *with* representation!

and a similar attitude pervades much subsequent writing, at least up to the time of the Colwyn Committee in 1927.[2] Such a view was encouraged by the fact that the conventional form of budget statement, on which these authorities had to rely, exaggerated the importance of government debt and debt interest. In particular, they included payments of debt interest by one government agency to others, and such intragovernmental payments were not inconsiderable. Moreover, the budget statements were only concerned with the expenditure of the central government and not with total government expenditure, and excluded the accounts of the various social insurance schemes. We should expect the significance of debt in the growth of total expenditures to become less marked when these matters were taken into account.

Even if we accept the inflated official figures of debt expenditures, we find that while debt expenditures never became negligible in absolute size, they declined in importance relative to expenditures of other types from the end of the Napoleonic Wars onwards. This confirms, for Britain, the argument of Wagner and other Continental writers whose researches covered a number of countries, that war debt alone could not serve as a general explanation of government expenditure growth, at least during this earlier period.

In Britain during our own period, debt interest payments have become of smaller relative importance than ever before, although just after World War I they rose again for a time to almost 30 per cent of total government expenditure. The evolution can be seen from Tables 3 and 4, but the place of debt interest payments in total government expenditure is perhaps most easily understood from Charts 8, 9 and 10, which show what happens to the curve of government expenditure, and its relation to national income, when national debt interest and other war-related expenditures are omitted.[3] The curve of government expenditure less debt interest shows a displacement at the same periods as total expenditures, whether we use statistics of total money expenditures or of real expenditures per head. Thus, this residual curve starts at a much higher "real" level after 1918 (Chart 9), declines at a faster rate than the total expenditure curve up to 1923, and thereafter follows a more quickly rising trend than total expenditure up to 1939. This is the result of the

---

[2] See, for example, C. F. Bastable, *Public Finance*, 3rd ed., London, 1903, pp. 70–72; J. Stuart Mill, *Principles of Public Economy* (Ashley edition), London, 1909, Book 5, Chapter 7, pp. 788–880; and the *Colwyn Committee Report on National Debt and Taxation*, H.M.S.O., Command Paper 2800, 1927. For an interesting review of that committee's views on debt burdens, see also J. M. Keynes, *Economic Journal*, June 1927, pp. 208–212.

[3] It will be noted that only the total government expenditure curve is complete for the war years; the peaks are omitted in the residual curves because no very satisfactory breakdown of the wartime expenditure statistics is possible (see Appendix, "Central Government," p. 162). However, this does not preclude using the charts for information about the plateaus.

CHART 8
Total Government Expenditure and Its War-Related and Defense Components, in Relation to Gross National Product, at Current Prices, 1890–1955

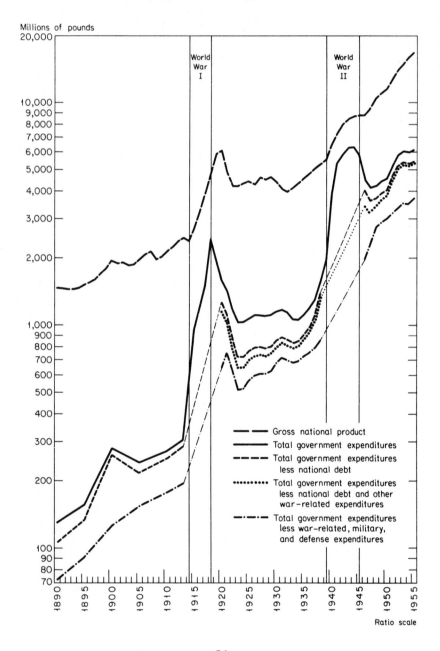

Millions of pounds

World War I

World War II

Gross national product
Total government expenditures
Total government expenditures less national debt
Total government expenditures less national debt and other war-related expenditures
Total government expenditures less war-related, military, and defense expenditures

Ratio scale

54

TABLE 3

TOTAL GOVERNMENT EXPENDITURE, AND EXPENDITURE FOR WAR-RELATED AND DEFENSE PURPOSES, AT CURRENT PRICES, SELECTED YEARS, 1890–1955

(millions of pounds)

Expenditures	1890	1900	1910	1920	1928	1933	1938	1950	1952	1955
1. Total government	130.6	280.8	272.0	1,592.1	1,094.7	1,066.0	1,587.0	4,539	5,777	6,143
2. National debt	23.8	19.6	20.2	324.8	305.1	228.4	212.5	507	609	707
3. (1) minus (2)	106.8	261.2	251.8	1,267.3	789.6	837.6	1,374.5	4,032	5,168	5,436
4. Other war-related	—	—	—	104.7	57.5	45.5	39.4	194	154	119
5. (3) minus (4)	106.8	261.2	251.8	1,162.6	732.1	792.1	1,335.1	3,838	5,014	5,317
6. Defense	34.9	134.9	74.3	519.7	125.1	112.4	469.0	836	1,641	1,606
7. (5) minus (6)	71.9	126.3	177.5	642.9	607.0	679.7	866.1	3,002	3,373	3,711

SOURCE: Appendix Tables A-7 and A-9.

TABLE 4

Total Government Expenditure, and Expenditure for War-Related and Defense Purposes, per Head of Population, at 1900 Prices, Selected Years, 1890–1955
(pounds per head. Index, 1900 = 100)

Expenditures	1890	1900	1910	1920	1928	1933	1938	1950	1952	1955
1. Total government										
At 1900 prices	3.6	6.8	5.9	12.9	12.2	13.2	17.9	23.8	26.0	25.7
Index	53	100	87	190	179	194	263	350	382	378
2. National debt										
At 1900 prices	0.6	0.5	0.4	2.7	3.4	2.8	2.4	2.7	2.8	3.0
Index	120	100	80	540	680	560	480	540	560	600
3. (1) minus (2)										
At 1900 prices	3.0	6.3	5.5	10.2	8.8	10.4	15.5	21.1	23.2	22.7
Index	48	100	87	162	140	165	246	335	368	360
4. Other war-related										
At 1900 prices	—	—	—	0.8	0.6	0.6	0.5	1.1	0.8	0.5
Index	—	—	—	—	—	—	—	—	—	—
5. (3) minus (4)										
At 1900 prices	3.0	6.3	5.5	9.4	8.2	9.8	15.0	20.0	22.4	22.2
Index	48	100	87	149	130	156	238	317	356	352
6. Defense										
At 1900 prices	1.0	3.3	1.6	4.3	1.4	1.4	5.3	4.5	7.6	6.9
Index	30	100	48	130	42	42	161	136	230	209
7. (5) minus (6)										
At 1900 prices	2.0	3.0	3.9	5.1	6.8	8.4	9.7	15.5	14.8	15.3
Index	67	100	130	170	227	280	323	517	493	510
Gross National Product										
8. Index	85	100	97	105	106	108	126	128	132	146

Source: Appendix Tables A-8 and A-10.

56

CHART 9

Total Government Expenditure and Its War-Related and Defense
Components, in Relation to Gross National Product, per Head of
Population, at 1900 Prices, 1890–1955

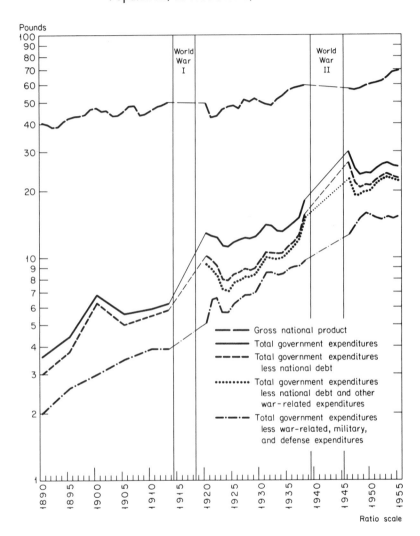

heavy burden of debt interest after 1918 resulting from the debt policies
of World War I, the significance of debt being greatest around 1924, then
reducing gradually up to around 1934, and more rapidly thereafter as a
result of the debt conversion operations of 1932 and 1934 (see Tables 3
and 4 and A-7 to A-10). While, therefore, the curve fluctuates somewhat

57

more than that for total expenditures, the residual expenditures never approach their earlier level after 1918, and describe a rough plateau at the new higher level over the period of the interwar years.

CHART 10

Indexes of Total Government Expenditure and Its War-Related and Defense Components, in Relation to Gross National Product, per Head of Population, at 1900 Prices, 1890–1955

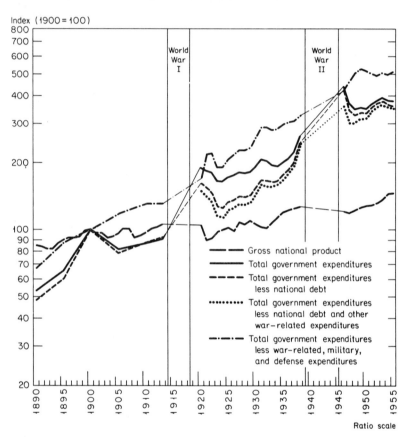

Index (1900 = 100)

Gross national product

Total government expenditures

Total government expenditures less national debt

Total government expenditures less national debt and other war−related expenditures

Total government expenditures less war−related, military, and defense expenditures

Ratio scale

The upward shift in the plateau is even more striking after 1945, and the sympathetic movement of the total expenditure curve and the curve of expenditures excluding debt interest is much more marked. This must be attributed first to wartime debt policy, which led to a much smaller increase (in real terms) in the size of debt during World War II than during World War I, second to the postwar "Dalton era" of cheap money which kept interest rates and debt service charges low, and third to the postwar inflation which has reduced the real significance of payments fixed in money terms. In relation to national income, the removal of debt interest must of course reduce the share of expenditures in total income, but the trend of that share is still an increasing one, as the residual grows much faster over the period than does GNP. The respective rates of growth can be seen from Table 4, by comparing the changes in GNP index and the "residual" indexes, and (perhaps more easily) from Chart 10, which plots indexes (1900 = 100) of GNP, government expenditure, and so on, per head at 1900 prices on a log scale. The increasing share of government expenditure less national debt is clearly shown by the rises in the relevant curve as compared with the curve of GNP per head, and the association of change with war is demonstrated by the fact that it is after the wars that the distance between the two curves widens.[4]

However, national debt interest is not the only type of war-related expenditure. Governments also incur obligations through war for such items as war pensions and war damage compensation. Could not the aggregation of these three items account for the time pattern that we are trying to explain? The magnitude of these other war-related expenditures can be seen from the tables, and their influence upon the displacement effect is brought out by the charts, which include a curve of total government expenditure excluding war pensions and war damage compensation as well as debt interest payments.[5] In fact, these additional items are relatively insignificant; the curve of expenditures excluding them differs little from the curve excluding debt interest only. All the conclusions reached by examination of the latter curve thus continue to hold; specifically, the displacement effect still appears in the new residual curve.

Defense Expenditure

There remains a further problem. The expenditures discussed so far are in a direct fashion the consequences of war. They take no account of expenditure upon war itself, or of peacetime military expenditures for the defense of the realm. It is very difficult to distinguish military and other types of government expenditures in wartime, and even more difficult to distinguish, even conceptually, between military spending

[4] The relation between the index of GNP and the indexes of government expenditure in the period before 1914 may perhaps require elucidation. The base year, 1900, is in the period of the South African War, so that some decline in government expenditures is to be expected in the following years of peace. Also, as explained earlier, the statistics for this period are at five-year intervals only; the divergencies between the curves would probably be smaller if annual data were available.

[5] No statistics for these other war-related expenditures were computed for the period before 1914. There is no reason to believe, however, that they were any more significant then than in later years.

concerned specifically with the prosecution of war and other kinds of defense spending which occur in both war and peace. Fortunately, our interest is in the influence of war upon peacetime government activities rather than in the detailed composition of actual government expenditures in wartime; for study of the displacement effect we can therefore concentrate our attention upon peacetime defense spending. Even so, the appropriate interpretation of defense expenditures in relation to the displacement effect is not easily decided. From one point of view, there are strong arguments for treating all defense spending as being exogenously determined in a sense that other government expenditures are not. The size of such expenditures clearly depends to an important extent upon world political conditions and upon the government's interpretation of its own security needs in the light of those conditions.[6] Consequently, it could be argued that influences (such as views about tolerable levels of taxation) that might be significant in determining the level of expenditures of other kinds would have much less direct effect on the level of defense spending. To the extent that this is so, any displacement effect of war on government expenditures in general would show more clearly if we eliminated both defense spending and more directly war-related expenditures from total spending, and studied the behavior of the residual.

On the other hand, peacetime defense expenditure clearly does not lie as completely outside the influences that affect expenditures of other types as do wartime military expenditure and other war-related expenditures. Politicians try to take account of the financial implications of proposals for defense policy, rather than simply accepting the views of military experts. In Peel's words: "If you adopt the opinion of military men, we are never safe."[7] Like all other expenditure, defense spending requires the raising of revenues, and the governments of many countries (including Britain) are answerable to the electorate for defense spending. Even if it is accepted that increases in defense expenditure are less easy to control in such ways than expenditures of other types, nevertheless, peacetime expenditure on defense constitutes a part of the total tax burden that the community is called on to bear. From this point of view defense expenditure is no different from any other expenditure; it is the total that is of prime importance to a government. Hence, acceptance of the need to spend more on defense in peacetime may result not (or not only) in changes in the total of government spending, but rather in

---

[6] This interpretation will itself not be independent of a country's economic development. The richer a country, the more it may become an object of envy and greed and the more liable it will be to attack if not adequately protected.

[7] Quoted in D. H. MacGregor, *Public Aspects of Finance*, Oxford, 1939, p. 34, in a discussion of these questions, pp. 33–35.

reductions in expenditures of other types. Conversely, it can be argued that if in any peacetime period defense expenditures had been smaller, the likely result would have been increased spending of other kinds rather than (or as well as) reduced total spending, given existing notions as to the tolerable burden of taxation. It is probable, therefore, that in eliminating all defense expenditures we are eliminating altogether too much if we want the residual to reflect what government expenditures "would have been" in the absence of such spending.

Unlike the other war-related expenditures, defense expenditures are by no means negligible, as can be seen from Tables 3 and 4 and from the Appendix tables. In many years, indeed, defense spending has been larger than all other expenditures for war-related purposes, and for a number of years after World War II it was around twice the size of these other items. The charts show the results of eliminating defense expenditures as well as the other types of war-related spending from the global statistics of government expenditures. The new residual expenditures still show a displacement in periods of war (lowest curve, Charts 8 and 9), and the peacetime expenditure plateaus do not show any more marked fluctuations. Of course, the time pattern of those fluctuations is now different; there is no reason why defense spending and military expenditure of other types should change in any closely connected fashion in peacetime, and it is clear from the tables that they have not done so. It is also clear from the GNP and residual expenditure indexes in Chart 10 that the residual still takes an increasing share of GNP over our period as a whole, and that changes in this share are roughly associated with periods of war.

The cumulative evidence seems to justify the conclusion that the characteristic time pattern of government expenditures is not solely the accidental consequence of wars. Some further explanation is therefore needed, to be found by more detailed examination of the changes that have occurred in the nature of peacetime government expenditures, to which we now turn.

CHAPTER 5

Government Expenditure by Economic and Functional Categories

WE have now established that the secular growth in British government expenditures relative to GNP, and the pattern of displacement in that growth, cannot be completely explained by the "permanent" influences affecting government spending, or by the direct effects of war in making increased expenditures continuously necessary, or by these two influences operating together. We shall next examine the data from other points of view, in order to discover what further characteristics of the displacement effect have been important to the nature and timing of expenditure growth. To do this, we shall have to examine the statistics of government expenditure classified by economic categories (capital and current expenditure, goods and services, and transfer expenditure) and according to function, and try to account for the behavior of the statistics when so classified.

We hope with these reclassified statistics to learn something about the indirect effects of wars on government expenditures. However, the indirect character of these effects makes for difficulties in interpretation. The statement that an increase in war pension payments after a major war was "caused" by that war is unlikely to mislead anyone seriously. But can we say with equal clarity that the British Health Service, for example, was the consequence of World War II—inviting the inference that had the war not occurred, the Service would not have come into existence?

This difficulty was explained in Chapter 2. The impact of social disturbances upon the enduring level of public expenditures must be seen as the consequence both of the displacement effect generated by the disturbances (in releasing governments from the "bonds of the revenue," in creating new social ideas, and in stimulating innovation in the fiscal system) and of the pre-existent socioeconomic environment in which the disturbances occur. That is, the consequences of wars, for example, are dual in nature; they change the society in which they occur, but are themselves conditioned by the existing characteristics of that society. It is clear, therefore, that we must place our statistics against a background which brings out the relevant facts of history, bearing particularly upon the control of public expenditures and upon the attitudes of government and people to the functions of government and hence to the mechanics of such control.

"Expenditure Depends upon Policy"

We believe that the displacement effect of wars upon government expenditures, insofar as it is not explicable by changes of the kind discussed in the last chapter, must be the consequence of the wartime weakening of checks that inhibit the rate of growth of public spending in more normal times. Clearly, therefore, the importance of the displacement effect at any time depends partly upon the government's attitude toward public expenditures, which will influence its willingness to take advantage of the opportunities for expansion created by war, and partly upon how war affects the government's permanent ability to raise revenues, either by the changes it induces in the ideas of citizens as to what is tolerable or by its effects upon the technical scope of the government's revenue-raising activities. Associated with these influences, but distinct and important enough to require separate consideration, is the fact that the growth and pattern of expenditure may also be affected by changes in political organization which touch upon the control of expenditure. In each of these three respects—attitudes toward public expenditures, war-induced changes in social ideas about tax burdens and in technical revenue-increasing possibilities, and changes in political organization— the British economy has seen important developments over the last century.

The secular rate of growth of government expenditures relative to GNP during our period is in striking contrast with the relative rate earlier in the nineteenth century. Perhaps the contrast can be explained in part by the absence in the earlier period of major social disturbances, other than the Napoleonic Wars, and by the fact that the rapid rate of growth in community output in the second half of the century gave scope for increasing the absolute size of government expenditures without the need to increase the share of the public sector in total output. But this leaves unexplained the apparent failure of even the Napoleonic Wars to cause any observable permanent increase in the share of government. It might be argued that a displacement effect did occur but cannot be seen in the global statistics because of the great importance of debt interest payments in that period. Thus, when debt payments were later reduced after being inflated by the Napoleonic Wars, there was no equivalent fall in total expenditure, but some of the "slack" so created was taken up by increases in expenditures of other kinds. In the light of the statistics and reasoning set forth in Chapter 3, such an argument is plausible. But it does not provide a complete explanation of the difference between the periods. There have also been important developments in the attitude of the government to public spending. Minimization of expenditures was an aim widely accepted in Parliament in the nineteenth century, and Parliamentary differences were concerned rather with the methods to be used to raise revenues. This attitude to expenditures, exemplified in the view held by Gladstone and others that it was "a rule of finance that governments should reduce their expenditures," stemmed from a particular interpretation of the concept that "expenditure determines policy."[1] This statement, admittedly a truism, has been of great importance in the practical development of the British system of public finance. Its application as a doctrine of policy falls into two distinct periods, in which it was interpreted first as a concept of retrenchment and later as a doctrine of expansionist public finance. There was of course never complete agreement with either interpretation. On the one hand, there was always some opposition to the philosophy of retrenchment from those who gave at least limited support to what Harcourt castigated as "the fatalistic doctrine of progressive taxation." On the other hand, as late as the third decade of the twentieth century, when Harcourt's views had fallen generally into disfavor, Hilton Young (Lord Kennet) could still write in a well-known book that "all the financial operations of the State are an unmitigated evil which is, unluckily, necessary. It is an evil, although a necessary one, that the State should have to collect and spend a revenue. A tax is a bad thing and not a good thing . . . . Could we do without taxes altogether, we should all be better off."[2] But despite these exceptions, it is reasonably clear that until about the 1880's "expenditure determines policy" was for practical purposes a doctrine of retrenchment, and that it thereafter became a justification for the expansion of the public sector.

The doctrine of retrenchment did not, however, derive simply from an objection to "wasteful expenditure"; it was an operating principle of public finance and depended upon a particular theory of employment and the conclusions of that theory for tax policy.[2a] Incomes should be left large enough for people to meet their needs; taxes (i.e., indirect taxes) impose a burden upon productive industry and in so doing induce unemployment and poverty. Such a view, dependent as it is upon a deficient theory of the economic consequences of taxation and public expenditures, led naturally to the proposition that government expenditures should be kept to the minimum, and that economy rather than any conception of efficiency should be the yardstick for deciding upon any change in tax and expenditure policy.[3] In Gladstone's words, "the cost of any policy would generally be about the sole element in deciding its desirability."

[1] It is also well illustrated by Bright's abortive motion of 1870 that the budget should have an absolute limit of £70 million.

[2] E. Hilton Young, *The System of National Finance*, London, 1924, Chapter X, p. 221.

[2a] See B. A. Corry, "The Theory of the Economic Effects of Government Expenditure in English Classical Political Economy," *Economica*, February 1958.

[3] There is evidence that the notion of efficiency was considered as a positive threat to wise administration. Thus, Sir Winston Churchill writes of expenditure on military services "It may begin in all individual earnestness in a simple demand for the reduction of expenditure. That is the first stage. But in the process of the controversy, the movement has been insensibly and irresistibly deflected from the original object. It began in a cry for economy; it has become a cry for efficiency. That is the second stage. The third stage becomes an agitation in favour of an increase of expenditure and a more lavish establishment." *Lord Randolph Churchill*, new ed., London, 1952, Vol. II, p. 313.

Together with this general attitude, the doctrine of retrenchment incorporated a special element which is of peculiar interest from our point of view. This is the importance attached by the proponents of retrenchment to the consequences of war. They saw the possibility that the large expenditures necessitated by wars would be continued afterwards, because the government could always find uses for the extra money, and they regarded this as a danger to be guarded against. The doctrine of retrenchment thus not only helps to explain the slow secular growth of government expenditures when ideas of retrenchment prevailed as compared with later years, but also provides a reason why the displacement effect of wars should be less marked than it has since become; there was a demand in Parliament for restriction of the extent to which government revenues and expenditures should be allowed to be permanently influenced by war.

Dissatisfaction with the doctrine of retrenchment, and a new interpretation of "expenditure depends upon policy," developed in the 1880's, at the beginning of our period. Retrenchment was itself becoming a less plausible doctrine intellectually with the growth in importance of the income tax. This "temporary," almost accidental by-product of the repeal of the Corn Laws drove those who continued to inveigh against growing taxes and expenditures to shift their ground, first to the unsatisfactory effects of the income tax on enterprise and then to the wider discussion of concepts of taxable capacity. At the same time, a philosophy of expansion was being positively encouraged by the growth of the idea that government spending might actually generate incomes. This, in turn, was clearly related to the growth of "popular democracy" following the widening of the franchise in 1884, and to a wider interpretation of the functions of government. By the 1890's, Harcourt, whose support for retrenchment persisted, was saying that "a Chancellor preaching against extravagance is the voice of one crying in the wilderness," and Goschen could dismiss objections to the growth of expenditure simply as "bunkum." The era of "social socialism" had begun; there could be no more complete contrast with Gladstonian finance than Lloyd George's assertion in 1908 that "No one need be afraid of any taxes being taken off in my time." Prophetically, some Fabian socialists saw these developments in state activity as a danger to the growth of "industrial" socialism.[4]

The development of doctrines of expansionist finance did not mean, of course, that all desire to limit the size of government expenditures disappeared. Criticism of the new doctrines was continuous, and further evidence of disagreement is to be found, for instance, in the 1922 Committee on National Expenditure, which suggested (unsuccessfully) a scheme for rationing government departments to keep expenditures in

[4] Cf. Hubert Bland, "The Outlook," *Fabian Essays in Socialism*, 3rd ed., London, 1931.

check. More important, while policy was becoming more generally regarded as the significant matter and expenditure as its passive consequence, governments still had to take account of what citizens would tolerate by way of taxation. The important change thus lies in the government's attitude to public expenditures, in the relaxation of its desire for retrenchment for its own sake, and in the consequent shift in the effective restriction of the size of public expenditures away from what the government wished and toward what the electorate, broadened by the widening of the franchise, would allow (by tolerating the implied tax burden). From the 1880's, then, the notion of taxable capacity began to replace the doctrine of retrenchment as the effective curb on government expenditures. But it was a less concrete concept than retrenchment and hence a less severe curb—particularly in that it provided no similar check upon the upward displacement of expenditures by wars. In consequence, the secular rate of growth of government expenditures became much faster and continued so throughout our period. Wars, which were seen earlier as dangerous invitations to later extravagance, now became simply the periods in which community ideas about the tolerable burden of taxation underwent enforced revision. As Ursula Hicks puts it, "the high level of taxation which can be established in wartime, almost without protest, conditions taxpayers to permanently higher exactions."[5]

This revision of ideas is to be clearly seen over the period of the two World Wars. Sir Bernard Mallet has recorded that before World War I Sir Robert Giffen was thought by some authorities to be taking an extreme view in suggesting that 10 per cent of national income was a reasonable proportion to appropriate for public purposes.[6] After that war, as Mallet points out, an actual proportion of between two and three times that size did not excite general disapproval; the famous Colwyn Committee of 1927, for example, took the view that "the present taxation . . . is not one of the main causes of industrial difficulty."[7]

Since World War II, the proportion has approached 40 per cent, and while (as always throughout fiscal history) there has been no lack of complaint that the burden of taxation is too heavy, the objections have not yet persuaded any British government drastically to reduce the scope of its activities. It is consequently not easy to find an answer to Mallet's wry comment that "percentages are never so convincing as practical experience."[8] During this later period, indeed, the doctrine of expan-

[5] Ursula K. Hicks, *British Public Finances, 1880–1952*, Oxford, 1954, p. 13. See also A. M. Cartter, *Redistribution of Incomes in Post-War Britain*, New Haven, 1954.

[6] See Sir Bernard Mallet and C. O. George, *British Budgets*, 3rd ser. (1921–22 to 1932–33), London, 1933, p. 464.

[7] *Report of the Committee on National Debt and Taxation*, H.M.S.O., Command Paper 2800, 1927. The detailed argument is to be found in the Majority Report, paragraph 702.

[8] Mallet and George, *op. cit.*, p. 465.

sionist finance has been further encouraged by the growing acceptance (connected with war, as we shall later show) of government action in directions formerly considered outside its scope, and by the encouragement given to ideas of "income generating" expenditures by the interwar depression years. Expenditure is now no longer a matter of defraying the expenses of government; it has become an instrument of economic policy. Finally, over the period of World War II, we find the doctrine of retrenchment being stood completely on its head, with the acceptance of the "new orthodoxy"—the Keynesian doctrine which sees government expenditure not as a source of unemployment but as a possible instrument for its cure.

It is clear, then, that changes in government attitudes have been of great importance in encouraging an increased rate of growth of British public expenditures. Also, this examination of the first of the three influences singled out for study on page 63 has thrown some light upon the second—the influence of war on the government's ability to raise revenues. Perhaps the most reliable of economic predictions at any time is that citizens will dislike being asked to pay more taxes. Nevertheless, we have seen that, once governments ceased actively to oppose the growth of government expenditures, the views of citizens about tax burdens were not alone enough to prevent such growth. Whenever wars effectively destroyed existing ideas about tax burdens, the government, now that it had a mind to, was able to increase the scope of its exactions. Also, the changing ideas about the role of government, already referred to, affected citizens as well as governments. Despite the ability of individuals to hold incompatible views about the scope of government activities and about the tolerable burden of taxes, these changing ideas can have made the acceptance of successively higher postwar tax levels at least no more difficult. In particular, the widening of the franchise increased the political importance of the group most likely to believe that public expenditures should be increased for their benefit, but that the necessary revenues should be raised from others (the richer) by such means as progressive taxation. Finally, revenue raising (and hence the growth of expenditures) has been facilitated by wars in a technical fashion, by the widening of the tax opportunities of governments and the consequent reduction of the difficulties of expansion. The tax system, indeed, provides a special and important instance of the "inspection effect" of war. The exigencies of periods of crisis make possible the general revision of the tax system, producing far-reaching permanent changes, and experimentation with new tax sources also becomes possible. In our period, the result has been to produce a considerable widening of the fiscal system, making taxes easier to raise and expenditures easier to envisage. To illustrate, experience obtained during World War I in the techniques and administrative problems of assessing lower income groups for income tax provided the foundation for the permanent extension of that tax. Similarly, the pay-as-you-earn system, through which a considerable proportion of the population now has income tax deducted at source, was introduced during World War II. It was also during this later period that the purchase tax was first introduced—as a "temporary" expedient—and the revenue-raising potentialities of the tobacco tax came to be fully appreciated. These changes are merely illustrative and could be multiplied without difficulty.

It remains to consider the third influence on the nature and importance of the displacement effect, namely, the character of, and changes in, Parliamentary institutions and organization. Continental writers have interpreted the changes described so far as an illustration of a general development common to many countries; they are seen as the British manifestation of the evolution of the public sector from a "participating system" (*Anteilsystem*) into a "control system" (*Kontrollsystem*).[9] One of the reasons suggested for this evolution, to which Schmölders in particular pays attention, is the growth of a "favorable attitude of Parliaments towards spending."[10] The position of parliaments (the representatives of the people) *vis-à-vis* the governments (the executive bodies) has been reversed, it is argued, by changes in the nature of the parliamentary decision-taking process. In their earlier manifestations, parliaments operated as a brake on the tendency of the sovereigns to increase expenditure. Nowadays, it is usually governments that need to try to prevent parliaments from introducing spending that would necessitate additional revenues. This is a not unrealistic description of what has happened in Britain, although the powers of the Sovereign in money matters had been considerably curtailed before the beginning of our period. Rather, what has now changed is the position of the Chancellor of the Exchequer in the government, and the position of Parliament in relation to both.

British Chancellors of the Exchequer have always complained that the House of Commons exercised its influence in favor of increasing rather than reducing government expenditures; it is natural that the propensity of individuals to consume public services should encourage their representatives in Parliament to press for such services.[11] So long as it persisted, however, the doctrine of retrenchment kept this influence in check. There

---

[9] See F. K. Mann, *Die Staatswirtschaft unserer Zeit*, Jena, 1929, and G. Schmölders, *Finanzpolitik*, Berlin, 1955, pp. 132–133. H. Laufenburger, *Finances comparées*, Paris, 1952, describes the evolution as from the "*État gendarme*" to the "*État providence*" and then to the "*État faustien*"!

[10] "*Ausgabenfreudigkeit der Parlamente*," ibid., pp. 138–139. On this point, see also Drees, *op. cit.*, pp. 67–69.

[11] See D. H. MacGregor, *Public Aspects of Finance*, Oxford, 1939, Part I, especially pp. 62–65.

were few items of policy involving expenditure about which disagreement was possible, and in such circumstances close centralized control over the spending departments could be exercised by the permanent officials of the Chancellor's own department, the Treasury. Indeed, in the days of broad agreement about expenditure policy, Treasury control could be more continuous than the governments themselves, since successive Chancellors, even when of different parties, tended to accept the same permanent Treasury view.[12] At the same time, the Treasury and the Chancellor stood at the center of the system of cabinet government. "It used to be the distinguishing feature of the British administration," said Parnell, "that the Treasury was its heart . . . the other departments were necessarily subordinate." This placed the Chancellor in a special position, for "the control of the Treasury is neither more or less than the personal influence of the Chancellor upon the Cabinet."[13] Such a situation, possible while the public economy remains a participating system based upon the doctrine of retrenchment, meets difficulties as retrenchment is abandoned and a widening scope of public activities (the control system) becomes acceptable. Thus in 1919 Mr. Baldwin, Financial Secretary to the Treasury, could point out that a minister appealing to the Cabinet against a decision of Mr. Gladstone would have met a hostile Cabinet, ". . . which in nine cases out of ten would back the Treasury. The whole outlook to-day is changed . . . and all large items are controlled, not by the Treasury, but by the policy of the Government, and if the Chancellor raises objection, and the Minister takes the matter to the Cabinet, the natural bias will not be against the expenditure but in favour . . . . the House of Commons itself would in nearly every case support the Government which was spending the money on purposes of social amelioration." That is, the "changed attitude of Parliaments to public spending" is really in the case of Britain a reduction in the powers of the Chancellor of the Exchequer to prevent such spending. Formerly those powers and the efficacy of the Treasury control which flowed from them could render any Parliamentary pressure for increased spending ineffective. To-day, while the Chancellor is still one of the most important members of the Cabinet, his prime duty is to propose the means by which the revenues needed to implement government policies should be raised. His authority over expenditures is limited to the support he can obtain in Cabinet discussion.[14] As a corollary, the nature of Treasury control has altered. It has become less concerned with "the saving of candle ends" and more with the "efficient" allocation of resources as between public and private

---

[12] Churchill, *op. cit.*, pp. 179–180.
[13] *Ibid.*, p. 184.
[14] The resignation of Mr. Thorneycroft in early 1958 is a case in point.

uses,[15] thus remedying the deficiency complained of by Sir Robert Giffen.[16] This is not to suggest, of course, that the traditional functions of the Treasury have completely disappeared; they are still manifested, for example, in the Treasury examination of departmental projects to be included in the Annual Estimates so as to ensure "value for money." But the Chancellor and the Treasury no longer have their former authority or efficiency in curbing the growth of public spending; the only important obstacles to such growth now are the fear of political consequences of the concomitant need to raise more taxes, and the possible economic (incentive) consequences of that need. Clearly, such a situation enhances the possibility of upward displacements at times of social disturbance.[17]

In the light of this review of parliamentary and social history, we turn to the actual expenditure statistics, classified by economic and functional categories. Clearly, we cannot hope to see the changes in social ideas, in fiscal techniques, and in political control over spending reflected in neat and unambiguous fashion. We must expect them to affect both the secular behavior of expenditures and the displacement generated by periods of social disturbance, and the precise explanation of displacement in particular cannot be free from speculation. How far wartime displacement has been in some sense the fundamental cause of expenditure growth and how far it has operated only upon the growth's timing cannot be determined by statistics. The most we can hope for is that the data will lead us toward those further facts of history that are of relevance to an understanding of the growth in British public expenditures, and it is by its success in this that the displacement hypothesis should be judged.

Expenditure by Economic Categories

Two broad divisions of government expenditure invite examination: expenditures on goods and services and upon transfers, and on capital and current account.

EXPENDITURE ON GOODS AND SERVICES AND ON TRANSFERS

Not all government expenditures imply the exercise of direct claims on the country's real resources, since some part of the expenditure consists of transfer and subsidy payments. Consequently, a study of "resource

[15] Sir Edward (now Lord) Bridges, in "Treasury Control," Stamp Memorial Lecture, 1950, p. 9, ascribes this change to the effects of World War I on traditional ideas about government spending.
[16] See Chapter 3, first section.
[17] Further and illuminating discussion of the development of political and ideological views in Britain, and of the changing character of British government, is to be found in Moses Abramovitz and Vera F. Eliasberg, *The Growth of Public Employment in Great Britain*, Princeton University Press for National Bureau of Economic Research, 1957.

TABLE 5

GOVERNMENT RESOURCE USE AND GROSS NATIONAL PRODUCT, AT CURRENT AND 1900 PRICES, SELECTED YEARS, 1890–1955

(amounts in millions of pounds; index, 1900 = 100)

Government Expenditures	1890	1900	1910	1920	1928	1933	1938	1950	1952	1955
1. On goods and services										
Money, current prices	96.9	244.6	216.9	989.6	560.6	527.4	1,041.4	2,508	3,689	3,810
Index	40	100	89	405	299	216	426	1,025	1,508	1,558
Real, 1900 prices	98.9	244.6	211.1	348.6	285.1	306.4	556.3	646	819	796
Index	40	100	86	143	117	125	227	264	335	325
2. On transfers and subsidies										
Money, current prices	33.7	36.2	55.1	602.5	534.1	538.6	545.6	2,031	2,088	2,333
Index	93	100	152	1,664	1,475	1,488	1,507	5,610	5,768	6,445
Real, 1900 prices	34.4	36.2	52.5	216.7	269.7	309.5	294.9	549	492	513
Index	95	100	145	599	745	855	815	1,517	1,359	1,417
3. (1) as percentage of GNP										
Money	7	13	10	16	12	13	20	22	26	23
Real	7	13	10	16	12	13	20	21	26	23
4. (1) as percentage of total expenditure										
Money	74	87	80	62	51	50	66	55	64	62
Real	74	87	80	62	51	50	65	54	63	61

SOURCE: Appendix Tables A-11 and A-12.

CHART II
Government Expenditure on Goods and Services, and Gross National Product, at Current Prices, 1890–1955

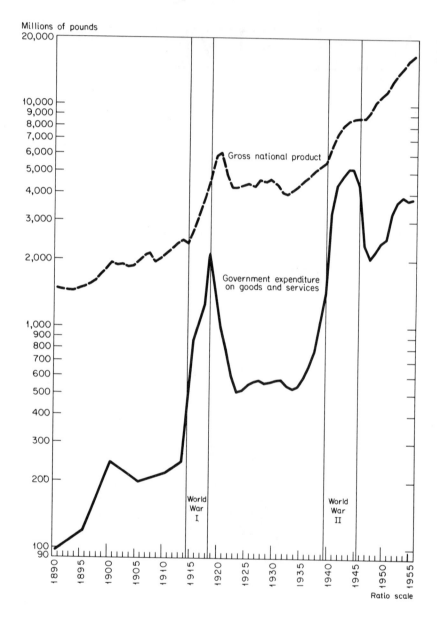

using" and other expenditures is a useful first step toward elucidating the residual elements of the displacement effect.

The relevant material is contained in Table 5 and Charts 11 to 14 and in Tables A-11 and A-12. From these, it is clear that the secular rate of growth of the government's direct claims on community product (as measured by its expenditures on goods and services) is still impressive, if somewhat less than the rate of increase in government expenditures as a whole. The index of money expenditures on goods and services per head of population rose from 43 in 1890 (1900 = 100) to 381 in 1920 and 1,258 in 1955. In real terms, a similar index moves from 100 in 1900 to 263 in 1955. Over the whole period, this rate of increase is a good deal faster than that of GNP; the proportion of expenditure on goods and services to GNP was 7 per cent in 1890 and 23 per cent in 1955. Further, the statistics and Charts 11 to 14 also suggest that expenditure on goods and services at least shared in the upward displacement of wars, although

CHART 12

Indexes of Government Expenditure on Goods and Services, and Gross National Product, per Head of Population, at 1900 Prices, 1890–1955

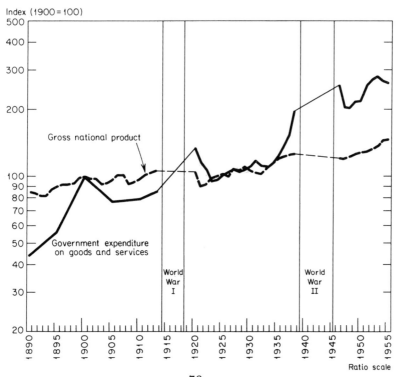

it did not of course account for all of it. Government expenditure on goods and services was taking about 7 to 10 per cent of GNP up to World War I and 12 to 15 per cent between the two wars (until the rearmament campaign in the late 1930's which preceded the outbreak of World War II). Since World War II, the proportion has risen to well over 20 per cent for most of the years recorded. The effect of social disturbance upon spending on goods and services, that is, was less marked at the period of World War I than at that of World War II.

The reason for this contrast is to be found in the changing relative importance of government expenditures on goods and services and on transfers. We have already observed the great importance of transfer payments (chiefly interest on the national debt) during the nineteenth century. Such payments had begun to take a smaller part of total expenditures, however, well before the turn of the century, as debt interest payments began to decline in relative importance. This growing importance of spending on goods and services continued between 1890, when such spending accounted for 74 per cent of all government expenditures, and 1900, when the proportion was 87 per cent (Table 5, Chart 13). Thereafter, transfers became of rather greater significance once more; by 1913 only 81 per cent of all expenditure was for direct government consumption. Following this, there was a quite marked increase in the relative importance of transfers over the period of World War I. As against 19 per cent of total government spending going to such purposes in 1913, as much as 45 per cent of government expenditure was for transfers in 1921 and a half of all spending was of this kind in 1923. That is, the time of World War I saw an important growth in government activities involving transfers, since these took less than one-fifth of all spending before the war and around one-half after it. It is not difficult to identify some of the kinds of expenditure that must have helped cause the change. One cause we have observed earlier and discuss further below: debt interest payments again became a significant part of total expenditure. But to a considerable extent, also, the change must have been due to the great extension in the coverage of unemployment insurance, from two and one-quarter million workers before 1914 to nearly twelve million after the Unemployment Insurance Act of 1920, and to the increased scope and higher real benefits of health insurance which became relevant around the same time. This in turn provides an interesting commentary upon the effects of unemployment on public expenditures. Periods of depression may have changed social ideas, but it is after a period of war that we see those ideas translated into effective social action.

By way of contrast, the pattern since World War II shows the share of expenditures taken by goods and services as being similar to that of the interwar years up to 1950, and higher and more variable thereafter.

Certainly there has been no change comparable to that after 1918; the displacement effect in this later period implied a general increase in the claims of government rather than a relative growth in either transfer or resource using activities. This difference is partly but not completely

CHART 13

Percentage Distribution of Total Government Expenditure, by Economic Category, at Current Prices, 1890–1955

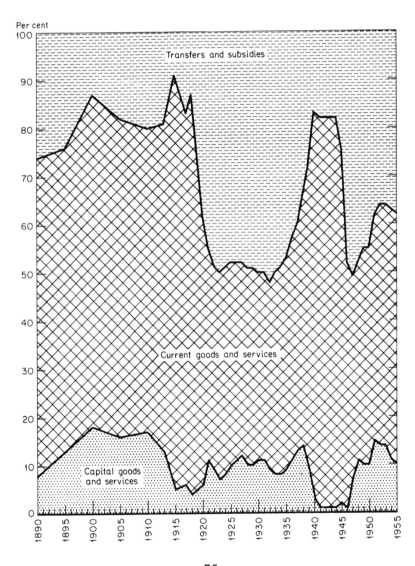

explained by the continuous full employment that Britain has experienced since World War II, with the consequent minimization of unemployment transfer payments.

Finally, from a secular point of view, resource-using expenditures, while much larger in absolute size, constitute a smaller proportion of all government expenditure at the end of our period than at the beginning.

CHART 14

Indexes of Total Government Expenditure, by Economic Category, per Head of Population, at 1900 Prices, 1890–1955

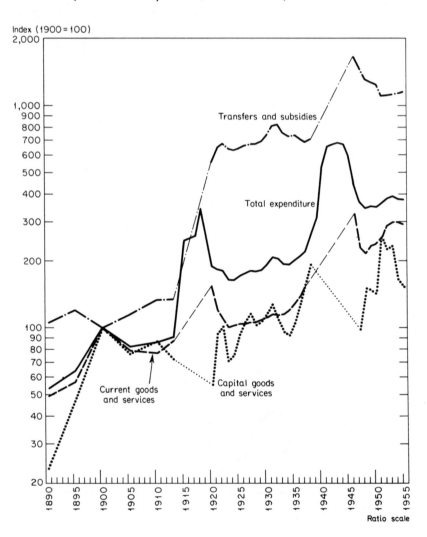

EXPENDITURE ON CURRENT AND CAPITAL ACCOUNT

Table 6 and Charts 13, 14, and 15 show that government expenditure on current account, both in total money terms and in real terms per head, rose during our period at a much faster secular rate than GNP. Such expenditures were 8 per cent of GNP in 1890 and 35 per cent (in real terms) in 1955. Chart 15 also shows clearly that the rise follows the now familiar pattern of displacement: the share of government current expenditures was between 8 and 11 per cent up to 1913, 22 to 26 per cent between the wars, and 38 to 35 per cent after World War II.

Capital expenditure behaved rather differently. During the period 1900–55, when the index of real current government expenditure per head was rising from 100 to 425, a similar index of expenditure on capital account rose only from 100 to 152, not much faster than that of real GNP. But the comparison is a little misleading; four years earlier the index of capital expenditures had been 70 per cent higher, at 258. In fact, capital expenditures followed a less regular trend than expenditures of other types, and changes in their importance bear a less neat relation to the incidence of wars. This is clearly brought out in Chart 13, in the curve showing the percentages of total government expenditures devoted to current and capital purposes.

This irregularity of capital spending suggests that expenditure on current account explains most of the phenomenon of displacement; this was in any case inevitable since current expenditures have at no time accounted for less than 82 per cent of all government spending. The irregularity of expenditure on capital account is itself not particularly surprising. By definition, capital expenditures create durable assets, and such expenditures must, therefore, tend to occur irregularly. Also, the well-known phenomenon of "bunched investment" can affect public as well as private investment, and there are two sorts of reasons for expecting it to do so. First, the idea that spending on capital projects might help the unemployed did not begin with Keynes, though he gave it intellectual plausibility. The direct effects of capital spending are obvious enough, and after the breakdown of the doctrine of retrenchment there was no overwhelming argument against such spending. Consequently, over most of our period we find growing pressure for capital spending in time of unemployment. When such spending occurs it tends to reduce the volume of investment spending required later. In contrast with current relief payments in time of unemployment, for example, it is a transfer of expenditure in time rather than a simple addition to the total of government spending. Thus, investment spending shows a fluctuation over time, and this may then be perpetuated by the periodicity with which the assets so created require replacement.

TABLE 6

GOVERNMENT EXPENDITURE ON CURRENT AND CAPITAL ACCOUNT, AND GROSS NATIONAL PRODUCT,
AT CURRENT AND 1900 PRICES, SELECTED YEARS, 1890–1955
(amounts in millions of pounds; index, 1900 = 100)

Government Expenditures	1890	1900	1910	1920	1928	1933	1938	1950	1952	1955
1. On current account										
Money, current prices	120.4	230.4	226.9	1,490.2	986.0	977.5	1,368.3	4,102	4,978	5,525
Index	52	100	98	647	428	424	594	1,780	2,161	2,398
Real, 1900 prices	122.9	230.4	216.1	536.0	497.9	561.7	739.6	1,109	1,174	1,214
Index	53	100	94	233	216	244	321	481	510	527
2. On capital account										
Money, current prices	10.2	50.4	45.1	101.9	108.7	88.5	218.7	437	799	618
Index	20	100	89	202	216	176	434	867	1,585	1,226
Real, 1900 prices	10.4	50.4	47.5	29.3	56.9	54.2	111.6	86	137	95
Index	21	100	94	58	113	108	221	171	272	188
3. (1) as percentage of GNP										
Money	8	12	11	25	22	24	26	35	36	33
Real	8	12	11	25	22	24	26	37	37	35
4. (1) as percentage of total expenditure										
Money	92	82	83	94	90	92	86	90	86	90
Real	92	82	82	95	90	91	87	93	90	93

SOURCE: Appendix Tables A-13 and A-14.

CHART 15
Government Expenditure on Current Account, and Gross National Product, at Current Prices, 1890–1955

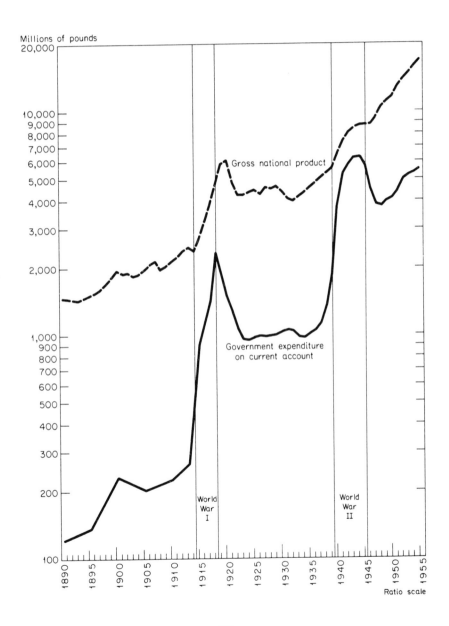

The second and perhaps less obvious possible reason for bunchiness is to be found in the phenomenon of displacement. There is evidence that new projects introduced over periods of displacement have their immediate effect on the level of current expenditures, but that in course of time such new current obligations involve the government in the need to under-take new capital projects also. Consequently, while capital expenditures do not follow the time pattern of other government expenditures, their own irregularity over time is probably influenced by that pattern. The growing problems of providing the requisite school and hospital accommodation in Britain to cope with the post-World War II expansion of these services illustrates the point.

Expenditure by Function

The discussion in Chapter 4 of one important government service—defense—which might account for the displacement effect yielded the conclusion that no complete explanation was possible along such lines. This suggests that a classification of all government expenditure by functions, apart from illuminating further the process of economic change, is also necessary in order to provide further understanding of the influence of war on government expenditure. In this section, then, we classify expenditure in the following categories:[18] (1) general administration (including the costs of tax collection), (2) national debt service, (3) law and order, (4) overseas services (excluding defense), (5) military and defense, (6) social services, (7) economic services, and (8) environmental services.

TABLE 7

GOVERNMENT EXPENDITURE, BY FUNCTION AND ECONOMIC CATEGORIES,
AT CURRENT PRICES, SELECTED YEARS, 1890–1955
(millions of pounds)

Year	Total	*Goods and Services* Current	Capital	Transfers
		ADMINISTRATION AND OTHER		
1890	15.8	14.7	0.6	0.5
1900	16.5	13.6	2.0	0.9
1910	22.1	18.4	2.2	1.5
1920	71.5	64.2	4.7	2.6
1928	49.1	45.5	2.7	0.9
1933	44.3	40.9	3.0	0.4
1938	60.6	53.3	6.7	0.6
1950	175.0	118.0	18.0	39.0
1952	167.0	123.0	16.0	28.0
1955	182.0	138.0	18.0	26.0

[18]The exact content of these categories is explained in the Appendix under the same headings.

TABLE 7 (continued)

Year	Total	Goods and Services Current	Capital	Transfers	Subsidies
		NATIONAL DEBT			
1890	23.8			23.8	
1900	19.6			19.6	
1910	20.2			20.2	
1920	324.8			324.8	
1928	305.1			305.1	
1933	228.4			228.4	
1938	212.5			212.5	
1950	507.0			507.0	
1952	609.0			609.0	
1955	707.0			707.0	
		LAW AND ORDER			
1890	9.0	8.2	0.3	0.5	
1900	9.8	9.2	0.2	0.4	
1910	12.9	12.1	0.2	0.6	
1920	33.3	32.3	0.4	0.6	
1928	30.8	28.7	0.4	1.7	
1933	30.9	29.0	0.4	1.5	
1938	38.7	35.4	2.0	1.3	
1950	79.0	72.0	7.0	—	
1952	96.0	85.0	10.0	1.0	
1955	115.0	103.0	10.0	2.0	
		OVERSEAS SERVICES			
1890	0.4	0.2	—	0.2	
1900	1.0	1.0	—	—	
1910	1.1	0.9	0.2	—	
1920	2.5	0.2	—	2.3	
1928	1.3	0.5	—	0.8	
1933	1.7	1.1	—	0.6	
1938	3.0	0.7	—	2.3	
1950	179.0	39.0	—	140.0	
1952	77.0	40.0	—	37.0	
1955	80.0	41.0	—	39.0	
		MILITARY AND DEFENSE			
1890	34.9	32.7	1.5	0.7	—
1900	134.9	118.0	16.2	0.7	—
1910	74.3	55.5	16.5	2.3	—
1920	519.7	499.1	10.6	8.0	2.0
1928	125.1	120.5	4.1	0.5	—
1933	112.4	107.0	3.5	1.9	—
1938	473.2	418.6	52.2	2.4	—
1950	836.0	822.0	5.0	9.0	—
1952	1,641.0	1,469.0	155.0	17.0	—
1955	1,606.0	1,523.0	59.0	24.0	—

TABLE 7 (concluded)

Year	Total	Goods and Services		Transfers	Subsidies
		Current	Capital		
SOCIAL SERVICES					
1890	27.3	17.6	1.9	7.8	—
1900	50.6	28.6	7.6	14.4	—
1910	89.1	52.4	6.6	30.1	—
1920	411.8	167.0	49.1	193.7	2.0
1928	434.8	161.2	54.3	218.8	—
1933	497.2	167.1	36.9	293.2	—
1938	596.3	206.7	85.8	303.8	—
1950	2,094.0	781.0	336.0	815.0	162.0
1952	2,438.0	896.0	442.0	989.0	111.0
1955	2,739.0	1,070.0	417.0	1,205.0	47.0
ECONOMIC SERVICES					
1890	14.4	10.2	4.0	0.2	—
1900	36.4	16.4	19.8	0.2	—
1910	37.8	21.6	15.8	0.4	—
1920	203.2	102.7	34.0	1.9	64.6
1928	117.1	71.3	40.4	0.8	4.6
1933	111.8	66.0	34.7	0.7	10.4
1938	151.4	72.6	59.7	1.8	17.3
1950	572.0	169.0	44.0	120.0	239.0
1952	629.0	194.0	139.0	76.0	220.0
1955	531.0	220.0	68.0	44.0	199.0
ENVIRONMENTAL SERVICES					
1890	5.0	3.1	1.9	—	—
1900	12.0	7.4	4.6	—	—
1910	14.5	10.9	3.6	—	—
1920	25.3	22.2	3.1	—	—
1928	31.9	24.2	6.8	0.9	—
1933	39.3	27.8	10.0	1.5	—
1938	51.3	35.4	12.3	3.6	—
1950	97.0	70.0	27.0	—	—
1952	120.0	83.0	37.0	—	—
1955	183.0	97.0	46.0	40.0	—
ALL SERVICES					
1890	130.6	86.7	10.2	33.7	—
1900	280.8	194.2	50.4	36.2	—
1910	272.0	171.8	45.1	55.1	—
1920	1,592.1	887.7	101.9	533.9	68.6
1928	1,094.7	451.9	108.7	529.5	4.6
1933	1,066.0	438.9	88.5	528.2	10.4
1938	1,587.0	822.7	218.7	528.3	17.3
1950	4,539.0	2,071.0	437.0	1,630.0	401.0
1952	5,777.0	2,890.0	799.0	1,757.0	331.0
1955	6,143.0	3,192.0	618.0	2,087.0	246.0

SOURCE: For totals, see Appendix Table A-15. From 1890 to 1918 subsidies are included in transfers.

In Table 7, the growth of expenditure by function at current prices is illustrated, and in Table 8 the real growth per head of population. Government expenditure, both in money terms and in real expenditure per head of population, rose for all categories of expenditure over the period 1890 to 1955. Moreover, as Table 9 shows, the rate of growth of

TABLE 8

GOVERNMENT EXPENDITURE, BY FUNCTION AND ECONOMIC CATEGORIES,
PER HEAD OF POPULATION, AT 1900 PRICES,
SELECTED YEARS, 1890–1955
(pounds per head)

| Year | Total | Goods and Services | | Transfers |
		Current	Capital	
ADMINISTRATION AND OTHER				
1890	0.4	0.4	—	—
1900	0.4	0.3	0.1	—
1910	0.5	0.4	0.1	—
1920	0.6	0.5	—	—
1928	0.5	0.5	—	—
1933	0.6	0.5	—	—
1938	0.7	0.6	0.1	—
1950	0.9	0.6	0.1	0.2
1952	0.8	0.6	0.1	0.1
1955	0.8	0.6	0.1	—
NATIONAL DEBT				
1890	0.7			0.7
1900	0.5			0.5
1910	0.4			0.4
1920	2.7			3.4
1928	3.4			3.4
1933	2.8			2.8
1938	2.4			2.4
1950	2.7			2.7
1952	2.9			2.9
1955	3.0			3.0
LAW AND ORDER				
1890	0.2	0.2	—	—
1900	0.2	0.2	—	—
1910	0.3	0.3	—	—
1920	0.3	0.3	—	—
1928	0.3	0.3	—	—
1933	0.4	0.4	—	—
1938	0.4	0.4	—	—
1950	0.4	0.4	—	—
1952	0.4	0.4	—	—
1955	0.4	0.5	—	—

TABLE 8 (continued)

Year	Total	Goods and Services		Transfers	Subsidies
		Current	Capital		
		OVERSEAS SERVICES			
1890	—	—	—	—	
1900	—	—	—	—	
1910	—	—	—	—	
1920	—	—	—	—	
1928	—	—	—	—	
1933	—	—	—	—	
1938	—	—	—	—	
1950	1.0	0.2	—	0.8	
1952	0.4	0.2	—	0.2	
1955	0.4	0.2	—	0.2	
		MILITARY AND DEFENSE			
1890	1.0	0.9	—	—	—
1900	3.3	2.9	0.4	—	—
1910	1.6	1.2	0.4	0.1	—
1920	4.3	4.1	0.1	0.1	—
1928	1.4	1.3	0.1	—	—
1933	1.4	1.3	0.1	—	—
1938	5.4	4.8	0.6	—	—
1950	4.5	4.4	—	0.1	—
1952	7.5	6.9	0.6	0.1	—
1955	6.9	6.6	0.2	0.1	—
		SOCIAL SERVICES			
1890	0.7	0.5	0.1	0.2	—
1900	1.2	0.7	0.2	0.4	—
1910	1.9	1.1	0.2	0.6	—
1920	3.3	1.4	0.3	1.6	—
1928	4.8	1.8	0.6	2.4	—
1933	6.2	2.1	0.5	3.6	—
1938	6.7	2.4	0.9	3.5	—
1950	10.9	4.2	1.4	4.4	0.9
1952	10.8	4.2	1.5	4.6	0.5
1955	11.3	4.6	1.3	5.2	0.2
		ECONOMIC SERVICES			
1890	0.4	0.3	0.1	—	—
1900	0.9	0.4	0.5	—	—
1910	0.8	0.5	0.4	—	—
1920	1.6	0.8	0.2	—	0.5
1928	1.3	0.8	0.5	—	0.1
1933	1.4	0.8	0.5	—	0.1
1938	1.7	0.8	0.6	—	0.2
1950	3.0	0.9	0.1	0.7	1.3
1952	2.8	0.9	0.5	0.4	1.0
1955	2.1	1.0	0.1	0.2	0.9

TABLE 8 (concluded)

Year	Total	Goods and Services		Transfers	Subsidies
		Current	Capital		
		ENVIRONMENTAL SERVICES			
1890	0.1	0.1	0.1	—	—
1900	0.3	0.2	0.1	—	—
1910	0.3	0.2	0.1	—	—
1920	0.2	0.2	—	—	—
1928	0.4	0.3	0.1	—	—
1933	0.5	0.3	0.1	—	—
1938	0.6	0.4	0.1	—	—
1950	0.5	0.4	0.1	—	—
1952	0.5	0.4	0.1	—	—
1955	0.7	0.4	0.2	0.2	—
		ALL SERVICES			
1890	3.6	2.4	0.3	0.9	—
1900	6.8	4.7	1.2	0.9	—
1910	5.9	3.6	1.1	1.2	—
1920	12.9	7.3	0.7	4.4	0.6
1928	12.2	5.0	1.3	5.9	0.1
1933	13.2	5.4	1.2	6.5	0.1
1938	17.9	9.4	2.4	6.0	0.2
1950	23.8	11.2	1.7	8.8	2.2
1952	26.0	13.5	2.7	8.2	1.6
1955	25.7	13.8	1.9	9.0	1.1

SOURCE: For totals, see Appendix Table A-16.

expenditure per head has been higher than that of the gross national product for all categories except administration, whose share remained roughly constant. This is not to say, of course, that the growth has been regular or that its rate has been uniform for each type of expenditure.

As we see from Chart 16, the rate of growth of real expenditure per head on national debt interest and on social services has exceeded that for government expenditure as a whole. By the same measure, the rate of growth of economic services has roughly kept pace with that of expenditure as a whole, but the rates of growth of expenditures for military purposes, environmental services, and law and order have been slower. Expressing the most important of these categories as percentages of total government expenditure, as in Chart 17 and Table 9, we observe that social services expenditure did not fall below 30 per cent of total expenditure after 1910 and remained well above 40 per cent after 1930, apart

TABLE 9

PERCENTAGE DISTRIBUTION OF GOVERNMENT EXPENDITURE BY FUNCTION, SELECTED YEARS, 1890–1955
(percentage of totals at current prices)

Year	Administration and Other		National Debt		Law and Order		Overseas Services		Military and Defense	
	GNP	Expenditure	GNP	Expenditure	GNP	Expenditure	GNP	Expenditure	GNP	Expenditure
1890	1.1	12.1	1.6	18.2	0.6	6.9	—	0.3	2.4	26.7
1900	0.8	5.9	1.0	7.0	0.5	3.5	0.1	0.4	6.9	48.0
1910	1.0	8.1	0.9	7.4	0.6	4.7	0.1	0.4	3.5	27.3
1920	1.2	4.5	5.4	20.4	0.5	2.1	—	0.2	8.6	32.6
1928	1.1	4.5	6.7	27.9	0.7	2.8	—	0.1	2.8	11.4
1933	1.1	4.2	5.5	21.4	0.7	2.9	—	0.2	2.7	10.5
1938	1.1	3.8	4.0	13.4	0.7	2.4	0.1	0.2	8.9	29.8
1950	1.5	3.9	4.4	11.2	0.7	1.7	1.5	3.9	7.2	18.5
1952	1.2	2.9	4.4	10.5	0.7	1.7	0.6	1.3	11.8	28.4
1955	1.1	3.0	4.2	11.5	0.7	1.9	0.5	1.3	9.6	26.1

Year	Social Services		Economic Services		Environmental Services		All Services	
	GNP	Expenditure	GNP	Expenditure	GNP	Expenditure	GNP	Expenditure
1890	1.9	20.9	1.0	11.0	0.3	3.8	8.9	100.0
1900	2.6	18.0	1.9	13.0	0.6	4.3	14.4	100.0
1910	4.2	32.8	1.8	13.9	0.7	5.3	12.7	100.0
1920	6.8	25.9	3.3	12.8	0.4	1.6	26.2	100.0
1928	9.6	39.7	2.6	10.7	0.7	2.9	24.2	100.0
1933	12.0	46.6	2.7	10.5	0.9	3.7	25.7	100.0
1938	11.3	37.6	2.9	9.5	1.0	3.2	30.0	100.0
1950	18.0	46.1	4.9	12.6	0.8	2.1	39.0	100.0
1952	17.5	42.2	4.5	10.9	0.9	2.1	41.5	100.0
1955	16.3	44.6	3.2	8.6	1.1	3.0	36.6	100.0

SOURCE: Appendix Tables A-15 and A-17.

CHART 16
Indexes of Total Government Expenditure, and Expenditure by Function, per Head of Population, at 1900 Prices, 1890-1955

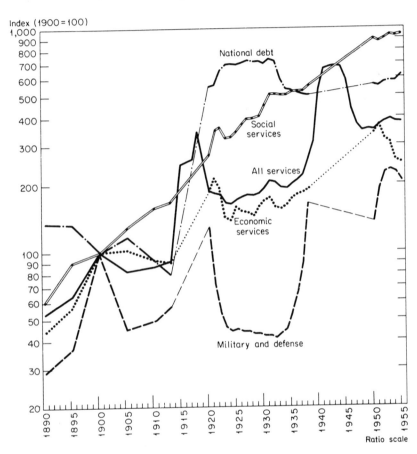

from war periods.[19] Military and defense expenditure in peacetime varied from about 25 to 30 per cent of total expenditure before World War I, dropped significantly in the 1920's and 1930's to nearer 12 per cent, but returned to well over 20 per cent after 1950. Of course, in wartime it rose significantly, although we cannot specify a percentage for World

[19] During wartime the fall in percentage is rather misleading, because many forms of social service, such as hospital treatment and housing, would be undertaken for the armed forces and would appear under the category of military expenditure. All statistics of wartime expenditures by subclassifications need cautious handling, for similar reasons. Because of this, only intermittent statistics are given for such periods (Appendix, "Government Expenditure," 1939-45).

War II. The relative changes in the different categories can also be seen in Chart 18, which shows real expenditures in a block diagram.

The percentage of expenditure on debt interest shows some interesting variations. It fell significantly between 1890 and World War I, rose to

CHART 17
Percentage Distribution of Total Government Expenditure, by Function, at Current Prices, 1890–1955

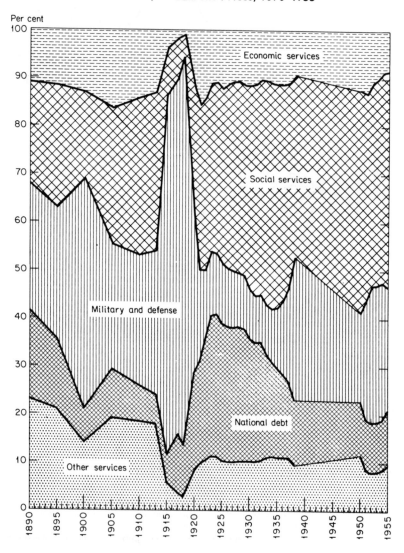

over one-quarter of government expenditure in the interwar years, falling again in the 1930's after the important conversion operations in 1932 and 1934. Despite World War II, the percentage fell in the post-1945 period. These changes reflect the greater efficiency of war finance during World War II, and they illustrate once again why war-related expenditure is not sufficient to account for the displacement effect.[20] They also help account for the greater relative importance of transfer payments in that displacement effect over the period of World War I.

The only remaining category of significance covers economic services. Expenditure per head in real terms for this category rose five times between 1890 and 1955. Apart from periods of war, when such services were reduced, and during immediate postwar periods, when reconstruction was just beginning, the percentage of total government expenditure on such services varied very little, falling slightly over the whole period under review.

Next to be considered is the relation between expenditures classified by economic and by functional categories. Tables 7 and 8 give money and real per capita expenditures by both categories. Table 9 shows functional categories as a proportion of GNP. We find that the growth of social services is even more marked in the case of capital as distinct from current expenditure. In 1900, the capital expenditure on social services was about 15 per cent of total government gross capital formation. In 1928, it averaged 50 per cent, and reached about 67 per cent in 1955. Capital expenditure for military purposes and for economic services became relatively much less important; in the case of military and defense spending, gross capital formation fell from 32 per cent of government gross fixed capital formation in 1900 to around 9 per cent after World War II. The economic services were the most important category so far as government capital investment was concerned at the turn of the century, but by 1955 they had given way to the social services, their share in government gross fixed capital formation having fallen from about 39 per cent to 11 per cent over the period.

In the case of transfer expenditures and subsidies, only social services and debt interest payments are of major importance. Debt interest payments were more than half of total transfer payments in 1900, but less than one-third in 1955, while social services paid out around 40 per cent of all transfers at the turn of the century but more than half the total in 1955. We have here the explanation of the secular behavior of expenditures on goods and services and on transfers which we described earlier. The decline of transfers for debt interest has been offset by the growth in transfer expenditures on social services, so that the share of

[20] See R. S. Sayers, *Financial Policy*, 1939–45, London, 1956, Chapter I.

CHART 18
Total Government Expenditure, by Function, at 1900 Prices, 1890–1955

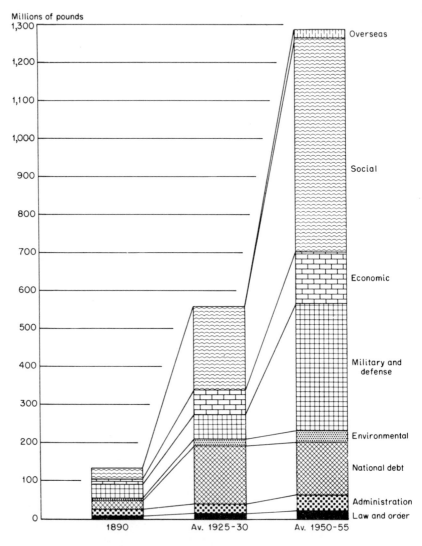

transfers in total government expenditures was larger in 1955 than at the turn of the century.

The picture of displacement that we are now left with is by no means simple. But we have seen, on our way through this chapter, how the successive classifications direct attention towards the most important characteristics of change. Now this final analysis (of functional and economic categories together) takes us one step further. Complex as the final picture is, it yet points clearly enough toward two kinds of expenditures, which by their magnitude and evolution must have been of fundamental importance in displacement.

The first of these is war-related and military and defense spending. It was shown in Chapter 4 while such spending may be an important element in displacement (as e.g., debt interest undoubtedly was over the period of World War I), it cannot alone provide a complete explanation of the phenomenon. Examining the nature of military and defense expenditure in a little more detail will be useful here, however, as a means of illustrating the complications that lie behind the simple statistics of expenditure growth. At the beginning of the period under review, aircraft had not been invented; and during World War I, they were lightly built structures made of wooden frames powered by engines of some forty horsepower. That the airplane was an offensive force to be reckoned with was not demonstrated until the Spanish Civil War, and expenditure on the Royal Air Force first assumed importance during the rearmament campaign of 1936. By the end of World War II the picture was altered, and with it the proportions of expenditure between the different armed forces. Thus in 1920, 24 per cent of military expenditure was for the Royal Navy, 56 per cent for the Army, and 6 per cent for the Royal Air Force. In 1956 the percentages were 24, 33, and 30 respectively (the remaining 13 per cent representing expenditure by the Ministry of Supply on such items as weapons research, stockpiling of strategic raw materials).

The second group of expenditures that the analysis shows to warrant further study is social services. The wartime displacements in social service expenditures can be clearly seen in the statistics already given; not much more than 4 per cent of GNP up to World War I, social service spending accounted for at least one-twelfth of community output every year until World War II, and after that war experienced another upward shift, to take around one-sixth of GNP in the 1950's. The character of this change can be seen in greater detail by considering Table 10, which gives social service expenditures by types from 1920 on, together with the inferences already drawn from the statistics in the earlier section of this chapter about the period before 1920. The great increase after World War I must have been due in part to the considerable extension of social benefits of a "cash transfer" character (i.e., health and unemployment benefits), so that in 1920 we find insurance and assistance accounting for more than one-half of all social service expenditures. This proportion fell gradually up to the Great Depression, when the stimulation of these social transfer payments and the coincident checking or reduction in other

TABLE 10

GOVERNMENT EXPENDITURE ON SOCIAL SERVICES, BY TYPE,
AT CURRENT PRICES, 1920–55
(millions of pounds)

Year	Education	Health	Social Insurance and Assistance	Housing	Food Subsidies	Total
1920	97.4	48.8	212.8	52.8		411.8
1921	106.8	55.8	227.2	100.9		490.7
1922	97.3	54.1	206.1	65.7		423.2
1923	91.4	52.2	183.2	31.9		358.7
1924	92.7	54.0	182.6	35.7		365.0
1925	97.1	56.7	185.7	49.8		389.3
1926	99.4	62.4	194.9	67.7		424.4
1927	101.9	67.1	190.3	76.7		436.0
1928	104.8	66.4	202.5	60.6		434.3
1929	108.0	69.0	207.5	53.5		438.0
1930	113.4	71.9	247.9	51.5		484.7
1931	115.7	74.3	272.8	54.0		516.8
1932	110.2	74.5	278.9	47.5		511.1
1933	107.5	75.2	268.7	45.8		497.2
1934	111.0	75.7	266.4	45.2		498.3
1935	118.3	78.8	271.4	50.7		519.2
1936	125.2	83.3	264.9	59.3		532.7
1937	131.8	90.1	262.1	70.5		554.5
1938	138.9	98.9	278.2	80.3		596.3
1950	440.0	478.0	674.0	340.0	162.0	2,094.0
1951	497.0	497.0	707.0	368.0	165.0	2,234.0
1952	552.0	510.0	825.0	440.0	111.0	2,438.0
1953	581.0	524.0	916.0	496.0	71.0	2,588.0
1954	621.0	542.0	923.0	472.0	53.0	2,611.0
1955	675.0	582.0	1,015.0	420.0	47.0	2,739.0

social service spending produced a new increase in their relative importance after 1929. This change is perhaps typical of the behavior of transfer
and other social service payments between the wars. Their proportions
were not changing sharply as the result of new government policies or of
the operation of permanent causes, but were affected over short periods
by the "built-in stabilizer" inherent in the social insurance schemes.
Displacement over the World War II period had a different character.
The post-1945 period has been marked by a relative decline in social
security services to about one-third of total social service expenditure;
in 1954, expenditure on unemployment benefits was almost the same

in money terms as in 1938. To-day the bulk of social insurance benefit payments represents old-age pensions; the problem of poverty in Britain has become that of the old rather than of the unemployed or of the prolific. Inside the faster growing environmental social services, the most spectacular increase has been in expenditure on health. During the period 1920 to 1938, expenditure on health grew at about the same rate as for all social services, but between 1938 and 1954 expenditure in money terms increased nearly sixfold while that for all social services only increased about fourfold.

We have now discovered as much as possible by statistical methods about the association of the growth in British social service expenditures and the periods of war. It remains to seek a more qualitative answer to the question that this association invites: Why should wars affect social policy in such a fashion? Britain's wars since the turn of the century have more and more affected all sections of the community, both by way of the demands of military service and through the removal of the front line from foreign countries to the surrounding coast and air above the homeland. The conduct of war, therefore, has increasingly instituted a general inspection process for the whole population and economy, which has revealed much about social conditions. It has taken the catastrophe of war to bring home to those in power that economic progress does not automatically disseminate the benefits of education and health. As Titmuss has recalled, it was after the Battle of Waterloo in 1815 that Lord Brougham's committee was set up to consider "the Education of the Lower Orders."[21] The Crimean War of 1855–57 did much to improve conditions within the military services, but it was the Boer War of 1899–1902 that drew attention to the physical condition of the civilian population through medical reports on servicemen. Of course, investigators like Charles Booth, the Webbs, and later Seebohm Rowntree had quite independently confirmed these conditions, and Abramovitz and Eliasberg, in the companion volume on British government employment, have stressed the role of social statistics in drawing attention to social conditions.[22] But it has required major wars to stimulate public opinion and obtain general consent to the extension of social policy.

The evolution of public social services was again accelerated by the events of World War I; as we have seen, its conclusion brought a much wider scope of unemployment benefits and health insurance, the development of subsidized housing schemes with the Housing Act of 1919, and the extension of public elementary education. It is also noteworthy that

[21] Richard M. Titmuss, "Problems of Social Policy," *History of the Second World War,* U.K. Civil Series, No. 1, London, 1950, p. 507.
[22] See Abramovitz and Eliasberg, *op. cit.,* pp. 30–31.

governments had become much more willing after World War I to commit their successors, by the introduction of social benefits which were payable as a right but which were to a considerable degree a charge on the Exchequer, and of housing subsidies—those "intractable items in the national expenditure,"[23] which, even if the service were to be discontinued at any time, would still require liquidation over many years. Despite warnings about growing expenditures from a succession of Parliamentary committees, notably the Geddes Committee of 1921 and the May Committee, the view that social services had a positive contribution to make to economic progress was too strong.[24] The latter committee was well aware that its suggested reduction in expenditure made in 1931 would be difficult to carry out "so heavily loaded are the dice in favour of expenditure."

Titmuss carries the story to the present day in his penetrating analysis of the growth of social services during World War II. As he shows, the social services during this period were an integral part of the war effort.[25] We must look, for example, for the birth of the National Health Service in the aftermath of the bombing of London which brought about the development of emergency state health measures on a large scale. We must view the plans for reconstruction after the war, especially the famous Beveridge Plan, as a real part of the war effort.[26] Also, as our statistics have led us to expect, the emphasis and interest in this last period of displacement shifted away from the simple amelioration of poverty toward that provision of specific services in kind that constitute an important part of what is to-day popularly called the Welfare State.

We have shown the importance of the displacement effect to any explanation of the growth of British public expenditures, and we have now shown the importance of war-related and social service expenditures to the explanation of displacement. It would be tempting to conclude that, war-related expenditures apart, the wartime displacements have

[23] The words of the May Committee on National Expenditure, Command Paper 3920, 1931, p. 10.

[24] There was strong support for this view among Labour supporters in public life. Particularly noteworthy is Dalton's *Principles of Public Finance* (the first edition appeared in 1922), which criticized the negative attitude of previous British writers to public expenditure. His views have their counterpart in the minority report to the May Committee written by two Labour supporters, Mr. Pugh and Mr. (later Lord) Latham, who argued that the "growth in social services is a natural corollary to the development of industry and commerce and it cannot be denied that these have profited materially from services narrowly regarded as amenities, and it is not an overstatement of the case to say that improved health and sanitation, better education, wider and cleaner roads, quicker communications and even open spaces and playing fields are essential to modern large-scale industry," Command Paper 3920, 1931, p. 226.

[25] Titmuss, *op. cit.*, Chapter XXV, *passim*.

[26] On this point, see also W. K. Hancock and M. M. Gowing, "British War Economy," *History of the Second World War*, Civil Series, No. 1, London, 1949, Chapter XIX.

been caused by the influence of wars upon social policy. Such a conclusion would be dangerous, in that we do not know what the level of spending on social services would have been had the wars not occurred. Further, we know of no statistical techniques that might throw further light on such a question. It is obviously very difficult to trace a particular social policy change to its exact time of origin. We have tried to make clear our belief that we should be on very shaky ground if we ascribed any new social service introduced after a war purely to circumstances occurring during that war. Moreover, there is a difficulty in defining what precisely is meant by a "new" service. In terms of organization the National Health Service was an innovation introduced after World War II, but it nevertheless embraces a variety of services and duties that were part of the public sector long before it existed. Yet again, after the wars the jump in social services expenditure often took the form, as in unemployment benefits after World War I and sickness benefits after World War II, of an increase in the scope and standard of service. How great an expansion of existing services should one take to constitute a new activity? In these circumstances, we cannot hope to carry our statistical analysis further by an extension of the method used earlier to eliminate war-related expenditures. We do not know what to eliminate as being in some sense the consequence of war, and what to retain as due to other causes. This is a difficulty that bedevils all attempts to reach precise conclusions about cause and effect in economic life when the "universe" under consideration involves the entire economy and the questions to be answered are concerned with "what might have been."

We shall be content, therefore, with a more limited conclusion. It would be difficult to deny that the climate of opinion during the twentieth century has been increasingly favorable to the extension of public and social services. But it would be equally foolish, in the light of our statistics, to ignore the influence of war in actually stimulating changes both in ideas and in actual policies. We would hope that our hypothesis of displacement, by bringing these two influences together, has helped us to illuminate the nature of expenditure growth as a whole and the role of the social services therein, and in doing so has directed attention to some neglected aspects of British fiscal history.

CHAPTER 6

Central and Local Government Expenditures

WE have examined the pattern of growth of government expenditures from the points of view of the behavior of global expenditures and of expenditures of particular types and economic characteristics. We turn next to changes in the size and character of expenditures by central and local government authorities respectively. In this examination we shall keep two questions in mind. First, how have the spending activities of the different authorities changed over time, in relation to government activity as a whole and to GNP? The question includes consideration of how the displacement effect is manifested in the expenditures undertaken at different levels of government. Second, in what way have any changes in the relative importance of central and local authorities come about?

In Chapter 2 we envisaged the possibility that economic and social change might bring with them a change in effective responsibility for public expenditures, with higher authorities growing in importance relative to lower ones.[1] The incidence of this—the concentration process—is not likely to be completely independent of the displacement effect and of the incidence of wars or other social disturbances. We have observed that it is not easy to show the precise character of the displacement effect in statistical series. Since the concentration effect is similar in its general nature to the displacement effect, it will cause no surprise to discover that here also our statistics provide no more than the most general evidence. In considering the concentration process, therefore, we once again use our statistics as a guide for interpreting history—in this case, the history of central–local relations during our period.

There is an additional interpretative difficulty in identifying the responsibility for expenditures. The authority which actually spends money is not necessarily the authority effectively responsible for decisions about the size and nature of expenditures. The complex division of real responsibility is reflected in the legal and political relations between local authorities and the central government, and also in the means by which locally administered services are financed. During our period, local authority income has come partly from local taxation and partly from a system of central government grants provided subject to a diversity of conditions. Such grants may be unconditional, in that they can be used for any purpose for which the local authority could use its own tax revenues. This leaves decisions about the *character* of spending with the local authority, though it could be argued that the central authority

---

[1] The statistics of expenditures by nationalized industries are excluded from the main body of the study but are examined separately in Chapter 7. Consequently, the only authorities studied in this chapter are central and local governments.

can influence the *total size* of local expenditures if it alone determines the size of the grant. At the other extreme, grants may be for specific amounts and provided for payment of specific expenses. If the expenditure is obligatory, the local authority would seem to have no real influence upon either the extent or direction of the public expenditures concerned. If it is optional, local discretion is limited to a decision as to whether or not to spend money provided by the central authorities. Between these extremes, grants can take a wide variety of forms. In fact, both the size and character of grant aid have changed during our period in ways that are important for local autonomy in expenditure matters.

With this in mind, we endeavor in the following section to provide a background for the later discussion of the expenditure statistics by explaining and discussing the character and history of central–local relations, first from a legal and constitutional viewpoint and then from the viewpoint of sources of local authority income. This provides some insight into the changes that have occurred in local financial independence and in the scope of local functions, and from it we can derive some initial, though restricted, ideas about how the concentration process may have operated. The local authority expenditure statistics presented in the subsequent section provide some further understanding of the operation of the concentration process and displacement effect at the local level. In the final section, the conclusions suggested by the statistics as a whole are used to interpret the historical evolution of central and local authority activities.

The Character and Financing of British Local Government

LEGAL AND POLITICAL RELATIONS

The relations between central and local governments in Britain are discussed in the companion study to this volume, in the special context of the problems of public employment.[2] Here we provide only such additional information and comment as are necessary for continuity and for discussion of the questions just raised.

For purposes of local government, England and Wales and Northern Ireland are divided into administrative counties and county boroughs. The administrative counties are further divided into three types of county districts: the municipal or noncounty boroughs, urban districts, and rural districts. Except in Northern Ireland, these districts are subdivided into parishes. Each of these regions is administered by an elected local council, set up by Act of Parliament and deriving its powers from Parliament. The overall pattern is complicated by a separate legal code governing

2 See Moses Abramovitz and Vera F. Eliasberg, *The Growth of Public Employment in Great Britain*, Princeton University Press for National Bureau of Economic Research, 1957, Chapter 5.

the local authorities for London, and by distinct arrangements for local government in Scotland.[3]

As with so many British political institutions, the actual relations between the central government and the local authorities differ markedly from their formal constitutional position; the conventions that affect the true situation are as important as the legal background. In law, the duty of local councils is to administer policies prescribed by Parliament. These policies are sometimes obligatory, sometimes permissive, they may be special to the authority concerned, which has initiated enabling legislation by the passage of a Private Bill through Parliament. It might appear from this that the local governments are simply the spending agents of the central government, and that discussion of local "responsibility" for expenditures has no point. Certainly, local councils are obliged by legislation to carry out certain duties and to make certain expenditures, and they cannot undertake activities except for purposes for which they have been granted legal authority.

Nevertheless, such a view would be oversimple; the scope and activities of British local authorities are less different from those of their counterparts in the United States, for example, than such a formal statement of their legal position suggests. While local authorities are the creatures of Parliament, they are in no sense under the absolute control of the central government's administrative departments. Ministries exercise control over local authorities only to the extent that specific legislation permits; there are no general powers of interference. Indeed, local governments can introduce Private Bills into Parliament, concerned with their own

---

[3] The authorities in existence in 1955 were:

England and Wales
County councils (61)
County borough councils (83)
Noncounty borough councils (309)
Urban district councils (571)
Rural district councils (476)
Parish councils (7,000), or
Parish meetings (4,100)

London
The London County Council
The Corporation of the City of London
The metropolitan borough councils (28)

Northern Ireland
County councils (6)
County borough councils (2)
Noncounty borough councils and municipal town councils (8)
Urban district councils (28)
Rural district councils (32)

Scotland
(The local authorities in Scotland are regulated by the Local Government (Scotland) Act, 1947)
County councils (31)
Counties of cities: Edinburgh, Glasgow, Dundee, and Aberdeen
Town councils:
Large burghs, over 20,000 population (20)
Small burghs (173)
District councils (199)

activities, and for this purpose have direct access to Parliament without reference to departments.[4] This has not been a negligible power; the history of government activity in Britain is to an important degree a history of the evolution of services by individual local governments, the successful experiments later being taken up and generalized by legal action of the central government. The development of the present education and public health services, for example, owes a great deal to the initiative of pioneering local councils that stimulated the central government to encourage emulation elsewhere. This kind of activity was especially important in the nineteenth century, when, as Abramovitz and Eliasberg point out, public enterprise obtained its most ready acceptance at the local level.[5] This is reflected in the statistics of local expenditures before 1890, given in Chapter 3. Further, both the central government and the local councils are elected bodies, and the electorate as a whole can be greatly influenced by policies implemented at the local level (such as the present education and housing policies). This limits the extent to which the central government can ignore the broad wishes of local governments and electorates, and emphasizes the importance that local authorities may have in policy making—and hence in the evolution of public expenditures—at least in certain directions.

SOURCES OF LOCAL AUTHORITY REVENUES

The one important source of income under the direct control of local authorities is the local rate, a tax levied by them upon the annual value of land and buildings.[6] Such an independent source of income serves as an important means for maintaining the freedom of action of local authorities, and its existence provides a further argument against the view that local authorities are simply agents of the central government in expenditure matters. The relevant statistics of the changes in local rate income during our period are given in Table 11 and in Appendix Tables A-18 and A-19. Rate and other local income has grown over the period covered from £31.3 million in 1890 to £461 million in 1955.[7] These are statistics of revenues at current prices; the real rate of increase was of course much slower.

[4] In fact, consultation with the ministries likely to be concerned with the activities envisaged by a bill is usual, for obvious administrative reasons. But it is not obligatory, and no consent is required.

[5] *Op. cit.*

[6] Local authorities also have some direct income from trading and other services. If imputed rent income is not included, the size of these items is not large enough to warrant our attention in the present context.

[7] There are other sources of local income apart from grants and rates. But since income from trading services is excluded, the column "Other Revenues" in the tables is comprised almost entirely of rate income and is an accurate measure of the growth of such income.

TABLE 11
PERCENTAGE DISTRIBUTION OF TOTAL LOCAL GOVERNMENT CURRENT EXPENDITURE, BY FUNCTION AND REVENUE SOURCE, SELECTED YEARS, 1890–1955

Year	Administration and Other		Law and Order		Civil Defense[a]		Social Services	
	Allocated Grants	Other Revenues[b]	Allocated Grants	Other Revenues[b]	Allocated Grants	Other Revenues[b]	Allocated Grants	Other Revenues[b]
1890								
1900								
1910								
1920	5	95	47	53			39	61
1928	3	97	48	52			37	63
1933	3	97	48	52			28	72
1938	3	97	48	52	63	37	28	72
1950	8	92	47	53	(100)	—	56	44
1952	6	94	49	51	(100)	—	56	44
1955	6	94	49	51	(100)	—	56	44

Year	Housing		Economic Services		Environmental Services		All Services		
	Allocated Grants	Other Revenues[b]	Allocated Grants	Other Revenues[b]	Allocated Grants	Other Revenues[b]	Allocated Grants	Unallocated Grants	Other Revenues[b]
1890								25	75
1900								30	70
1910								31	69
1920	34	66	12	88	1	99	29	1	70
1928	81	19	29	71	4	96	34	2	64
1933	82	18	20	80	7	93	28	18	54
1938	77	23	20	80	6	94	28	16	56
1950	68	32	23	77	3	97	43	9	48
1952	67	33	24	76	1	99	44	9	47
1955	73	27	25	75	2	98	46	8	46

SOURCE: Appendix Table A-19.

[a] Official sources show grants for civil defense as larger than total expenditures for that function in some years. This is an accounting problem. The figures are given in parentheses to avoid confusion.

[b] Rate income and other miscellaneous (nontrading) revenues.

100

In fact, the increase in rate income has been slower than the rate of increase of local expenditures. It can be seen from Table 11 that 75 per cent of all local current expenditures was met by rate income in 1890 and 64 per cent in 1928. By 1938 only 56 per cent was coming out of rates, and in 1955 more than one-half of local expenditures was financed by other means. One reason for this decline must be that the local rate has become a less fruitful source of revenue since the 1930's as a consequence of the derating of agricultural premises and the partial derating of industrial premises by central government decree. As a corollary, wars seem to have had less effect upon the local rate than upon government revenues as a whole. The most striking example of this is the period of World War II. Rate revenues rose only from £206.2 million in 1938 to £315 million in 1947 (Table A-18), which means that local authority rate income was probably smaller in real terms in the latter year. Over a similar period, central government revenues increased about 3½ times. In sum, it would appear that one manifestation of a shift in responsibility toward the central government (i.e., of a concentration process) over our period has been a decline in the dependence of local authorities upon their own tax source, and this decline has occurred at least in part by the failure of rate revenues to share in the general expansion of government revenues as a whole at the time of World War II.

The decline in the relative importance of rate income has been associated with a growth in local dependence upon central government grants. The general position can be seen from Tables A-18 and A-19, which give details of grant income in relation to local government current expenditure.[8] In these tables, grants are divided into two groups, allocated and unallocated, following the classification in the *Blue Book*. Broadly, allocated grants are paid to meet local expenditure on specific functions, more or less narrowly defined, while unallocated grants are made available to meet any local authority expenses. It will be seen from Tables 11 and A-19 that grants as a whole provide for a steadily increasing proportion of local expenditures up to the 1930's, when little less than one-half of local government current expenditure was being financed by grants, as against 30 per cent in 1920. From 1940, grants failed to provide for as much as one-half of all current expenditure in only one year, and the proportion has been roughly constant between 50 and 54 per cent since

[8] The tables give details of current grants and current expenditure only. Grants for capital purposes have been relatively unimportant (£14 milion in total, including war damage compensation, in 1954) and can be ignored for present purposes. The central government has in fact used measures to encourage capital creation by local authorities, but primarily by provision of grant assistance to meet the current obligations entailed rather than by direct grants for capital development. The actual financing of local authority capital development has been done by stock issues or, particularly since World War II, by borrowing at favorable rates from the Public Works Loan Board, a Treasury agency.

1948. Unallocated grants have been less significant than allocated through-out the period. They are of greatest importance during the 1930's, after the introduction of the General Exchequer Contribution, which was the first large general grant-in-aid from the central government to local authorities and was intended at least in part to make up for the losses of local revenue caused by the derating measures. More recently, unallo-cated grants have declined in importance again as a consequence of further changes in the grant system. The General Exchequer Contribution was replaced after World War II by the Exchequer Equalization Grant. Unlike the grant it replaced, this did not accrue to all local authorities but only to those whose weighted rateable value per head was below the national average. The more restricted scope of this new general grant is reflected in the statistics; unallocated grants provided for only 8 per cent of local expenditure in 1955 as against 18 per cent in 1933.

Taken together with our analysis of rate income, the increased depend-ence of local authorities upon central government grants strengthens the inference that local autonomy, and with it the importance of local government as an influence on public spending, has diminished during our period. But for an adequate appreciation of the significance of the changes in grant aid, and hence of the changes in central–local relations, it is necessary to examine the statistics of grant aid a little more closely. We have just seen that the amount of grant aid provided in unallocated grants has varied in importance over the period. It can plausibly be argued that such grants interfere less than other types with the freedom of action of local authorities, since they demand the performance of no specific service. Even though unallocated grants are always a relatively minor part of all grant aid, therefore, they nevertheless vary sufficiently in importance from year to year for comparisons of grant aid at different times to need careful handling. Thus, in 1928 grants provided for 36 per cent of local expenditures, and less than 6 per cent of local grant income was unallocated. In 1933, grants amounted to 46 per cent of a slightly larger total expenditure, but almost two-fifths of all grant aid was unallo-cated. That is, local dependence on grants increased between the two years, but the form of the grants changed in a way that might give the central government less control over their spending. In addition, the division of grants into the two groups so far used is not entirely satis-factory, in that the allocated group includes grants for a wide diversity of purposes and subject to a variety of conditions. This diversity is a reflection of the multiple and sometimes conflicting aims of the govern-ment in making grants, and also of changes in those aims, and in the activities of local governments, over time. To illustrate, grants for a particular service may be conditional, in that their payment depends upon the performance of specified duties, or, less often, unconditional.

They may be completely specific—as for expenses such as salaries of specified employees[9]—or they may be general or unallocated in the sense just discussed. They may be fixed or variable in amount and the variability may take a number of forms.[10] Finally, their size may or may not be related to the means (rate resources) of local authorities; the Exchequer Equalization Grant was directly related to rate resources.[11] Most combinations of these attributes are to be found in one grant formula or another, and the general pattern has varied from one type of local government function to another. The evolution of types of grant aid over time, in terms of these characteristics, reflects the changes in the relations of central and local authorities in an interesting way. Briefly and very broadly, the pattern has progressed from allocated to unallocated grants. Initially grants have been made to stimulate the attainment of a general minimum standard in some particular service. Such grants tend to be conditional, more or less specific, and variable in some fashion with total expenditure on the service concerned. As their purposes are achieved, legal minimum standards can be prescribed and maintained by use of the administrative apparatus. The financial assistance can then become less specific in nature. "Encouragement" grants thus tend to be replaced by general grants, made subject only to much broader conditions. Then, as a further step toward autonomy, grants conditional only upon the willingness of local governments to meet their general legal obligations appear—the unallocated grants.

This evolution, and the changing character and importance of grant aid generally, is also reflected in the statistics of grant aid to particular services. Tables 11, A-18, and A-19 give details of allocated grants classified by function, in accordance with the method used generally in this study for expenditures. It is apparent that allocated grants have been of varying importance for financing different services. The importance of such grants to the social services is striking. Those functions (including housing, shown separately in the tables for convenience and comparability) have always absorbed the greater part of the allocated grants and, compared with other functions, have depended upon them to a great and increasing degree. We shall see later that education expenditure has grown to dominant importance in local social service

[9] Thus, before 1921, detailed grants were given to aid the teaching of cookery.
[10] The grant may be proportionate, for example, to expenditure of a particular type, as with the main grant for education, or to the physical amount of a service provided, or a variant of either of these.
[11] This classification follows that given in D. N. Chester, *Central and Local Government: Financial and Administrative Relations*, London, 1951, Chapter V. This is a valuable book for readers wishing to examine central–local relations in more detail. There is also a useful short survey: Central Office of Information, *Local Government in Britain*, 3rd ed., London, 1957.

spending during our period. The largest allocated grants in recent years have been the education main grants, which by 1954 accounted for one-half of all local authority grant aid (including unallocated grants) and around one-quarter of all local current expenditure.

The conclusions of this highly condensed survey of local revenues might be summarized in this way. We have found some sign of a concentration process in the growing importance of central grants and the declining importance of rate income. The latter change is fairly continuous over the whole period, but it also shows some particular relation with the period of displacement of World War II. The loss of local responsibility entailed by growing dependence on grants has perhaps been mitigated over some periods by the more general form of the grant aid. On the other hand, particular functions—especially in the field of social services—have come to depend very heavily upon fairly specific grants.

So far, however, we have information only about the financing of local expenditures and not about their absolute size. The discussion provides little evidence that the concentration process has been associated with a general decline in the relative importance of local authorities in the scheme of government activity, as distinct from a decline in their overall financial independence. For information about this, we turn now to the statistics of central and local government expenditures.

Central and Local Government Expenditures

Here, the statistics of expenditures by particular authorities are presented and considered against the background sketched in above. To explain our procedure, some short preliminary observations are necessary about the method adopted to present the statistics of central and local spending, the treatment of local housing expenditures, and the derivation of data of real expenditures.

The emphasis in this chapter is upon the development of local authority activities. Although the financial transactions of the central government are of greater quantitative importance, there would be no point in placing them at the center of attention here. Further, we are interested, among other things, in the concentration process, which is most simply understood by consideration of the changes in local expenditures and responsibilities. However, any conclusions reached by a study of local authority expenditures in the context of government expenditures as a whole must provide, by implication, information about the expenditures of the central government also.

From the point of view of statistical presentation, our approach lends itself to a method we have used elsewhere; we show the relation of local expenditure and its components to total government expenditures, to

GNP, and to appropriate components of government expenditure as a whole. For exposition, this method is adequate. But used alone it might be deficient from the point of view of some readers, in that the local statistics can be presented without giving central government expenditures directly; they could appear only implicitly, as differences between total and local expenditures. Since this chapter is concerned with both central and local government expenditures, statistics of both central and local expenditures are given in all text and appendix tables where useful, but only local expenditures are shown in the form of ratios, indexes, and so on. To show these for central government expenditures also would add nothing to our understanding.

The treatment of housing expenditures differs from that in the official statistics, in that such spending is treated here as a local social service, not as a trading service. This is explained in detail in the Appendix notes.[12] However, to avoid confusion, and because of the great importance of housing in some contexts, housing expenditures are shown separately in text and Appendix tables wherever appropriate. A final difficulty is how to deflate the statistics of local expenditures in order to give information about real expenditures per head, a problem dealt with in Chapter 5. Here a similar procedure is used. We give deflated and per head statistics only in contexts where meaningful, and only where the computation has value because separate price indexes are available. This procedure causes no serious problems, since much of our interest is in the comparative development of local expenditures in relation to public expenditures as a whole. For this purpose it is unlikely that the relative price changes in the goods and services purchased at the central and the local level have been different enough to affect our results significantly.

TOTAL EXPENDITURES

Tables 12, 13, and A-20 give details of central government expenditure, and of local government expenditures in relation to GNP and total government expenditures, in money and real terms. The relative changes in magnitudes can also be seen from Charts 19 and 20. In money terms, local government expenditures in 1928 and 1933 were around three times the 1910 figure and about eight times the 1890 figure; the 1955 expenditure was four times the 1933 figure. But as we know, these money figures are misleading. The growth of local expenditures in real terms can be seen from Chart 19 and from Appendix Table A-20. The index of real expenditures (1900 = 100) reads 52 in 1890, 206 in 1928, 230 in 1933, and 311 in 1955—almost a sixfold growth over the whole period. This

[12] See Appendix, "Government Expenditure."

TABLE 12

CENTRAL AND LOCAL GOVERNMENT EXPENDITURES, BY FUNCTION, AT CURRENT PRICES, SELECTED YEARS, 1890–1955
(millions of pounds)

Year	Administration and Other			National Debt			Law and Order			Overseas Services		
	Total	Central	Local	Total	Central	Local	Total	Central	Local	Total	Central	Local
1890	15.8	8.6	7.2	23.8	23.8	—	9.0	3.9	5.1	0.4	0.4	—
1900	16.5	7.8	8.7	19.6	19.6	—	9.8	3.7	6.1	1.0	1.0	—
1910	22.1	11.4	10.7	20.2	20.2	—	12.9	4.1	8.8	1.1	1.1	—
1920	71.5	50.5	21.7	324.8	324.8	—	33.3	11.5	21.8	2.5	2.5	—
1928	49.1	29.7	19.4	305.1	305.1	—	30.8	6.7	24.1	1.3	1.3	—
1933	44.3	27.6	16.7	228.4	228.4	—	30.9	6.4	24.5	1.7	1.7	—
1938	60.6	36.3	24.3	212.5	212.5	—	38.7	7.5	31.2	3.0	3.0	—
1950	175.0	122.0	53.0	507.0	507.0	—	79.0	17.0	62.0	179.0	179.0	—
1952	167.0	115.0	52.0	609.0	609.0	—	96.0	18.0	78.0	77.0	77.0	—
1955	182.0	124.0	58.0	707.0	707.0	—	115.0	23.0	92.0	80.0	80.0	—

Year	Military and Defense			Social Services			Economic Services		
	Total	Central	Local	Total	Central	Local	Total	Central	Local
1890	34.9	34.9	—	27.3	7.9	19.4	14.4	0.9	13.5
1900	134.9	134.9	—	50.6	13.5	37.1	36.4	1.2	35.2
1910	74.3	74.3	—	89.1	28.9	60.2	37.8	1.6	36.2
1920	519.7	519.7	—	411.8	238.2	173.6	203.2	126.9	76.3
1928	125.1	125.1	—	434.3	212.3	222.0	117.1	13.7	103.4
1933	112.4	112.4	—	497.2	278.8	218.4	111.8	18.9	92.9
1938	473.2	469.0	4.2	596.3	291.2	305.1	151.4	30.6	120.8
1950	836.0	834.0	2.0	2,094.0	1,379.0	715.0	572.0	434.0	138.0
1952	1,641.0	1,638.0	3.0	2,438.0	1,506.0	932.0	629.0	461.0	168.0
1955	1,606.0	1,603.0	3.0	2,739.0	1,686.0	1,053.0	531.0	336.0	195.0

(continued)

TABLE 12 (concluded)

Year	Environmental Services			All Services		
	Total	Central	Local	Total	Central	Local
1890	5.0	0.1	4.9	130.6	80.5	50.1
1900	12.0	0.2	11.8	280.8	181.9	98.9
1910	14.5	0.2	14.3	272.0	141.8	130.2
1920	25.3	0.7	24.6	1,592.1	1,274.8	317.3
1928	31.9	1.5	30.4	1,094.7	695.4	399.3
1933	39.3	2.1	37.2	1,066.0	676.3	389.7
1938	51.3	5.7	45.6	1,587.0	1,055.8	531.2
1950	97.0	7.0	90.0	4,539.0	3,479.0	1,060.0
1952	120.0	9.0	111.0	5,777.0	4,433.0	1,344.0
1955	183.0	48.0	135.0	6,143.0	4,607.0	1,536.0

SOURCE: Table 7 and Appendix Table A-23.

TABLE 13

TOTAL LOCAL GOVERNMENT EXPENDITURE AT CURRENT PRICES, AS PERCENTAGE OF ALL GOVERNMENT EXPENDITURE AND OF GROSS NATIONAL PRODUCT, SELECTED YEARS, 1890–1955

Year	Local Government Expenditure as Percentage of:	
	GNP	Total Government
1890	3.4	38.4
1900	5.1	35.2
1910	6.1	47.9
1920	5.2	19.9
1921	8.2	28.0
1928	8.8	36.5
1933	9.4	36.6
1938	10.0	33.5
1950	9.1	23.4
1952	9.6	23.3
1955	9.2	25.0

SOURCE: Appendix Table A-20.

real rate of growth was slower than that of central government expenditure over the period, and during the later part it was also somewhat slower than the growth of GNP. Comparison of the evolution of local expenditures, GNP, and total government spending during the period brings out sharply, in fact, the interrelation between the displacement

CHART 19
Indexes of Total and of Central and Local Government Expenditures, at 1900 Prices, 1890–1955

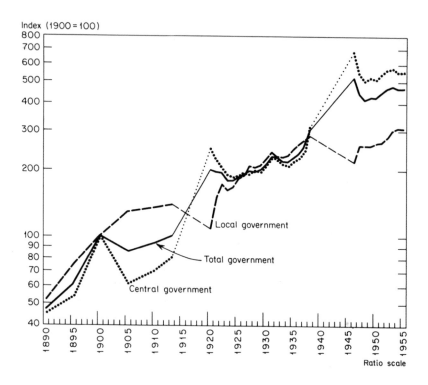

and concentration phenomena. This can be seen from Table 13 and, perhaps more clearly, from Charts 19 and 20 and the detailed statistics in Table A-20. Over the period as a whole, local government expenditure has taken an increasing part of GNP (3.4 per cent in 1890 and 9.2 per cent in 1955). During the same period the share of local authorities in total government spending has declined from 38.4 per cent in 1890 to 25.0 per cent in 1955. We have here a first indication of the existence and nature of a concentration process in British public expenditures. It occurred, not by diminution of local activities over the period, but by restriction to the central level of the important growth in government activities and responsibilities as a whole. As to displacement, the two wars also provide us with contrasting developments. In 1910, local expenditures were 6.1 per cent of GNP and almost 48 per cent of all government expenditure; in 1921, 8.2 per cent of GNP but only 28 per cent of total government spending. That is, local authority expenditures

108

did share in the displacement effect of World War I, but not to the same extent as the central government; the concentration process takes the form of a relatively more rapid growth of central responsibilities. Between the wars, the share of local expenditures in total government spending

CHART 20

Percentage Distribution of Total Government Expenditure, by Spending Authority, 1890–1955

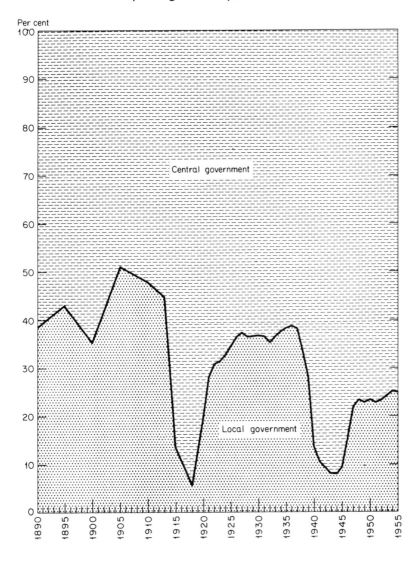

and its proportion of GNP remained roughly constant, as the charts show. Further, the share taken of GNP is little affected by World War II; it was 9.6 per cent in 1936 and 9.5 per cent in 1948. But over this same period the share of local spending in total government spending fell from 38.8 per cent to 23.4 per cent. Thus the displacement effect seems to have occurred entirely at the central level over the period of World War II. That period must also have been one of relative growth in central responsibilities as against local, with local activities failing to share in displacement at all. These findings confirm and extend the conclusions reached in the examination of local revenues in the previous section.

LOCAL EXPENDITURE BY ECONOMIC CATEGORY

Following the procedure used in Chapter 5, we shall discuss expenditures on goods and services and transfers, and on current and capital account.

The first point of interest suggested by Tables 14 and A-21 is the relative unimportance of local transfer payments (which include housing transfers). Transfer payments never account for much more than a tenth of all local expenditures, and the proportion is both more constant and much smaller than for government expenditure as a whole, of which transfers and subsidies were nearly two-fifths in 1955, around one-half in 1928, and 20 to 25 per cent before 1913. Local authorities have always been providers of local communal services rather than redistributors of income, as the statistics of transfer expenditures reflect. Nevertheless, over our period, local transfer payments have become rather more important. At the turn of the century, transfers were less than 4 per cent of all local spending, and around 10 per cent of all government transfer expenditure (Table A-21). Since World War II the proportion of transfers to all local spending has been between 7.5 and 10 per cent (3.5 to 6.3 per cent of all transfers).[13] The nature of transfer payments has also changed in a way that illuminates the changing character of local responsibilities. Table 14 shows that all local transfers were for social service functions during the period under review. Table A-22 shows how the different types of social service shared in total transfers payments. Up to World War I, transfers with negligible exceptions were for relief purposes. Housing and education transfers were introduced after that war, but local transfers continued to be primarily concerned with the relief of poverty and distress; as was indicated earlier, local authorities have played an important part in the development of this kind of social service. The situation was very different by the 1950's, all important relief activities

[13] These figures include the central government housing subsidy, for reasons discussed earlier. As this is a significant item in the context, it is shown separately for the relevant years in Table 14 and in Appendix tables.

110

TABLE 14
LOCAL GOVERNMENT EXPENDITURE, BY FUNCTION AND BY ECONOMIC CATEGORY, AT CURRENT PRICES, SELECTED YEARS, 1890-1955
(millions of pounds)

YEAR	ADMINISTRATION AND OTHER			LAW AND ORDER			CIVIL DEFENSE			SOCIAL SERVICES			
		Goods and Services			Goods and Services			Goods and Services			Goods and Services		
	Total	Current	Capital	Total	Current	Capital	Total	Current	Capital	Total	Current	Capital	Transfers
1890	7.2	6.9	0.3	5.1	4.8	0.3				19.4	14.3	1.9	3.2
1900	8.7	7.1	1.6	6.1	6.0	0.1				37.1	25.8	7.6	3.7
1910	10.7	9.2	1.5	8.8	8.7	0.1				60.2	49.2	6.6	4.4
1920	21.0	19.0	2.0	21.8	21.6	0.2				127.9	116.3	3.6	8.0
1928	19.4	17.7	1.7	24.1	23.8	0.3				162.8	133.5	9.8	19.5
1933	16.7	13.9	2.8	24.5	24.2	0.3				172.9	138.8	9.6	24.5
1938	24.3	18.6	5.7	31.2	29.5	1.7	4.2	3.5	0.7	225.1	171.6	28.2	25.3
1950	53.0	48.0	5.0	62.0	57.0	5.0	2.0	2.0	—	411.0	316.0	56.0	39.0
1952	52.0	47.0	5.0	78.0	69.0	9.0	3.0	3.0	—	526.0	401.0	77.0	48.0
1955	58.0	51.0	7.0	92.0	83.0	9.0	3.0	3.0	—	658.0	505.0	82.0	71.0

YEAR	HOUSING			ECONOMIC SERVICES			ENVIRONMENTAL SERVICES			ALL SERVICES			
	Goods and Services				Goods and Services			Goods and Services			Goods and Services		
	Total	Capital	Transfers	Total	Current	Capital	Total	Current	Capital	Total	Current	Capital	Transfers
1890				13.5	9.5	4.0	4.9	3.0	1.9	50.1	38.5	8.4	3.2
1900				35.2	15.5	19.7	11.8	7.3	4.5	98.9	61.7	33.5	3.7
1910				36.2	20.4	15.8	14.3	10.7	3.6	130.2	98.2	27.6	4.4
1920	45.7	43.8	1.9	76.3	42.7	33.6	24.6	21.5	3.1	317.3	221.1	86.3	9.9
1928	59.2	44.2	15.0	103.4	63.2	40.2	30.4	23.6	6.8	399.3	261.8	103.0	34.5
1933	45.5	27.0	18.5	92.9	58.3	34.6	37.2	27.2	10.0	389.7	262.4	84.3	43.0
1938	80.0	57.1	22.9	120.8	63.5	57.3	45.6	33.3	12.3	531.2	320.0	163.0	48.2
1950	304.0	264.0	40.0	138.0	91.0	47.0	90.0	63.0	27.0	1,060.0	577.0	404.0	79.0
1952	406.0	352.0	54.0	168.0	107.0	61.0	111.0	74.0	37.0	1,344.0	701.0	541.0	102.0
1955	395.0	318.0	77.0	195.0	127.0	68.0	135.0	89.0	46.0	1,536.0	858.0	530.0	148.0

SOURCE: Appendix Table A-23, for totals only.

(unemployment, health and old age insurance, and most medical care) being the responsibility of the central government and its organs. Even outdoor relief became the responsibility of the central government in 1948. Now, therefore, all local government transfers are for housing or education, services not related solely or directly to the amelioration of poverty. Housing subsidies accrue to tenants of local authority houses, a group by no means confined at present to the poverty stricken. Education transfers, which have increased greatly in relative size—almost 45 per cent of all local government transfers in 1954—accrue to all families with school-age children, being subsidy payments for school meals and milk.

The breakdown of expenditure by current and capital outlays in Tables 14 and 15 informs us about other aspects of the evolution of local expenditures. Current expenditure by local authorities has fluctuated less than expenditure on capital account. This would be expected in view of the nature of capital expenditures. It accords with the behavior of total government capital expenditure, discussed in the preceding chapter. However, capital expenditures are a more significant item in local than in central government spending. Whereas capital spending is never as much as 20 per cent of all government spending, its proportion in total local spending was higher than that in most years, reaching one-third in some years before 1938 and as much as 40 per cent in some years after World War II. For much of the period the explanation of the difference lies in the responsibilities of local authorities for housing, which from 1918 on has been easily the most significant item of local capital expenditure and has been growing in relative importance. Its growth accounts for the increased importance of capital expenditure in local expenditures over the period as a whole, and for a great deal of the displacement in local expenditures observed over the years of World War I. Negligible before 1918, housing capital expenditures were one-half of all local capital expenditures in 1920 and three-fifths in 1955.

The statistics of local capital formation are shown in Table A-21 in the context of total capital formation by government. Local governments were responsible for around 60 per cent of the (relatively small) government capital creation before 1914. After the war, with the growth in housing expenditures, they accounted for almost the whole of public capital formation until the mid-1930's. Since World War II, local governments have remained important in the process of government capital formation, but new types of central capital spending have developed, with the result that the share of local authorities in capital formation by government has fluctuated widely since 1948. It is noteworthy, however, that as recently as 1954 local authorities accounted for more than 90 per cent of the annual public capital creation.

112

TABLE 15

PERCENTAGE DISTRIBUTION OF LOCAL GOVERNMENT EXPENDITURE, BY FUNCTION AND ECONOMIC CATEGORY, SELECTED YEARS, 1890–1955

| | FUNCTION | | | | | | | ECONOMIC CATEGORY | | |
| | | | | | | | | Goods and Services | | |
YEAR	Administration and Other	Law and Order	Civil Defense	Social Services	Housing	Economic Services	Environmental Services	Current	Capital	Transfers
1890	14.4	10.2		38.7		26.9	9.8	76.8	16.8	6.4
1900	8.8	6.2		37.5		35.6	11.9	62.4	33.9	3.7
1910	8.2	6.8		46.2		27.8	11.0	75.4	21.2	3.4
1920	6.6	6.9		40.3	14.4	24.0	7.8	69.7	27.2	3.1
1928	4.9	6.0		40.8	14.8	25.9	7.6	65.6	25.8	8.6
1933	4.3	6.3		44.4	11.7	23.8	9.5	67.3	21.7	11.0
1938	4.6	5.9	0.8	42.4	15.1	22.7	8.6	60.2	30.7	9.1
1950	5.0	5.8	0.2	38.8	28.7	13.0	8.5	54.4	38.1	7.5
1952	3.9	5.8	0.2	39.1	30.2	12.5	8.3	52.1	40.3	7.6
1955	3.8	6.0	0.2	42.8	25.7	12.7	8.8	55.9	34.5	9.6

SOURCE: Appendix Tables A-21 and A-23.

Examination of local expenditures thus sheds a little more light on the character of the displacement effect and the concentration process at the local level. Most significantly, we have found in capital (housing) expenditures one of the important reasons why local authorities shared in the displacement effect over the period of World War I. Less important statistically, but valuable as a clue to the nature of the concentration process, is the discovery that local authorities seem to have lost one of their traditional (transfer) functions in the amelioration of poverty and distress. Transfers of a previously less characteristic kind have come to take a rather larger (though still not important) share of local expenditures in the period since World War I.

Here the statistical examination of central–local expenditures follows the functional classification used earlier. Table 12, for example, is derived in part from the corresponding Table 7 in Chapter 5.

Tables 12, 14, 15, and 16, the corresponding Appendix tables, and Chart 21 bring out the essential features about the evolution of central and local services respectively by functional categories. Expenditure on social services has been the outstanding element in local spending over the whole period of study, and has grown in relative importance. Social services including housing accounted for almost 40 per cent of all local expenditures in 1890, 46 per cent in 1910, 57 per cent in 1922, and around 56 per cent in 1933. In 1952 and 1955 the proportion had risen to almost 70 per cent (Tables 15 and A-23). Over the whole period, the share of social service expenditure in local government spending is greater than the share of such expenditures in the aggregate of public expenditures. But the growth in importance of such expenditures in the pattern of government expenditure as a whole (see Table A-15 and Charts 16 and 17) is much greater than their growth in relative importance at the local level. Further, the statistics for social services other than housing show that they took a smaller share of total local government expenditure after World War I and again after World War II. The concentration process, that is, has operated partly by the decline in relative importance of local authorities as purveyors of social services other than housing, even though it remains their most important group of activities.

The social service expenditure of local authorities is so important in the pattern of local expenditure as a whole that a more detailed examination is required. The global statistics of social service spending in fact conceal important developments, foreshadowed in the discussion of local revenues. The observed significance of housing expenditure for the growth of local capital spending has been paralleled in current spending by the growth in relative importance of education expenditure. In 1933, little

TABLE 16

LOCAL GOVERNMENT EXPENDITURE, BY FUNCTION, AS PERCENTAGE OF TOTAL GOVERNMENT EXPENDITURE ON EACH FUNCTION, SELECTED YEARS, 1890–1955

Year	Administration and Other	Law and Order	Military and Defense	Social Services	Housing	Economic Services	Environmental Services	All Services
1890	46	57		71		94	98	38
1900	53	62		73		97	98	35
1910	48	68		68		96	99	48
1920	29	65		35	100	38	97	20
1928	40	78		43	100	88	95	36
1933	38	79		38	100	83	95	37
1938	40	81	1	44	100	80	89	33
1950	30	78	—	23	89	24	93	23
1952	31	81	—	26	92	27	93	23
1955	32	80	—	28	94	37	74	25

SOURCE: Appendix Table A-24

115

more than one-half of local social service expenditure was on education; in 1953, the proportion had reached 73 per cent. Even when housing expenditure became important after 1920, it was never more than two-thirds the size of current spending on education until the years after

CHART 21

Percentage Distribution of Local Government Expenditure, by Function, 1890–1955

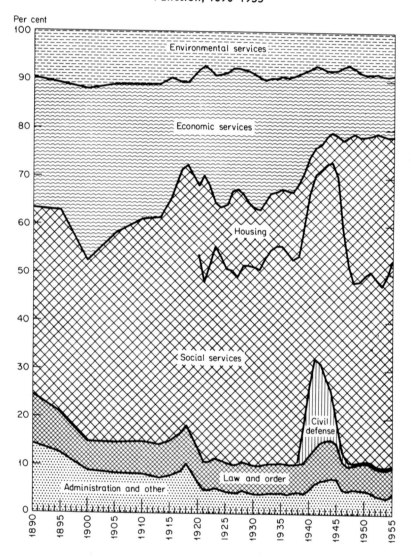

World War II. The importance of the growth can be seen in another way: current spending on education was almost one-fourth of all local expenditure in 1920, 1928, and 1933, and around two-thirds of the total after World War II. In contrast, expenditure on health was around one-sixth of local current expenditure in 1917 and 1920, one-fifth in 1933, and rather less than one-sixth in 1952. Poor relief, the remaining part of social service expenditure, was one-fifth of current local expenditure in 1920, and almost one-fourth in 1933. In 1952 it was less than one-thirtieth, and smaller in money terms than in 1917. The figures reinforce our earlier conclusion about the decline of local relief functions.

Of the other functions supported by local authorities, economic and environmental services are next in importance to social services for almost all of our period, but even together their significance is always much smaller than that of social service expenditure alone (Table 15). They are of greater importance in the pattern of local spending than in the pattern of government spending as a whole; for whereas at the local level they are the only functions of importance outside the social services, they account for a smaller share of central (and total) expenditure than either the national debt interest or military costs. Such war-related expenditures are of negligible importance at the local level. War debt interest does not exist at all,[14] and the military spending of local government, confined to civil defense, has been quite unimportant except in the actual years of World War II.

Finally, Tables 16 and A-24 bring out the importance of local spending on particular functions in the scheme of government activity as a whole. Apart from the social services, the most striking feature is the importance of local authorities as providers of environmental services—these are primarily basic amenities that are often specifically local in character. The total expenditure concerned, however, is never much more than one-tenth of total local expenditure. In contrast, the relative importance of local authorities as providers of economic services declined markedly after both wars—this again was to be expected, since those services are particularly likely to be affected by economic change and the widening of possible market areas, and hence are highly likely to show the effects of a concentration process over periods such as the one being studied.

General Conclusions

It is evident that considerable changes have occurred in the relative importance and broad responsibilities of central and local authorities during our period. These changes are revealed in many ways in the statistics, and particularly by the fact that growth in local spending,

[14] See Appendix, "Government Expenditure on Current Account."

117

while a little faster than growth in GNP over the whole period, has been much slower than growth in government expenditure as a whole. That is, there has been a change in the relative importance of central and local levels of government—described here as the concentration process. Further, the concentration process has been shown to have some relation to periods of war, as demonstrated by the failure of local authorities to share fully in the upward displacement in government spending after World War I, or to share at all in the displacement after World War II. The concentration process can be seen also in the failure of local authorities to increase their revenues over periods of war to the same degree as the central government has.

Some such association of the concentration process with wars was to be expected. Wars are times when the resources of the community have to be mobilized for specific purposes and by inevitably authoritarian methods, with slight regard for such issues as the desire to decentralize authority or to preserve local autonomy. Consequently, it is the central government that finds itself with expanded revenue sources in the aftermath of war. However, the relative inadequacy of local resources which arises in this way need not in itself imply a decline in the relative importance of local expenditure. Financing for local activities can be provided by the central government, so that local authorities are enabled to share in the general growth of government. We have indeed seen that local authorities have become increasingly dependent upon grants-in-aid; the reduced relative importance of local expenditures has occurred despite this. For further explanation we have to look to the character of the displacement effect. The effect of war on the level of expenditures, as well as upon the availability of revenues, is more likely to show itself at the central than at the local level. This is not only because war-related expenditures are outside the scope of local activities, so that to the extent that such expenditures affect the continuing level of total spending they must enhance the relative importance of the central government. It is also due to the fact that it is at the level of central rather than local government that the "inspection effect" of war is likely to influence social ideas, providing a bias toward central rather than local control of new government activities.

It would be a mistake, however, to overemphasize the importance of wars to the concentration process. They are by no means the sole factor involved, and the concentration process (unlike the displacement effect) is not confined to such periods (Chapter 2). A number of other influences, some of them conflicting, have also affected the scope of local government functions during the period under review.[15]

[15] For further discussion of influences upon the evolution of local government, see also Abramovitz and Eliasberg, *op. cit.*, pp. 21–23.

118

First, the *nature of the economic environment* in which local governments operate has changed greatly since 1890. Local governments have been particularly affected by rising standards of living and by the ease, speed, and convenience of transportation, and the associated growth in size of economic and social organizations and of conurbations. At the same time, the major and inescapable problems of urban life—the creation of basic amenities such as sewerage, general public health services, and so on— have been understood and largely solved during the period, leaving local governments with the relatively less onerous task of maintenance of established standards. Second, the simultaneous *change in social ideas* has also influenced expenditure and activity. Local governments have shared in the growing acceptance of government intervention, which has encouraged the development of government activity as a whole. But within that activity, there has been a general shift in emphasis from relief of outright distress (e.g., in the provision of indoor poor relief) to provision of public services on the basis of desirability (as education) and a growing consciousness (undoubtedly related to transportation developments) of the state as one community to which common standards should apply. Such environmental and social changes have been found reflected in our expenditure statistics, and especially in the functional expenditures of local government. There can be no doubting their importance in encouraging a concentration process, particularly when we consider that the economic and social changes under consideration have carried with them a diminution of interest in safeguarding local powers, autonomy, and responsibility—often, when pressure for common standards of service is involved, generating positive opposition to such autonomy.

The effects of changes in the economic environment and social ideas, together with the incidence of wars (as an influence on the timing of changes), have been felt in all types of local activity. It would be tedious to attempt to iterate them; we must be content with some examples. We have already seen how the introduction of public housing after World War I, for example, enabled local authorities to share in the displacement effect generated by that war. More recently, we can find important instances of shifts in functions, such as in 1948 the removal from local governments of their responsibility for poor relief and for general health services, and the loss of their important trading services to the nationalized industries. Local responsibilities for education, on the other hand, have expanded, but the dependence of this service upon central financing has also become greater than heretofore.

The loss by local governments of their traditional relief functions, associated with the extent of the dependence of their expanding social service activities upon central financing, prompts the view that the true extent of the concentration process has been even greater than it appears when measured simply by the decline in significance of local expenditures. Certainly, there has been growing concern in recent years about the decline in prestige and importance of local government, and pressure for increased local autonomy. From the point of view of the present discussion, it is of interest to observe that recent measures of reform, ostensibly intended to establish a grant system more consonant with such autonomy, have generated controversy precisely because they appeared likely to conflict with the social aspirations and economic facts that we have described as encouraging a concentration process, and with it a decline in the importance of local responsibilities and autonomy.

CHAPTER 7
The Nationalized Industries

THE public corporations as a whole differ from other public collective services in important respects. They make charges for their services, related broadly to the costs of provision, and preserve other characteristics of private trading. Notably, they retain control over the use of their reserves and have usually the power to issue stock; they may even be subjected to profits taxes, or be required to pay local rates, or both. On the other hand, the nationalized industries differ from private enterprises in being subjected to certain general (and often extremely vague) directives, laid down in the individual nationalization Acts. One such directive is ubiquitous: that the industries shall perform their functions so as to "secure that the combined revenues . . . are not less than sufficient to meet their combined outgoings properly chargeable to revenue account taking one year with another."[1] Most Acts also include a general exhortation to provide the services concerned "efficiently and cheaply," whatever that might mean. There is evidence that the enterprises have not always found these directives easy to fulfill or mutually compatible; the further general and vague requirement to act "in the public interest" has accordingly been used to interpret the other directives as the corporations might wish.[2]

It is not easy to provide statistics of nationalized industries' income and expenditure payments of a kind that will illuminate the evolution of these enterprises as a part of the public sector. There is, for example, no simple way to deal with the fact that some enterprises now nationalized were earlier in the hands of local authorities (and hence already in the public sector), while others were privately operated. The statistics we give are those directly available from official sources, and begin only in 1938. They nevertheless provide valuable information, since the post-1938 period is that of the great expansion of British public enterprise.

At first sight, it would appear that the nationalized industries cannot be fitted into our story of the operation of the displacement effect and the concentration process. This, indeed, was our own first impression. But even with inadequate statistical information it is still possible to see the traces of these effects in operation.

Our procedure is intended to show how this contention can be justified. This requires us to refer briefly to the history of nationalization and to

---

[1] The quotation is from Section 36 (1) of the Electricity Act, 1947. Similar phrases are to be found in other Acts. For a fuller discussion of the implications of these directives for price policy, see D. N. Chester, *The Nationalized Industries: an Analysis of the Statutory Provisions*, London, 1951, pp. 66–73.

[2] See, for example, the comments on this topic in the Annual Reports of the Raw Cotton Commission.

define the scope of the nationalized industries for purposes of statistical comparison over time. We then present the statistics of the income and expenditure payments of public corporations in order to demonstrate their considerable growth since 1938. Finally, we examine the change in the size and composition of public enterprise in the light of our general thesis.

Growth and Present Extent of Nationalized Industries

A study of this sort cannot embark upon a history of nationalization in Britain,[3] but a background knowledge will help to give us the necessary perspective in analyzing its development. For our purposes, what is most necessary is recognition of the fact that nationalization has a longer history than is generally realized. Not only are there examples of state enterprise before the period of our study, but there are also some important examples of industries that have been subject to close regulation by the state for a long time and have remained so up to the present, or have later been formally assimilated as part of the nationalized sector.

Although the General Post Office is not regarded as an independent public corporation in Britain (and hence is excluded from the statistics in this chapter), because of its financial dependence on the central government especially for its capital budget, it has been a government trading monopoly for 350 years. Its great period of development began with the introduction of the penny post by Rowland Hill in the 1930's, followed by the extension of its activities in the financial field through the money order system and savings bank facilities. Much later the Post Office became the organization responsible for the state monopoly of the telephone business. At the local government level, the public utility became the standard form of trading service in the nineteenth century, the most important examples being the provision of light and water. After World War I, there was close state control over railway rates and after the Great Depression a compulsory cartelization of the coal industry. These measures paved the way for further and more radical state intervention during and after World War II. The interwar period witnessed also the nationalizing of broadcasting and of overseas airways, these being less important in size but significant in character; they were both relatively new industries when taken into the public sector.

It is, however, true that the most important period of nationalization came after World War II with the assumption of public ownership of the Bank of England; coal, transport, electricity, and gas enterprises; and the temporary nationalization of iron and steel production during the last period of office of the Labour Government which ended in 1951.

[3] For further information, see W. A. Robson, *Nationalized Industry and Public Ownership*, London, 1960, and R. Kelf-Cohen, *Nationalization in Britain: the End of a Dogma*, London, 1958.

The significance of this change is clearly reflected in the income and expenditure figures for the nationalized industries presented in the next section.

The nationalized industries, or, as we term them following official practice, the public corporations, are listed below. The list and the classification, used also in our subsequent statistical analysis, are taken from the relevant *Blue Book of National Income and Expenditure.*

Fuel and Power Industries
   National Coal Board
   Electricity authorities
      Central Electricity Board
      Electricity Board of Northern Ireland
      North of Scotland Hydro-Electric Board
      British Electricity Authority and Area electricity boards
   Gas Council and Area Gas Boards

Iron and Steel

Transport and Communications
   Airways Corporations
      British Overseas Airways Corporation
      British South American Airways Corporation
      British European Airways
   British Transport Commission (covering railways and road services)
   Ulster Transport Authority
   Cable and Wireless, Ltd.[4]
   National Dock Labour Board.

Housing and New Town Corporations

Raw Cotton Commission

Other Corporations[5]

The list brings out the great diversity of activity of public corporations which has resulted from piecemeal nationalization. Compare, for instance, the functions of the Raw Cotton Commission (broadly, those of a raw cotton merchant and speculative trader) and the functions of New Town Corporations responsible for the complete planning and development of new urban areas. It also suggests some of the problems created by nationalization measures of this kind, such as those arising from competition between the nationalized undertakings, especially the coal, gas, and electricity industries.

[4] The name is that of the company to whom the enterprise formerly belonged.
[5] This group does not include all other "trading" activities of public bodies. For example, the General Post Office and the National Health Service are not classified as public corporations.

Income and Expenditure of Public Corporations, 1938–54

In social accounting terms, public corporations are normally treated as part of the enterprise sector so that payments for raw materials, and so on, represent intersector payments. Accordingly, since we are concerned with expenditure by national income categories (i.e., with resource use in the wide sense), the statistics we give do not comprehend all the expenditures of public corporations but deal only with expenditures that involve direct factor payments or payments for final output. The tables that follow therefore give details of income payments by public corporations; capital formation by public corporations as a group, both in absolute terms and as a proportion of total capital formation; and the breakdown of the same material by the industry groups set out in the classification above.

INCOME PAYMENTS

Table 17 gives details of the aggregate income payments of all public corporations. The table brings out the great increase in the incomes derived from the economic activities of such corporations as a consequence of the postwar nationalization measures, and also demonstrates the importance of such activities in the period since 1945. However, the increase in the share of total income payments deriving from public corporations from 0.5 per cent in 1938 to 10.9 per cent in 1955 does not represent a similar net enlargement of the public sector as a whole. The change reflected to an important extent a change in the form rather than the volume of public trading. For example, the nationalization of gas and electricity services increased the volume of public corporation activity, but it involved an important transfer of trading activities from the local authorities formerly responsible for the undertakings.[6]

Tables 17 and 18[7] together provide an interesting insight into the precise nature and effects of the postwar nationalization and denationalization measures. The statistics of most interest and importance are those concerned with incomes from employment. The nationalization program began in earnest in 1946, after the nationalization of the coal mines. Income from employment in public corporations as a percentage of total income from employment rose steadily until 1952; fuel and power, civil

---

[6] See Moses Abramovitz and Vera F. Eliasberg, *The Growth of Public Employment in Great Britain*, Princeton University Press for National Bureau of Economic Research, 1957.

[7] The statistics in Table 18 were provided by the Central Statistical Office. They are not fully comparable with those in Table 17, derived from published sources. Table 17 includes amendments received up to March 1956, and the classification is different (notably in including trading services). There are consequent differences in totals and minor discrepancies between the two tables.

TABLE 17

INCOME PAYMENTS OF PUBLIC CORPORATIONS, SELECTED YEARS, 1938–55
(amounts in millions of pounds)

| | *National Income Category* | | | | |
Year	Income from Employment	Rent	Interest and Dividends (gross)	Undistri- buted Profits (gross)	Total Income Payments
1938	17.0	—	9.0	4.0	30.0
% of totalª	0.5	—	1.4	1.4	0.6
1946	42.0	2.0	14.0	11.0	69.0
% of total	0.7	—	2.1	1.9	0.8
1948	673.0	6.0	80.0	59.0	818.0
% of total	10.0	1.4	11.7	6.0	7.8
1950	803.0	6.0	102.0	118.0	1,029.0
% of total	10.6	1.2	13.5	8.7	8.6
1952	1,139.0	6.0	159.0	143.0	1,447.0
% of total	12.5	1.1	18.5	13.7	10.5
1954	1,204.0	5.0	170.0	221.0	1,600.0
% of total	11.7	0.7	16.0	14.4	10.2
1955	1,220.0	5.0	164.0	187.0	1,576.0
% of total	10.9	0.7	14.1	11.3	9.4

ª Percentage of total domestic income of the same type before providing for depreciation and stock appreciation.

TABLE 18

INCOME PAYMENTS OF PUBLIC CORPORATIONS BY INDUSTRY GROUPS,
BY NATIONAL INCOME CATEGORY, 1948–54
(millions of pounds)

Year	Fuel and Power	Iron and Steel	Transport and Communi- cations	Housing and New Towns	Raw Cotton Com- mission	Other Corpo- rations	Total
		INCOME	FROM	EMPLOYMENT			
1948	366		300			6	672
1949	426		328			9	763
1950	452		335	1		14	802
1951	511	114	378	2		13	1,018
1952	581	139	402	3		13	1,138
1953	605	151	415	2		15	1,188
1954	638	114	432	3		16	1,203

TABLE 18 (concluded)

Year	Fuel and Power	Iron and Steel	Transport and Communications	Housing and New Towns	Raw Cotton Commission	Other Corporations	Total
			PURCHASES[a]				
1948	203		220	1	106	10	540
1949	306		227		114	10	657
1950	377		245	1	133	10	766
1951	436	262	249	2	199	13	1,161
1952	504	400	280	2	149	6	1,341
1953	549	452	296	3	89	12	1,401
1954	606	363	281	3	64	13	1,330
			RENT				
1948	1		1		1	3	6
1949	1		1		1	3	6
1950	1		1		1	3	6
1951	1		2		1	2	6
1952	2		1		1	2	6
1953	2		2		1	2	6
1954	3		2			1	6
			TAXES ON EXPENDITURE				
1948	12		6				18
1949	17		7				24
1950	18		8				26
1951	20		8				28
1952	21	1	8			1	31
1953	22	1	8	1			32
1954	25		9				34
			TRADING SURPLUS				
1948	73		37			5	115
1949	112		36		3	3	154
1950	128		54		15	−3	194
1951	125	65	69	1	−2	−2	256
1952	138	92	62	1	−23	3	273
1953	177	85	69		−9	−5	317
1954	190	74	85	1	3	−1	352
			TOTAL				
1948	655		564	1	107	24	1,351
1949	862		599		118	25	1,604
1950	976		643	2	149	24	1,794
1951	1,093	441	706	5	198	26	2,469
1952	1,246	632	753	6	127	25	2,789
1953	1,355	689	790	6	80	24	2,944
1954	1,562	551	809	7	67	29	2,925

[a] Adjusted for stock changes.

aviation, transport, and iron and steel changed ownership in the period. Between 1952 and 1954, steel and road-haulage industries were denationalized, and as a result incomes from employment by public corporations fell from 12.5 per cent to 11.7 per cent of all such incomes (Table 17). In contrast, income from employment derived from all central and local government activity, excluding public corporations, was approximately 10 per cent of all income from employment in the postwar years. Thus, from 1950 to 1954, public corporations provided a larger percentage of total income than all other government activity did. Twelve years earlier, in 1938, the proportion of total income provided by these corporations had been negligible (less than 1 per cent of the total). The growth is of course due to the character of the industries in the postwar nationalizations. Coal and transport, for example, though not necessarily prosperous when outside the public sector, had long been very large employers of labor.

Tables 17 and 18 also show an increase in the importance of income payments by public corporations for services other than employment. The underlying reason is, of course, the growth in the size and importance of the public enterprise sector; but the statistics also reflect both the actual conditions of nationalization and a diversity of trading experience from one industry to another. Thus the interest and dividends figures are aggregations of interest paid on borrowing by the individual corporations and of dividends on the securities issued by corporations (e.g., the electricity authorities) under the statutory powers conferred by the nationalization Acts. The profits figures for individual years are an amalgam of profits in some enterprises and losses in others, the outcome being affected by the changing composition of the public enterprise sector and by fluctuations in the fortunes of some of the corporations such as the National Coal Board and (on a smaller scale) the Raw Cotton Commission.

CAPITAL FORMATION

Fixed domestic capital formation of public corporations has grown enormously in importance, both in absolute terms and as a component of total capital formation by the public sector, as demonstrated in Table 19. Once more, the great absolute increase occurred after 1946; investment rose from £16 million in that year to £180 million in 1948. This is to be expected; in any advanced country, the great public utilities (railroads, electric light and power, gas, water, etc.) account for a large fraction of total invested capital, even by comparison with heavy manufacturing industries such as iron and steel.[8] The postwar nationalizations included enterprises of just that type. It is also noteworthy that the

[8] See Lawrence H. Seltzer, "The Mobility of Capital," *Quarterly Journal of Economics*, May 1932.

TABLE 19

GROSS DOMESTIC FIXED CAPITAL FORMATION OF PUBLIC CORPORATIONS
SELECTED YEARS, 1938–55
(amounts in millions of pounds)

	GROSS FIXED CAPITAL FORMATION					
	Public Sector				Public Sector as Percentage of Total	Public Corporations as Percentage of Public Sector
	Public Corpora- tions	Govern- ment	Total	Total		
1938	10	173	183	656	27.9	5.5
1946	16	259	275	925	29.7	5.8
1948	180	491	671	1,435	46.8	26.8
1950	288	531	819	1,700	48.2	35.2
1952	409	755	1,164	2,108	55.2	35.1
1954	537	762	1,299	2,549	51.0	41.3
1955	575	725	1,300	2,865	45.4	44.2

increase continued after 1948, despite the denationalizations referred to earlier. The share of the public sector as a whole in total gross capital formation fell from 55.2 per cent to 51.0 per cent between 1952 and 1954, but that was the consequence of the slower rate of increase of other public sector investment, which was £7 million higher in 1954 than in 1952, rather than of changes in the public corporations group, whose gross investment rose to £128 million over the same period.

The table also shows the extent to which public corporation investment has come to be the major component of gross fixed investment by the public sector by the end of our period. Less than 6 per cent of public sector investment in 1938 and in 1946 was made by public corporations; in 1954 they were responsible for more than 40 per cent of the total.

Table 20 breaks down capital formation (including changes in the value of stocks) by industry groups. The rise in the proportion of gross domestic capital formation originating in the public corporations to around one-fifth of all gross domestic capital formation since 1949 is shown to be due primarily to investment by the fuel and power group. Investment in fuel and power rose almost continuously during the post-war period and in 1953 still constituted much more than one-half of all domestic fixed capital formation by public corporations, despite an increase in investment by the other groups. Up to 1954, investment by the other three important groups (iron and steel while nationalized, transport, and housing), though significant in total amount, had always been smaller in total volume than investment in fuel and power alone.

The sources of funds for financing investment by public corporations can be seen from Tables 21 and 22. The items need some explanation.

TABLE 20

GROSS DOMESTIC CAPITAL FORMATION OF PUBLIC CORPORATIONS,
BY INDUSTRY CLASSIFICATION, SELECTED YEARS, 1938–54
(millions of pounds)

	Fuel and Power	Iron and Steel	Transport and Communications	Housing and New Towns	Raw Cotton Commission	Other Corporations	Total	Percentage of Gross Domestic Capital Formation
1938							10ᵃ	1.5
1948	126	—	65	10	10	1	212	13.2
1949	193	—	76	13	13	2	297	18.0
1950	194	—	74	14	18	2	302	20.3
1951	253	52	85	22	29	2	443	17.9
1952	299	83	84	34	−48	2	454	21.0
1953	280	59	81	58	−34	3	447	18.1
1954	343	34	80	55	−29	3	486	15.4

ᵃ Almost entirely capital formation by London Passenger Transport Board.

TABLE 21

FINANCING OF PUBLIC CORPORATION INVESTMENT, SELECTED YEARS, 1948–55
(millions of pounds)

	1948	1950	1952	1953	1954	1955
Undistributed incomeᵃ	59	118	143	175	221	187
Capital transfersᵇ	4	3	5	6	6	12
Loans from central governmentᶜ	63	29	73	39	100	142
Stock issued less stock redeemed	109	163	228	219	205	371
Additions to tax and interest reservesᵈ	−23	−11	5	8	−46	−126
Total	212	302	454	447	486	586
Gross domestic capital formation Fixed capital formation	180	288	409	478	537	575
Increase in value of stocks and work in progress	32	14	45	−31	−51	11
Total	212	302	454	447	486	586

ᵃ Before providing for depreciation and stock appreciation.
ᵇ Net receipts.
ᶜ Net.
ᵈ Less net acquisition of other financial assets and net investment abroad.

TABLE 22

FINANCING OF PUBLIC CORPORATION INVESTMENT, BY MAJOR INDUSTRY GROUP, SELECTED YEARS, 1948–54

(millions of pounds)

1948

	Fuel and Power	Iron and Steel	Transport and Communications	Housing and New Towns
Undistributed income[a]	49	—	4	—
Capital transfers[b]	2	—	—	2
Loans from central government[c]	−1	—	—	2
Stock issues less stock redeemed	111	—	−2	—
Additions to tax and interest reserves[d]	−35	—	63	—

1950

	Fuel and Power	Iron and Steel	Transport and Communications	Housing and New Towns
Undistributed income[a]	87	—	17	—
Capital transfers[b]	2	—	—	1
Loans from central government[c]	−15	—	—	11
Stock issues less stock redeemed	163	—	—	—
Additions to tax and interest reserves[d]	−43	—	57	2

1952

	Fuel and Power	Iron and Steel	Transport and Communications	Housing and New Towns
Undistributed income[a]	90	48	23	—
Capital transfers[b]	3	—	—	2
Loans from central government[c]	42	—	—	31
Stock issues less stock redeemed	168	—	60	—
Additions to tax and interest reserves[d]	−4	35	1	1

1954

	Fuel and Power	Iron and Steel	Transport and Communications	Housing and New Towns
Undistributed income[a]	128	47	41	1
Capital transfers[b]	5	—	1	—
Loans from central government[c]	59	26	—	37
Stock issues less stock redeemed	110	—	95	—
Additions to tax and interest reserves[d]	41	−39	−57	17

a Before providing for depreciation and stock appreciation.
b Net receipts.
c Net.
d Less net acquisition of other financial assets and net investment abroad.

Broadly, the statistics exclude items concerned with the transfer of economic activities from private to public ownership, and are restricted to the trading operations of the corporations once in existence. Thus, stock issued (less stock redeemed) does not include stock (securities) issued as compensation to former owners. Gross domestic capital formation does not include increases in assets resulting from the transfer of assets from the private to the public sector. The figures in Table 22, which gives a breakdown by industrial groups, are not directly comparable with the overall figures in Table 21, because only the major groups are included in the detailed table.[9]

The chief sources of financing have been the corporations' own resources (undistributed income), loans from central government, and the issue of securities (Table 21). The aggregate statistics, which appear to indicate the growing importance of stock issues and corporation funds as sources of financing, conceal a good deal of diversity between industrial groups, and in any case cover too short a span of years to provide a reliable indication of a trend. From Table 22, we discover that during the period of study the preponderant fuel and power group depended to a relatively small extent upon government loans, but raised a growing amount of capital by stock issue and (to a smaller extent) from its own resources. In contrast, investment by the housing and new towns corporations was financed almost exclusively by central government loans, which have also been important in financing investment by the Raw Cotton Commission and by the other-corporations' group.

Public corporations have become increasingly important as buyers of particular types of capital goods. Only sparse data are available. The few figures we have suggest that by the end of our period the public corporations had become so important in some sectors (they purchased 34 per cent of all plant and machinery in 1954) that they may well have acquired monopolistic powers in some markets. The extent of these powers and the use that has been made of them have perhaps received less attention from economists than they deserve.

The Timing of Nationalization

It is commonly believed outside Britain that the extensive nationalization program carried out after World War II represents the realization of a Socialist program of long standing. Certainly, there had been a long period of discussion of, and support for, nationalization measures inside the Labour Party and among Fabians and other social reformers. The Labour Party program had incorporated extensive public ownership at

---

[9] Further information about the meaning of the items is given in the *Blue Book on National Income and Expenditure*, 1957, p. 48.

least as far back as 1918, and questions of the organization and control of individual industries had been discussed for many years. Nor had the idea of nationalization as a solution to the problems of particular industries been entirely anathema to other political groups. For example, the Sankey Commission, whose members could hardly be labeled as Labour apologists, had suggested as early as 1919 that nationalization was the only practicable solution for the problems of the coal industry, given the parlous state of that industry after World War I. Thus it could plausibly be argued that the timing of the nationalization measures reflects the accession to power of a Labour Government with a firm majority rather than the "inevitable" effects of the major war that preceded this unique situation in British political history.

Without straining our thesis too far, however, it is possible to argue that World War II cannot be dismissed as an irrelevance. True, there "might have been" a Labour Government during the 1940's, perhaps with a smaller majority, had the war not occurred. But we have already accepted the futility of speculation about such matters. World War II is part of our history, and it had such an important influence on our society that it produced a postwar situation in which no party coming to power, whatever its political character, could have afforded to neglect either the effects of the structure of the wartime economy on postwar policy or the effects of the war itself upon the organization of such major industries as coal and transport. We would offer two arguments in particular to bolster this general claim.

First, the Second World War, much more than the First, meant a very considerable depreciation in the fixed equipment and plants of major industries such as transport and fuel and power. Inevitably, therefore, the problem of rehabilitation was immense, necessitating some form of official intervention, if only in the form of subsidies. Further, the waging of a total war which required the complete reorganization of these industries to meet the needs of the war economy, involving the centralization of production and distribution decisions, left an administrative legacy similar to that already described in the case of the social services. Thus the combination of the necessity for state assistance and of the existence of an apparatus of state control imposed by wartime conditions invited nationalization as a solution.

Second, as acceptance of nationalization relies on the opinions of the electorate, one has to account for the strong electoral support given *for the first time* to nationalization measures by the election in 1945 of a Labour Government with a firm majority. While we do not know what "might have been," and while it is notoriously difficult to trace cause and effect in the translation of views and opinions into practical politics, it nevertheless seems plausible to suggest that the experiences of the war

132

engendered a new and profound—if mistaken—respect for the efficiency of collective physical planning and for large-scale government intervention.[10] As two war historians stated in another context, "perhaps the most insidious legacy of war was a habit of mind. The reckonings of national achievement to which people had accustomed themselves had been in physical terms. Finance had lost its traditional significance as a criterion and method of control. . . . For the British people, as well as for their defeated enemies, a painful and dreary course of 're-education' lay ahead."[11]

We are not concerned here to argue that the British nationalization measures after World War II were good or bad in themselves. But however sympathetic one might be, for example, to the view that nationalization offered the only possible solution for the problems facing the fuel and transport industries, the fact remains that no economist would put forward wartime experience as providing satisfactory technical evidence for the necessity or value of continuing the use of wartime "planning" methods in time of peace. Nevertheless, much of the initial postwar political support for planning and hence for nationalization rested in good measure upon such a false analogy between wartime and peacetime conditions. To this extent, and notwithstanding the long earlier history of pressure for nationalization measures from particular groups, it seems clear that the growth of this part of the public sector has shared in the displacement effect of war that we have found important to the evolution of government activities of other kinds.

[10] See, for example, Lionel C. Robbins, *The Economic Problem in Peace and War*, London, 1947, Lecture 2; and Roy F. Harrod, *Are These Hardships Necessary?*, London, 1947, pp. 111–114.

[11] W. K. Hancock and M. M. Gowing, "British War Economy," *History of the Second World War*, Civil Series, No. 1, London, 1949, p. 553.

CHAPTER 8

Possible Future Trends in Government Expenditure

In this study, we have tried to present the statistics of British government expenditure in a fashion that might be of value in the study of public expenditures in other countries or during other periods. We are conscious that the structure we offer does not have the formal symmetry or analytical rigor that might be obtained, for instance, by use of welfare economics. But, as we have pointed out, welfare analysis applied to the problems of government economic activity involves highly unrealistic assumptions about the nature of the aims of governments and consequently is of negligible value as a means of explaining the facts of history. We would claim for our approach that any sacrifice of rigor is more than compensated by the realism it makes possible, and indeed that flexibility is essential for any approach that is to be of value outside the immediate context of one country or period. We do not wish to establish a new "law," but we do hope to have evolved a method that will be of use to others interested in similar problems. At the same time, we believe our approach is not restricted to the interpretation of history. It can also contribute to our understanding of the processes that determine the size and character of public spending, and hence interest those whose concern is with economic policy and with the development of the public sector in the future.

At first sight, the last claim may seem implausible. We have placed great emphasis in earlier chapters upon the operation of the displacement effect and the concentration process. Our general argument would therefore seem to suggest that forecasting the future of public expenditures requires prediction of the dates of future wars or other social upheavals. But the policy maker and the student of economic policy cannot abdicate their task because they do not know whether or when there will be a war or an earthquake. They must postulate such an occurrence, or its absence. And it is within this context that our approach is relevant; it can help us make projections of public expenditure of a kind that provide information about the broad range of possibilities that are likely to face the government, and about the relation between these and the possible evolution of particular kinds of public spending, in the absence of major social disturbances.

The contribution of our study to projection problems has two aspects, one general and the other specific. The general contribution concerns the use we have made of the concept of the tolerable burden of taxation. If we assume that there will be no social disturbances during the period for which a projection is made, then our earlier argument and the historical evidence would suggest that we might expect to find some broad relation between the growth of community wealth (GNP) and the size of the total taxes that the government might feel itself able to raise. We do not suggest that the relation is a very precise one; it depends, for example, upon the form taken by people's views about tax burdens, and upon such things as the nature of the tax structure. For example, a progressive income tax and surtax will produce a tax yield that grows faster than money GNP, with constant tax rates. This may or may not be accepted by the community, depending upon whether those who find growing proportions of their real income being taken in tax are stimulated to protest. But while such matters affect the precise relation over time between GNP and government revenues, they are unlikely to be important enough to make it pointless to use the broad constancy of that relation as an indicator of the potential scope for public spending.

The second, and specific, contribution is more directly concerned with expenditures. Our historical study has provided us with information about the development of public spending for particular purposes, and there seems no reason why this material and method of classification should not be used as the basis for statistical speculation about future possibilities. Thus we can make explicit assumptions as to the evolution of particular groups of expenditures, and show what would happen to public spending over the period under review on the basis of those assumptions. Many of the difficulties that we have encountered in offering an *ex post facto* explanation of the development of government activities will be found to be equally relevant to the problem of analysing future growth.

Both of these procedures, of course, are intended to do no more than give an indication of possibilities of a kind that might inform discussion; we cannot emphasize too strongly that we do not believe ourselves to be forecasting what British Government expenditures are actually going to be in the future. With this proviso, the most interesting method of presenting the projection would seem to be first to derive expenditure estimates directly, for groups of services and on defined assumptions, and then to see how the totals compare with the scope for expenditure that GNP estimates suggest to be likely.

In the next section, then, we offer a projection of government expenditure for years up to 1981, and a detailed explanation of the specific assumptions on which it is based. The projection is limited to the magnitude and broad composition of current government expenditure, excluding nationalized industries. It is not offered as a prophecy, but rather as a means of narrowing the discussion of public expenditures and directing attention to the issues of significance for policy purposes.[1] We

[1] If we appear to labor this point, the experience of others who have made similar projections justifies that emphasis. How often must Nicholas Kaldor (Appendix C in

[*footnote continued on page 136*]

start out from the fundamental assumption that the period of the projection will be free from random disturbance by wars or other social upheavals; we do not concern ourselves, at least in our statistical projection, with any potential displacement effect. On this basis, we proceed by dividing up expenditures into three groups (expanding, contracting, constant), the division being dictated by our historical findings in earlier chapters, as modified by such specific considerations as seem to us relevant in respect of individual types of expenditure. Within each group, this fundamental assumption leaves us free to examine such "permanent" influences upon expenditure as changes in the size and structure of population as the possible determinants of the future size and composition of government spending.

Our projection is also based upon another general assumption, sufficiently important to require careful explanation. This is that there will be no major changes in public policy affecting the broad general scope of government spending. The justification for such an assumption is not simply that there are no policy differences between the major political parties, though in recent years there has in fact been a wide measure of agreement about the scope of social services and (to a lesser and decreasing extent) defense requirements, both of which are important from an expenditure point of view. Quite as important is the fact that the volume of "irrevocable" expenditure, at least in money terms, is such that even radical changes in government policies might take a considerable time to become effective in their influence on expenditures. A government that decided to discontinue subsidies to local housing projects, for example, could hardly stop payment of existing subsidies, to which it might be committed for as long as sixty years. Indeed, in recent years we have seen a considerable weakening in Britain of the principle that "no government can bind its successor." Postwar governments have introduced services, notably in the field of national insurance, in respect of which such officials as the Government Actuary are obliged to make projections of expenditure for as far ahead as twenty-five years. The planning period of the education and health programs is no longer identical with the expected period of office of the government in power. This development, in our view, makes our general assumption a reasonable one to use as the basis for our projection.

W. H. Beveridge, *Full Employment in a Free Society*, London, 1945) have been quoted in terms that suggest he was making a forecast?

To be quite clear: We do not expect our estimates of particular magnitudes for particular years to be borne out by events. Other qualifications apart, our assumption of constant prices would make such an outcome unlikely. Our figures are intended solely as a means of setting out the important issues and relative magnitudes, and we would not wish to have them quoted in any other context.

It may be objected that this assumption prevents us from taking account of actual plans and proposals that have been made for the extension of public services and expenditures in particular directions; influential proposals have been made, for example, for extended public education and health facilities. We have two answers to this objection. First, it is in the nature of political life that there are always in existence plans for the provision of more and better public services of a wide variety of kinds. If we assumed that all such plans would be implemented, and estimated the expenditure involved, we should get a total indicating a very much more rapid rate of growth than the one given by our actual projection. But we have discussed the political aspects of expenditure growth in earlier chapters; it should be enough to say here that, while we would agree that there has been a weakening in the procedure by which control over public expenditure has traditionally been exercised in Britain, we are still far from a position in which governments regard the growth of such expenditure as a matter of no concern at all: they are still aware of the need to raise the necessary taxes. This being so, to proceed simply by adding up the expenditures implied by existing proposals to extend government services would in our view be quite unrealistic: no one expects all such proposals to be implemented.

Second, we would refer yet once again to the nature of our exercise. We are concerned to make a projection, on assumptions that are explained. We may in the process ignore possibilities of expansion, and so on, in particular directions that other economists believe to be important. If so, they can modify our estimates, and perhaps our conclusions, accordingly. We shall be satisfied if our statistical exercise can be used to provide the theme around which others interested can furnish their own variations.

A Projection of Current Government Expenditure, 1953–81

Table 23 presents our projection. All figures are expressed at 1956 prices, and types of expenditure are classified according to whether they will expand, remain stationary, or contract.

The method of compilation is most easily explained by considering the questions that must be answered in order to make such a projection, and then giving the answers that we have used as the basis for this one— i.e., the specific technical and operational assumptions that we have made. The important questions are concerned with technical coefficients of production, with the standards of provision of public services, with changes in the size and composition of population, and with the future behavior of expenditures for a miscellaneous (but not insignificant) group of services that do not lend themselves easily to the general method of treatment adopted for the rest.

TABLE 23

PROJECTION OF TOTAL UNITED KINGDOM GOVERNMENT EXPENDITURE ON
CURRENT ACCOUNT, AT 1956 PRICES, SELECTED YEARS, 1953–81
(amounts in millions of pounds; index, 1956 = 100)

Type of Expenditure	Recent Years		Projection		
	1953	1956	1961	1971	1981
Expanding					
Education	473	543	557	535	545
National health	584	618	632	664	687
National insurance benefits	618	680	770	928	1,053
Other	589	640	654	688	712
Total	2,264	2,481	2,613	2,815	2,997
Index	83.2	100.0	105.3	113.5	120.8
Contracting					
Family allowances	125	116	117	113	115
National assistance	177	165	140	130	120
War pensions	87	84	80	73	55
Agriculture and food subsidies	306	254	210	285	185
Other	127	105	100	90	80
Total	822	724	647	591	555
Index	113.5	100.0	89.5	81.6	76.7
Stationary					
Defense	1,827	1,662	1,662	1,662	1,662
National Debt	738	725	725	725	725
Housing	106	107	107	107	107
Other	155	150	150	150	150
Total	2,826	2,644	2,644	2,644	2,644
Total current expenditure	5,912	5,849	5,904	6,050	6,196
Index	100.1	100.0	100.9	103.4	105.9

SOURCE: For 1953 and 1956 statistics, see *Blue Book,* 1957.

TECHNICAL COEFFICIENTS OF PRODUCTION

To project the future course of government expenditure, we need to
know what it is going to cost at any time to maintain any specified
standard of service for a given number of people. There is no reason why
the cost should remain constant, or why the provision of the same "real"
standard in a particular service for the same number of people in 1956
and in 1981 must involve the same amount of expenditure at constant
1956 prices. As pointed out in Chapter 2, statistical and other difficulties
are created by the fact that relative scarcities of resources can change
over time as a consequence of changes in technical coefficients of production and in the character of demand. The significance of these changes
in the present context is that they may change the nature and cost of
the "input mix" needed to produce a service or to increase its output.

As a result, changes over time in the volume of consumption of a service may not imply equivalent changes in the amount of expenditure at constant prices.

These changes in the technical coefficients of production are likely to be of special interest over periods when the process of technical change has different significance for the private and the public sector. But the changes are not easy to predict, for obvious reasons, nor does a projection of our type lend itself to the use of very complex propositions about them. It therefore seems best to assume fixed and constant technical coefficients, so that doubling the amount of a service provided implies doubling the amount of labor, materials, and so forth, purchased. Put in another way, the expenditure on a service, if standards of provision remain constant, is assumed to increase proportionately with the number of individuals for whom it is provided. This assumption is operationally convenient, but it will clearly call for further comment when we come to evaluate the projection in which it is used.

STANDARDS OF SERVICE

The volume of expenditure upon any government service must depend upon the standard of service to which the government commits itself. We have assumed for the projection that the standards of service provided in 1956 will be maintained. At first sight this might seem a simple matter to define. For transfer payments it is; we need only assume that such payments as retirement pensions and family allowances will be maintained at a level providing constant purchasing power for their recipients. This procedure involves us in some of the conceptual difficulties already discussed, but is otherwise unambiguous.

The difficult problems arise in dealing with government services given in kind rather than money, such as health and education. These provide a special and extreme case of the problems of technical coefficients and demand, just explained. What does the maintenance of a given standard mean in the context of services of this kind? Consider the case of health expenditures. Maintaining the same standard of service should really be discussed in terms of maintaining the health of the community as reflected in such things as mortality and morbidity rates. To try to reflect such a constant standard in, for example, a constant expenditure at 1956 prices per qualified individual for each year being studied is a dubious procedure. Tuberculosis is a good illustration. Twenty-five years ago it was one of the major causes of death. To-day many tuberculosis hospitals in Britain are closing down. Thus the real expenditure per individual necessary to maintain the same "output" of health from this particular point of view has declined; there is a changed relation between factor input and product output, in a wide sense of those terms. However, we have no satisfactory means of establishing a relationship through time—of a kind that might be used in our projection—between real expenditures per head and standards of provision in such services as health and education. For these two services (the major items of current expenditure for services in kind), therefore, we must fall back on the formula that maintaining the 1956 standard of service per individual can be equated with maintaining real expenditure per individual (1956 prices) at the 1956 level. That is, the fixed coefficients assumption explained above is applied here also. Some such assumption is unavoidable; we are aware that it is unsatisfactory and that this will need to be borne in mind when we assess our results.

A particular problem arises in the case of defense expenditure. Not only is it difficult, if not impossible, to define what precisely is meant by maintaining the 1956 standard of defense, but also it is impossible to attribute the benefits of defense to particular individuals in any meaningful fashion. Rather than attempt to define defense output and to allocate its benefits arbitrarily to individuals, we have chosen to adopt the assumption that defense expenditure remains fixed in real terms at the 1956 level. Once again, our projection must be interpreted and evaluated in the light of this procedure.

POPULATION

Given our assumptions about technical coefficients and standards of provision, the outstanding general determinant of the level of government expenditure becomes the size and character of the country's population, upon which it is reasonable to suppose that future expenditures on economic, environmental, and social services must depend. The problem thus becomes largely one of projecting future population and of relating expenditures on the various services to that projection. In economic and environmental services, we have ignored changes in population composition, writing up expenditures in proportion to changes in total population size. This procedure, unsatisfactory even for these services, would be much more so for the far more important social services. For these, a more complex procedure makes use of a previous study, adjustments being made for changes in standards of service since 1952, the year to which that study refers.[2] The statistical procedure is not described in detail here, since it is available in the cited paper. Essentially, it takes into account the fact that the expected aging of our

---

[2] See F. W. Paish and A. T. Peacock, "Economics of Dependence, 1952–82," *Economica*, November 1954. In this study detailed projections of the size and composition of population were based on Projection 14 of the Statistics Committee of the Royal Commission on Population. In our present study, we have adopted the projections of the Registrar General in the *Annual Abstract of Statistics*, 1957.

population, combined with a very slow rate of population growth, should bring with it a change in average expenditure on those services per head of population, because there is good reason to believe that the cost per head of social services may be higher for the retired population than for those of working age or for children.

EXPENDITURES REQUIRING DIFFERENT TREATMENT

There remains to be considered the treatment of certain other types of expenditure that cannot plausibly be assumed to be closely related to population changes, such as national debt interest, food and agricultural subsidies, and war pensions. The perplexing problem of debt interest is that it represents a commitment in money terms and not in real terms. The problem of projecting price changes so that one could express future debt interest payments in real terms is difficult enough, but there is another important factor at work. Even assuming no change in the size of national debt, conversion operations will be necessary, given the present structure of the debt. Debt interest payments will depend on future interest rates. When an earlier projection of government expenditure was made by one of us, it seemed at the time reasonable to assume that debt interest in real terms would fall.[3] Now it seems more satisfactory to assume a stationary total of debt interest payments in real terms. Like the previous estimate, this is pure guesswork. It will be recalled that a similar assumption was made in the case of defense. With food and agricultural subsidies, we have assumed that the remaining food subsidies will disappear, but that the various agricultural subsidies will remain constant in real terms. Housing subsidies are also assumed to remain constant in real terms. The real standard of provision of war pensions is assumed constant, which implies that, with the gradual reduction in the number of recipients, total real expenditure for this purpose will diminish. National assistance in the form of poor relief of various kinds is also likely, as assumed, to diminish in size, given constant standards of service, because of the increasing coverage of the contributory retirement pensions scheme after 1958.

Interpretation and Critique

The projection shows a 6 per cent increase in government expenditure at 1956 prices over a period of twenty-five years. At first sight, this may seem a surprisingly slow rate of growth, particularly in view of the fears often expressed about the potential growth of social service expenditures. True, the expanding types of expenditure (first group in Table 23) include such services, and on the assumptions of the projection they would

[3] See A. T. Peacock, "The Future of Government Expenditure," *District Bank Review*, June 1955.

increase by over 20 per cent in real terms over the period. But there are some forms of social expenditure that the projection shows to remain constant or to decline. More important, there are other great items of expenditure that are no more significant in 1981 than in 1956 (third group in Table 23). Consequently, the overall rate of growth in expenditures is very much less than that of the expanding social services.

We shall later discuss the effects on our projection of some variations in our operational assumptions. For the moment, let us accept the conclusions as realistic and consider what they imply. For this purpose, we can adopt the procedure used earlier in the study of comparing the projected expenditure growth with the growth of GNP.

There is no easy way of assessing the likely size of GNP by 1981, but it is possible to make calculations of varying degrees of sophistication. One would be to extrapolate the rate of growth recorded over, say, the last ten years. At the other extreme, another would be to try to work out capital-output ratios in a large range of industries, make some assumption about the rate of capital formation and the growth of the labor force, and, after prodigious effort, produce the resultant growth rate. But, whatever degree of sophistication is indulged in, the difficult problem has to be faced that the rate of growth of national output is not independent of the size and character of the public sector. Ideally we should provide a separate calculation of GNP for each of a series of projections of public expenditures, based on different answers to the questions examined earlier. In this way, we could approach the policy problem by comparison and assessment of the results of these separate exercises. Such a labor seems hardly worth the effort, in the light of the conceptual problems in making projections, already discussed, and of the added difficulties that would arise in making the GNP computation— including the major difficulty that, while there is certainly likely to be a relation between the growth of the public sector and the growth of GNP, we do not know what the relation is nor can we assume that it will not change over a period as long as twenty-five years.

Since our object, as already stated, is simply to provide a framework for policy discussion, to indicate possible future developments, and to direct attention to the issues that our analysis suggests to be most significant for future policy, we have taken the view that a complex procedure such as the one just described could provide us with more statistics, but would scarcely make the interpretative problem any easier or more certain. We have therefore adopted a less elaborate procedure, which enables the expenditure projection to be interpreted without need for elaborate calculations about GNP. We ask simply: What rate of increase of GNP would be necessary to keep the share of government in GNP constant?

142

Given the slow rate of increase of total expenditures indicated by the projection, the rate of growth of GNP required for the share of government to be no larger in 1981 than in 1956 would be modest indeed; and any larger—and more likely—rate of growth would leave scope for reducing the relative burden of taxation. A rise in GNP of only 2 per cent per annum, which is not a fantastic rate of increase on any reasonable criteria,[4] would reduce the percentage of current government expenditure out of GNP from 33 per cent in 1956 to 21 per cent in 1981.[5]

Put in another way, the projection suggests a future degree of scope for maneuver on the part of the government—whether by way of reduced tax burdens, acceptance of increased defense commitments, or increases in the range of public services—much greater than is generally assumed in current discussion. It remains to be seen whether this conclusion will need modification in the face of further consideration of the operational assumptions upon which the projection is based.

The assumption of fixed technical coefficients has already been admitted to be dubious. This kind of blanket assumption is certainly going to be wrong in particular instances; for example, it is unlikely that maintaining given standards in education requires that the number of teachers must necessarily increase proportionately with the number of pupils, or the ratio of nurses to patients in hospital. Indivisibilities are bound to be important in the provision of some services of that kind. Against this, we have to remember that our projection is restricted to current government expenditure and therefore is not concerned with expenditure on such things as school and hospital building or on local authority housing. It seems reasonable to expect this to make the fixed technical coefficients assumption less seriously misleading. The fundamental question is whether the technical conditions of production in the public and private sectors are likely to change in the next twenty-five years in so drastic a fashion as to make a projection based on fixed coefficients completely implausible. From this point of view (and granted that the assumption may be inaccurate in particular instances), it is still plausible to argue that the assumption is at least as realistic as any alternative general proposition about the public sector as a whole.

4 There are no officially accepted projections of GNP, but the Government Actuary, for his *Report on the Financial Provisions of the National Insurance Bill*, 1959, was asked to assume an increase in earnings of 2 per cent per annum in making his estimates of future wage-related contributions and benefits, under the proposed scheme. The report does not state whether the percentage related to money or real earnings.

5 It is interesting to compare the results of this projection with those of Otto Eckstein in his *Trends in Public Expenditure in the Next Decade*, New York, 1959. Using similar assumptions about political attitudes and the internal situation, he finds that his "medium" projection would result in a rate of growth of federal expenditures of about 2.7 per cent per annum up to 1968, which would be "less than the expected growth of GNP on moderate assumptions (3 per cent a year)."

Such a position is perhaps less tenable when we turn to the related proposition that the maintenance of real standards in particular social services can be equated with the maintenance of expenditures per head at 1956 prices. It is particularly so, if we admit the additional problem that the form of output required to maintain a given standard of health, for example, must be expected to change over time.

In any case, the whole treatment of standards of service can be objected to. In the light of our earlier arguments, it is unrealistic to assume that standards of provision will not change in the next fifteen years. As suggested in Chapter 2, there is a clear possibility that a rising real product per head will produce a rise in standards of service, affecting especially social service spending. This may come about through a "demonstration effect," operating through a desire to keep standards of provision in the public sector abreast of economic development in the private sector.[6] To illustrate: if standards of living improve in the private sector as the real national product rises, then the standards of provision in hospitals and schools, for example, are bound to be affected. If there are television sets in the home, there will be strong pressure to have them in hospitals—as indeed there is now. The gradual widening of the differential between wage rates and social security benefit rates has brought with it strong pressure from pensioners and from within the ranks of the Labour Party to make pensions proportional to income and to link benefits not only with price changes but also with productivity changes. Thus, under the National Superannuation Plan sponsored by the Labour Party, the assumption of a doubling of real national product between 1960 and 1980 would lead to an increase in the pensions bill in real terms from £775 million to £1,700–1,900 million, an increase of two and one-half times.[7] And if retirement pensions rise, unemployment and sickness benefits, war pensions, and workmen's compensation benefits cannot be expected to lag far behind. The demonstration effect is all the more important in Britain to-day because of the size of the welfare budget within the total of government expenditure. Finally, while the effect is brought about by taxpayers' comparisons of standards of services in the private and public sector, it is likely to be supplemented by the further desire, also discussed in Chapter 2, to improve collective services

[6] It is well known that the term demonstration effect was originally applied to the case of less developed countries, whose consumption standards are supposed to be a function of their contact with Western standards. This effect is supposed to explain the relatively high marginal propensity to consume of these countries.

[7] *National Superannuation: Labour's Policy for Security in Old Age*, 1957. As this passage was being written the Conservative Government introduced its own plan for wage-related contributions and benefits for old age, which, if it differs in financial scope from the Labour party proposals, accepts the same principle. See Ministry of Pensions and National Insurance, *Provision for Old Age*, Command Paper No. 538, 1958; and the National Insurance Bill, 1959.

such as roads, public health facilities, and so on, as standards of living rise. To the extent that such an advance in standards should occur, the projection must give too low a figure for future government expenditure, notably, the 20 per cent increase in the expanding sector would have to be written up. Such an increase must, of course, reduce the scope for other measures, involving increased expenditures, if the share of government in GNP is not to rise, and must reduce the possibilities of a reduction in the burden of taxation.

There is no way of deciding how important the rises in standards of services are likely to be, but we can establish their quantitative importance, and so indicate the range of possibilities, by a fairly simple exercise. Let us suppose that the standard of provision for the expanding services grows at the same rate as GNP. Thus if GNP in 1981 were 25 per cent higher than in 1956, the total expenditure for that group in Table 23 would be 25 per cent higher in 1981 than the figure in the table. This means an increase of roughly £750 million in those expenditures and in total government expenditure, and increases the total expenditure index for 1981 by about 13 per cent. Even on such a pessimistic assumption about the rate of increase of community output, we find that a rate of increase of expenditure on expanding services keeping pace with the increase in GNP still would leave total government expenditure expanding less quickly than output (19 per cent by 1981 as against the 25 per cent increase in GNP). If output should increase faster, as seems likely, the government's scope for increasing its activities without increasing its share of GNP would become greater.

Next we turn to the behavior of population. Keynes once remarked that population changes were the one thing we could predict with "reasonable safety."[8] It is doubtful if our experiences with population projections since Keynes wrote on the matter confirms his *obiter dictum*. We may be fairly sure that, short of some very large changes in immigration or emigration, our population will age, and to this extent we may be sure that the scales will be weighted in favor of larger social expenditures per head, as our projection assumes. However, even in the course of only six years the highest official estimates of fertility rates have proved to be too low. In the *Report of the Statistics Committee of the Royal Commission on Population,* sixteen projections were made for the period 1947–2047.[9] The highest projected figure for average annual births was 731,200 per annum for the period 1952–57. The recorded figure for average annual births for the same period was 838,000. Since these projections were published, single official projections have begun

[8] J. M. Keynes, "Some Economic Consequences of a Declining Population," *Eugenics Review*, April 1937, pp. 13–17.
[9] Vol. II of the Papers of the Royal Commission on Population, H.M.S.O., 1950.

to appear in the *Annual Abstract of Statistics*, the first in 1956. The second, published in 1957, is the one used here; the notes to that projection table record that the second projection had to be modified to take account of the maintenance of the unexpectedly high birth rate over the preceding five years.[10] While no one would deny the usefulness of population projections, it is clear that they are not completely free from uncertainties. The most we can say is that the population projection we have used is the most satisfactory one available, and that on present evidence any change in it is most likely to be in a direction that would increase social service spending on the young in the intermediate years of our expenditure forecast. The nature of the changes that could occur before we reached 1981, however, is a good deal less certain.

Conclusion

It has become fashionable to argue that the test of the value of all economic analysis is its ability to predict accurately. By this test, the purpose of our survey of the factors governing the growth of public expenditure should be to find indicators of future trends which can be expressed in some model of economic growth capable of being tested by econometric techniques. This is not an argument we accept.

It follows that we would not justify our approach by adopting the standard defensive reply to the charge that economists cannot predict— that more refined techniques can be developed, given time. In the present context it would require the building of models which would enable us to predict wars, revolutions, and natural disasters. What we are prepared to say is that the *procedure* adopted provides a means of testing the consistency of assumptions made in any attempt to analyze the future. Moreover, since formulation of any consistent policy by a government or private economic organization requires forecasting of future developments, a procedure for this purpose cannot be developed and understood without knowledge of economic analysis. If all that our analysis of the evolution of government expenditures teaches us is that forecasting is likely to be supremely difficult, that forms a better foundation for judgments about future events than would an oversimplification of the issues.

However, our study as a whole suggests that we might do more than this; we hope that the present chapter has indicated some of the possibilities. We believe that the formulation we have used for the examination of future developments, and the conclusions derived from its use, should help those concerned with policy to avoid simple (but not uncommon) errors and to concentrate upon the issues of real importance. This can

[10] See *Annual Abstract of Statistics*, No. 94, London, 1957, p. 6.

be demonstrated by summarizing the position to which our projection and comment upon it has brought us, and by relating this to the earlier discussion (Chapter 5) of the evolution and present position of the control of public expenditures in Britain. The two together throw an interesting light on the problems of present-day expenditure policy, and upon the difficulties and scope of action of the Plowden Committee, which has been set up to make recommendations upon the Parliamentary control of expenditure.

The projection indicates the possibility of considerable growth in some types of expenditure (notably on social services) by 1981, given present standards of provision. Nevertheless, the importance of the contracting and stationary groups of expenditure is great enough to make this growth compatible with a much slower overall rate of growth in government expenditure. With any reasonable rate of increase of community output, that is, the overall rate of growth in expenditures might be expected to be compatible with either a reduction of the share of GNP taken by government or an increase in the scope of government activities without need to increase that share. If it is thought that standards of provision must increase, the "elbow room" is of course reduced, but our projection suggests that a rate of growth of expanding services as fast as the rate of growth of GNP would not remove all freedom of maneuver, even for a rate of increase of GNP as low as 1 per cent per annum. For faster (more likely?) rates of economic growth, the scope for a growing public sector would be correspondingly larger. Further, that scope seems adequate to meet foreseeable demands for increases in the range and standard of public provision. Although much can happen in twenty-five years, there is no present reason to expect (in the absence of social disturbances) the sort of rapid changes that, for example, produced a 50 per cent rise in the share of government in GNP between 1890 and 1910.[11] Failing radical changes in social ideas or technological requirements in the near future, it seems that demands for improved standards of provision, and so forth, may be well within the limits imposed by the burden of taxation which we have to accept.

These results are, of course, subject to the views we have taken about technical coefficients and about population change, and to the absence of social disturbances during the period under survey. As to the first two of these, we believe that our discussion indicates that the margin of error to which our assumptions leave us vulnerable is not such as to affect our

[11] That period not only differed from the present in social climate (it was a period of growing acceptance of the need for policies requiring increased public expenditures) and in the much smaller share of GNP being taken by government; it was also affected by the South African War, which, while less far-reaching in its effects than the later world wars, must have eased the process of change and probably facilitated a rate of growth more rapid than would otherwise have been possible.

conclusions substantially. Social disturbances are assumed absent; the possible consequences for our argument should such disturbances occur will be discussed below.

Our projection invites the conclusion, then, that the scope for expansion of government expenditures in Britain in the next quarter-century may be much greater than is generally believed. Certainly, we are led to question the realism of the view that government revenues and expenditures have now reached some critical limit beyond which it would be impossible, or at best foolish, to go. But this does not imply that we ourselves are content with a situation in which the government continues to utilize (directly) a quarter of the national product, or that the community at large will wish it to do so. We have not demonstrated that expenditures *must* increase at the same rate as GNP, but only the scope for public activity that such a ("tolerable") rate of increase would provide. It remains to ask: Why should we not expect the future to bring a reduction in the burden of taxation rather than an increase in the extent and standards of public provision? This is not, of course, a question to which our projection provides an answer of itself; but considered along with the rest of our study, it provides a useful basis for "informed speculation."

Certainly, there is much concern about the present size of public expenditures; this is demonstrated, *inter alia*, by the very appointment of the Plowden Committee. There is a considerable body of opinion, for example, supporting the view that the income-leveling effects of progressive taxation produced much more severe disincentive effects after 1945 than after 1918, and that these effects still continue. Also, opposition already exists to that "cult of welfare" which was so important a part of the displacement effect during the Second World War, and there are signs that this opposition is growing in importance and influence.

Nevertheless, it seems to us likely that the growth of public expenditures will continue to be restricted by existing notions of what is tolerable rather than by deliberate attempts to reduce (or check the rate of growth of) the public sector. There is in the first place no general agreement as to the desirability of such deliberate restriction. The Labour Party in particular is committed, if returned to power, to schemes that must surely make for a rate of growth of spending as rapid as the community will accept—including a great increase in government aid to underdeveloped countries. The Conservative Party, though more concerned about the size of public spending, has not proposed a radical reduction in spending on any major service, and has plans that would require increased spending in particular directions. At best, they would probably be content with an overall rate of growth of spending that involved no major changes in tax rates. These arguments about current attitudes are reinforced by the conclusions reached by our earlier historical survey.

Concern about public expenditures is not new, nor is the Plowden Committee the first one to consider the matter. Neither the concern nor the earlier committees seem to have had any lasting effect on the growth of public spending. Furthermore, the practical problems of expenditure control are now more difficult than ever before in British history; we explained in Chapter 5 that the authority of the Chancellor of the Exchequer in expenditure matters has declined with the decline in agreement as to the economic rationale of public spending. Without agreement on objectives, Parliamentary control seems bound to be ineffective. At the same time, even simple control over the *efficiency* of public spending has become more and more difficult: the Treasury's task in "the saving of candle ends" has become a matter of keeping check upon expenditure on great projects of uncertain cost and length of life.

We would conclude, therefore, that the rate of growth of public expenditures is likely to be such as at least to maintain the share of government in GNP broadly at present levels. If the Plowden Committee can find ways to improve "the saving of candle ends," it will have achieved a notable public service; if it can find means, in existing British conditions, to restore or replace the former broad authority over expenditure policy of the Chancellor of the Exchequer and the Treasury, it will have achieved a miracle. Failing such a miracle, we must expect the opportunities for change that a rising GNP must bring to result in a growing public sector rather than a declining tax burden. Nor would we expect this conclusion to be changed by the occurrence during the period under examination of an important social disturbance (such as a major war or a runaway inflation). Failing some great change in social attitudes and institutions, the arguments adduced above also provide support for the view that any displacement effect of such a disruption would most likely be upward, and there is certainly no sign at present that the burden of taxation itself is likely to lead to revolution!

Appendix

THIS appendix explains the statistical sources and the definitions used for our various statistical series. There are five basic series: (1) government expenditure, (2) national income, (3) price series relevant for the deflation of (1) and (2), (4) population, and (5) unemployment. We shall deal with population, price, national income, and unemployment series first to clear the way for a detailed examination of government expenditure statistics.

One general definition used throughout the investigation may be mentioned at the outset. Our statistics all relate to the geographical area of the United Kingdom. The United Kingdom now consists of three parts, England and Wales, Scotland, and Northern Ireland. Before 1921, however, it included the whole of Ireland. It might be thought a more reasonable procedure to try to compute figures solely for Northern Ireland for the period before 1921 in order to ensure geographical comparability over the period as a whole. However, apart from the considerable statistical problems which this would involve, there is the further point that we are interested in the relation between the growth of government expenditure and the political decisions which determine the extent and time pattern of that growth. This obliges us to consider only that area of the British Isles in which these political decisions are effective, and so we make no allowance for the change in the geographical extent of the United Kingdom during the period.

The general statistical procedure has been to round to what seemed to us the significant digit. Thus total government expenditure is given to £0.1 million up to 1938, but only to the nearest million pounds thereafter, so reflecting the increase in prices over the period. Per capita statistics are given to £0.1, and computed from the total statistics in the form just described. Where data of particular kinds are not available or are available only in an unsatisfactory form, the appropriate column is left blank—as for many series for the war years. The disturbances created by war make for difficulties in obtaining satisfactory comparable classifications of some types of expenditures for wartime and peacetime years, even when statistics are available. Since our concern is with the effect of wars on peacetime government activities rather than with the years of war themselves, we have thought it least misleading to give wartime statistics only in suitably broad aggregates. Where statistics have been computed, but the total is negligible, this is shown by a dash (—), meaning that the figure concerned was less than 0.5 of the last unit recorded in the column. Thus, if figures are given to £0.1, sums of less than £0.05 are shown by a dash.

Population

The population series used is shown in Table A-1.

TABLE A-1

POPULATION OF THE UNITED KINGDOM, 1890–1955
(numbers in thousands; index, 1900 = 100)

	Population			Population	
Year	Number	Index	Year	Number	Index
1890	37,485	91	1920	43,740	106
1891	37,796	92	1921	44,027	107
1892	38,104	93	1922	44,325	108
1893	38,490	94	1923	44,596	108
1894	38,859	94	1924	44,915	109
1895	39,221	95	1925	45,059	109
1896	39,599	96	1926	45,232	110
1897	39,987	97	1927	45,389	110
1898	40,381	98	1928	45,580	111
1899	40,774	99	1929	45,679	111
1900	41,155	100	1930	45,873	111
1901	41,551	101	1931	46,038	112
1902	41,961	102	1932	46,335	113
1903	42,371	103	1933	46,520	113
1904	42,793	104	1934	46,666	113
1905	43,221	105	1935	46,869	114
1906	43,361	105	1936	47,081	114
1907	43,738	106	1937	47,289	115
1908	44,124	107	1938	47,494	115
1909	44,519	108	1939	47,762	116
1910	44,961	109	1940	48,226	117
1911	45,268	110	1941	48,216	117
1912	45,436	110	1942	48,400	118
1913	45,648	111	1943	48,789	118
1914	46,048	112	1944	49,016	119
1915	46,390	113	1945	49,182	120
1916	46,520	113	1946	49,217	120
1917	46,620	113	1947	49,571	120
1918	46,550	113	1948	49,620	121
1919	46,450	113	1949	49,930	121
			1950	50,180	122
			1951	50,225	122
			1952	50,444	123
			1953	50,611	123
			1954	50,784	123
			1955	50,968	124

For our purposes the ideal series would be one of total population normally resident in the United Kingdom during the period 1890–1955.

However, the nearest possible approximation is the *de facto* population, which excludes H.M. Forces serving overseas and merchant seamen at sea, although figures of total population are available for certain years.

The statistics of *de facto* population (midyear figures) for the periods 1890–1914, 1921–40, and 1948–55 are those of the Registrar General published in the *Annual Abstract of Statistics*. For the period 1915–20 there are no comparable estimates, only estimates of civilian population except for Scotland. For England and Wales and Ireland we have divided the recorded increase between 1914 and 1921 equally between the intervening years. For the period 1939–47, we have taken recorded figures of total population, because of the large difference between *de facto* peacetime population and *de facto* wartime population caused by the considerable proportion of the population serving overseas or at sea. As already explained, figures up to 1920 include the whole of Ireland; thereafter Eire is excluded.

Gross National Product at Factor Cost

As explained in Chapter 1, we use, as indicators of economic growth, gross national product (or expenditure) at factor cost at current and constant prices; and gross national product (or expenditure) at factor cost per head of population at current and constant prices. These indicators are shown in Table A-2. The relevant price indexes are discussed below.

The latest series of national income and expenditure covering our period are provided by James B. Jeffreys and Dorothy Walters, "National Income and Expenditure of the United Kingdom, 1870–1952," in *Income and Wealth, Series V*, London, 1955. Statistics for the years following 1937 in this study are taken from the official estimates contained in the Central Statistical Office's annual *Blue Book on National Income and Expenditure* and, for the war years, in the *Statistical Digest of the War*.

For the years before 1938 we have adopted the Jeffreys–Walters figures for current expenditure on goods and services, overseas lending, changes in stocks, and net indirect taxes (this component being, of course, deducted in order to arrive at factor cost estimates). In the case of public authorities' current expenditure on goods and services, we have constructed a series from different sources, which is described in detail below and which we believe to be more accurate, especially for the years before World War I. Improved estimates of gross fixed capital formation for the years 1924–37 have been published by Philip Redfern in his article "Net Investment in Fixed Assets in the United Kingdom, 1938–1953," *Journal of the Royal Statistical Society*, Series A, Vol. 118, Part 2, 1955. We have constructed a separate series from Jeffreys and Walters,

TABLE A-2

Gross National Product at Current and 1900 Prices, 1890-1955
(index, 1900 = 100)

YEAR	GNP AT CURRENT PRICES Total £ mn.	Index	Per Head £	Index	GNP AT 1900 PRICES Total £ mn.	Index	Per Head £	Index
1890	1,472	76	39.3	83	1,508	78	40.2	85
1891	1,464	75	38.7	82	1,506	77	39.8	84
1892	1,442	74	37.8	80	1,470	76	38.6	82
1893	1,437	74	37.3	79	1,483	76	38.5	82
1894	1,468	76	37.8	80	1,590	82	40.9	87
1895	1,507	78	38.4	81	1,666	86	42.5	90
1896	1,548	80	39.1	83	1,712	88	43.2	92
1897	1,600	82	40.0	85	1,730	89	43.3	92
1898	1,705	88	42.2	89	1,776	91	44.0	93
1899	1,805	93	44.3	94	1,903	98	46.7	99
1900	1,944	100	47.2	100	1,944	100	47.2	100
1901	1,889	97	45.5	96	1,893	97	45.6	97
1902	1,910	98	45.5	96	1,922	99	45.8	97
1903	1,846	95	43.6	92	1,842	95	43.5	92
1904	1,872	96	43.7	93	1,871	96	43.7	93
1905	1,970	101	45.6	97	1,967	101	45.5	96
1906	2,074	107	47.8	101	2,067	106	47.7	101
1907	2,142	110	49.0	104	2,094	108	47.9	101
1908	1,969	101	44.6	94	1,924	99	43.6	92
1909	2,034	105	45.7	97	1,970	101	44.3	94
1910	2,143	110	47.7	101	2,057	106	45.8	97
1911	2,243	115	49.5	105	2,154	111	47.6	101
1912	2,379	122	52.4	111	2,198	113	48.4	103
1913	2,468	127	54.1	115	2,275	117	49.8	106
1914	2,380	122	51.7	110	2,275	117	49.8	106
1915	2,740	141	59.1	125				
1916	3,260	168	70.1	149				
1917	3,880	200	83.2	176				
1918	4,690	241	100.8	214				
1919	5,860	301	126.2	267				
1920	6,070	312	138.8	294	(2,168)	(112)	(49.6)	(105)
1921	4,860	250	110.4	234	(1,870)	(96)	(42.5)	(90)
1922	4,230	218	95.4	202	(1,917)	(99)	(43.3)	(92)
1923	4,230	218	94.9	201	(2,070)	(106)	(46.4)	(98)
1924	4,332	223	96.4	204	2,127	109	47.4	100
1925	4,435	228	98.4	208	2,172	112	48.2	102
1926	4,303	221	95.1	201	2,104	108	46.5	99
1927	4,594	236	101.2	214	2,315	119	51.0	108
1928	4,523	233	99.2	210	2,289	118	50.2	106
1929	4,628	238	101.3	215	2,366	122	51.8	110

(continued)

TABLE A-2 (concluded)

| | GNP AT CURRENT PRICES | | | | GNP AT 1900 PRICES | | | |
| | Total | | Per Head | | Total | | Per Head | |
YEAR	£ mn.	Index	£	Index	£ mn.	Index	£	Index
1930	4,386	226	95.6	203	2,296	118	50.1	106
1931	4,074	210	88.5	187	2,241	115	48.7	103
1932	3,973	204	85.7	182	2,229	115	48.1	102
1933	4,141	213	89.0	189	2,377	122	51.1	108
1934	4,326	223	92.7	196	2,484	128	53.2	113
1935	4,587	236	97.9	207	2,634	135	56.2	119
1936	4,804	247	102.0	216	2,718	140	57.7	122
1937	5,064	260	107.1	227	2,769	142	58.6	124
1938	5,294	272	111.5	236	2,829	146	59.6	126
1939	5,550	285	116.2	246				
1940	6,500	334	134.8	286				
1941	7,360	379	152.6	323				
1942	8,050	414	166.3	352				
1943	8,480	436	173.8	368				
1944	8,680	447	177.1	375				
1945	8,750	450	177.9	377				
1946	8,787	452	178.5	378	2,815	145	57.2	121
1947	9,387	483	189.4	401	2,796	144	56.4	119
1948	10,376	534	209.1	443	2,851	147	57.5	122
1949	11,057	569	221.4	469	2,961	152	59.3	126
1950	11,636	599	231.9	491	3,024	156	60.3	128
1951	12,793	658	254.7	540	3,053	157	60.8	129
1952	13,928	716	276.1	585	3,131	161	62.1	132
1953	14,858	764	293.6	622	3,269	168	64.6	137
1954	15,909	818	313.3	664	3,450	177	67.9	144
1955	16,784	863	329.3	698	3,505	180	68.8	146

using these estimates. Our gross fixed capital formation figures are now based on the following sources.

1890–1913: Jeffreys and Walters use the estimates of A. K. Cairncross, *Home and Foreign Investment, 1870–1913,* Cambridge, Eng. 1953. We have adjusted certain individual price series in Cairncross's estimates, using Redfern's price series in his above-mentioned article, in order to improve comparability with estimates for the later period.

1914–23: Jeffreys and Walters have no figures for these years. We have compiled very rough estimates by interpolation using as our guide the changes in national income at constant prices in Jeffreys and Walters, *op. cit.* These estimate figures are not very reliable, and we show them for the relevant peacetime years in Table A-2 only, for purposes of broad comparison.

1924–37: Redfern, *op. cit.*

1938–55: Central Statistical Office, sources quoted above.

Price Indexes

The price series used in order to deflate GNP at factor cost are shown in Table A-3.

TABLE A-3

INDEXES OF PRICES, SELECTED YEARS, 1890–1955
(1900 = 100)

Year	Current Goods and Services	Total Fixed Capital Formation	Government Fixed Capital Formation	General Indexes Gross National Product	Government Expenditure
1890	98	93	98	98	98
1891	98	88	95	97	
1892	99	88	95	98	
1893	98	84	90	97	
1894	93	84	90	92	
1895	91	84	91	90	91
1896	91	84	91	90	
1897	93	87	93	92	
1898	97	88	93	96	
1899	95	94	97	95	
1900	100	100	100	100	100
1901	100	98	99	100	
1902	100	94	95	99	
1903	101	94	94	100	
1904	101	92	94	100	
1905	101	92	95	100	100
1906	101	94	96	100	
1907	103	94	96	102	
1908	103	93	96	102	
1909	104	92	95	103	
1910	105	92	95	104	103
1911	105	92	95	104	
1912	109	97	94	108	
1913	109	102	98	108	107
1920	278		348		282
1921	255		297		259
1922	218		200		216
1923	205		189		204
1924	204	201	197	204	203
1925	204	206	204	·204	204
1926	204	209	206	205	204
1927	198	202	201	198	198
1928	198	194	191	198	197
1929	196	192	188	196	195

(continued)

TABLE A-3 (concluded)

Year	Current Goods and Services	Total Fixed Capital Formation	Government Fixed Capital Formation	Gross National Product	Government Expenditure
				General Indexes	
1930	191	191	184	191	190
1931	181	189	176	182	180
1932	178	181	170	178	177
1933	174	176	163	174	173
1934	174	175	166	174	173
1935	174	175	171	174	174
1936	176	182	181	177	177
1937	181	197	194	183	183
1938	185	204	196	187	186
1946	303	420	408	312	307
1947	324	446	442	336	332
1948	350	485	471	364	361
1949	359	492	473	373	369
1950	370	501	478	385	380
1951	402	554	543	419	415
1952	424	615	594	445	441
1953	433	618	591	455	449
1954	440	616	586	461	454
1955	455	642	614	479	469

As explained in Chapter 1, we have not been content to use a single price index, such as a wholesale price index, in order to deflate GNP. The aggregate GNP figures have been split into two parts—gross fixed capital formation, and all other components of GNP. Ideally, separate price indexes for current goods and services, stocks, and net investment abroad would have been preferable. However, it was not possible to compile them, and we have deflated all these items by the one index.

PRICE INDEX FOR ALL COMPONENTS OTHER THAN FIXED CAPITAL FORMATION

It has been assumed that an index of prices of consumer goods and services is a suitable deflator for current values of increases in stocks, current expenditure on goods and services, and net investment abroad. We computed a consumers' expenditure average value index comparable as far as possible with that found in the London and Cambridge Economic Service series. Data for the compilation of such an index exist only for the period from 1900 onwards. For years before 1900 we used Bowley's index of retail prices. Our full list of sources follows:

1890–1900: A. L. Bowley, *Wages and Income in the United Kingdom,*

APPENDIX

Cambridge (Eng.), 1937, p. 30. The original index gives 1914 as the base year. We have adjusted the index so that the base year is 1900.

1901–19: A. R. Prest, assisted by A. A. Adams, *Consumers' Expenditure in the United Kingdom, 1900–19*, Cambridge (Eng.), 1954, p. 175. Prest and Adams give an implied price index of total consumers' expenditure at market prices with 1900 as base year.

1920–56: London and Cambridge Economic Service Bulletins published quarterly in *The Times Review of Industry*. The latest issues do not give figures for 1940–44; for these years, see the March 1956 issue. This index is based on Prest and Adams, *op. cit.*, and J. R. N. Stone, assisted by D. A. Rowe (and others), *The Measurement of Consumers' Expenditure and Behaviour (1920–38)* for the period up to 1938, and on Central Statistical Office estimates as given in the annual *Blue Book* for the postwar period. Figures for war years are our own estimates based on the *Statistical Digest of the War*. The L.C.E.S. index has 1938 as base year. This index has been spliced with the Prest-Adams index for the period 1900–19 with 1900 as base year.

PRICE INDEX FOR FIXED CAPITAL GOODS

The considerable research into capital formation since 1870 by such writers as Cairncross and Redfern has been referred to earlier. Fortunately, we have available the index compiled by Philip Redfern (*op. cit.*, pp. 170–171) for the whole period covered, with the exception of the years 1914–23. We have merely changed the base year for the index to 1900, and have not attempted estimates for the missing years.

CONVERSION OF GNP TO CONSTANT 1900 PRICES

Having deflated gross fixed capital formation at current prices by the index in Column 2, Table A-3, and the other components valued at current prices by the index in Column 1, Table A-3, we arrive by simple addition for the relevant year at the figure for GNP at constant prices. For the sake of completeness, we have reproduced the implied "price" index as Column 4 in Table A-3. This index does not differ appreciably from the price index of current goods and services until after World War II, when the relative rise in prices of capital goods was particularly marked.

CONVERSION OF GOVERNMENT EXPENDITURE TO CONSTANT 1900 PRICES

The full details of the calculation of government expenditure at current prices are given below. It may be useful, however, to complete our statement of the calculation of real expenditure changes by indicating the method used to deflate government expenditure. From the very detailed calculations in Redfern, *op. cit.*, it was possible to construct a

157

separate price index for government capital formation by converting the Redfern estimates to the base year 1900. Government current expenditure on goods and services, transfers and subsidies, and the very small changes in stocks were all deflated by the current goods and services price index in Column 1, Table A-3. Again, for comparative purposes, the implied "price" index is recorded separately in Column 5 of Table A-3. This index differs more widely from that in Column 1 than the index for GNP does.

Unemployment Series

The unemployment series used is found in Table A-4.

Data on unemployment are important for the discussion in Chapter 3. An ideal series would be one which would yield the percentage of the total labor force unemployed, but this is only possible for the period from 1947 onward. For the period 1890–1921, it is possible to obtain only the percentage unemployed from the returns of trade unions paying unemployment benefits, so that the coverage is not wide enough. From 1923 to 1947 we can increase the coverage with figures for the percentage of total insured population who are unemployed. Because of the lack of comparability in the separate series, we preferred to use unemployment percentages rather than numbers unemployed in order to illustrate the connection, if any, between government expenditure and unemployment trends. The sources for our series follow.

1890–1921: W. H. Beveridge, *Unemployment—A Problem of Industry,* London, 1930, pp. 39, 432, 459.

1923–55: Central Statistical Office, *Annual Abstract of Statistics,* Vol. 88, 1938–50; Vol. 89, 1952; Vol. 94, 1957.

Government Expenditure

The discussion of the statistics of government expenditure is divided into three sections: (1) definitions, (2) the sources of statistical information, and (3) the figures in the tables of government expenditure from which the tables and charts in the text were compiled.

DEFINITIONS

We have attempted to produce statistical series which conform with the requirements laid down by social accounting principles.[1] One over-riding requirement, so far as government expenditure is concerned, is that there be no duplication of expenditures. The accounts of the various

[1] For full discussion of these principles as applied to the government sector, see, for example, United Nations, Department of Economic and Social Affairs, *A Manual for Economic and Functional Classification of Government Transactions,* New York, 1958, Part I.

TABLE A-4
PERCENTAGE AND INDEXES OF UNEMPLOYMENT,
SELECTED YEARS, 1890–1955

Year	Percentage of Unemployment	Indexes of Unemployment
1890	2.10	86
1895	6.0	245
1900	2.45	100
1905	5.25	214
1910	5.10	208
1911	3.05	124
1912	3.15	129
1913	2.10	86
1914	3.25	133
1915	1.0	41
1916	0.45	18
1917	0.6	24
1918	0.7	29
1919	2.5	102
1920	2.55	104
1921	15.6	637
1923	11.5	100
1924	9.7	84
1925	11.2	97
1926	14.4	125
1927	9.2	80
1928	11.6	101
1929	9.7	84
1930	16.2	141
1931	22.0	191
1932	22.8	198
1933	19.5	170
1934	16.7	145
1935	14.4	125
1936	11.7	102
1937	9.5	87
1938	12.1	105
1939	7.9	69
1940	5.0	44
1941	1.6	14
1942	0.7	6
1943	0.5	4
1944	0.5	4
1945	0.9	8
1946	2.5	22
1947	1.8	16
1948	1.4	100
1949	1.2	86
1950	1.3	93
1951	0.9	64
1952	2.0	139
1953	1.3	93
1954	1.1	79
1955	0.7	50

parts of the government sector are consolidated and no intra-governmental transactions appear. For example, in the United Kingdom the Exchequer provides local authorities with substantial grants. We should be double-counting if we showed these grants as part of central government expenditure and then showed the expenditure they finance as part of local government expenditure. Similarly, central government contributions to the national insurance system are not recorded as part of central government expenditure.

Allowing for certain exceptions listed below, we have adopted the definition of the public sector used by the Central Statistical Office, as found in the national income and expenditure *Blue Books*.[2] This aids comparability over time. In general terms, therefore, the public sector includes the central government, the national insurance system, and the local authorities of the United Kingdom.

The central government embraces a wide number of separate activities involving collective consumption. It also includes certain trading activities, although it excludes the nationalized industries. The nationalized industries are enumerated in Chapter 7. They can be distinguished from certain trading activities of the central government, notably the Post Office, by their financial independence, particularly in regard to borrowing powers. The inclusion of certain trading services in the central government sector. presents problems of classification of expenditures, considered below. The wide range of activities of the public sector will be discerned in the functional classification of expenditures and the division of these expenditures between central and local governments in Tables A-15 and A-20.

The British national insurance system (in contrast to those of other countries), which covers unemployment, sickness, retirement, and industrial injuries as well as other forms of benefits, is administered by a central government department that has no control over reserve policy. Contributions are paid to a central National Insurance Fund, making the system part of the central government's activities.

The definition of local authorities for our purpose corresponds to that found in Part XI of the Local Government Act, 1933. It includes all local governing bodies, other than companies trading for profit, that have the power to levy rates, tolls, or dues, or to require them to be levied. Our figures, therefore, cover the transactions of drainage boards, water boards, harbor boards (other than national bodies), the conservators of common land, the trustees of certain London squares, and other such bodies. The main activities of local authorities have changed markedly over the period in question, as made clear in Chapter 6.

---

[2] See *National Income Statistics, Sources and Methods*, C.S.O., 1956.

We now turn to certain questions associated with the nature of expenditures. Certain government nontrading services collect fees and other receipts for services rendered, for example the prescription fee under the National Health Service. These are deducted from expenditures in order to arrive at our final figures. Other fees and tax receipts are, of course, treated as government receipts and are not deducted. In the case of local government, any income other than government grants and local rates is deducted from total gross expenditure. Thus we deduct rents received by local authorities for housing from the total expenditure on housing. School fees, important during the period before World War II, are also deducted. On the other hand, government purchases of goods and services are valued at market prices and thus include a small proportion of taxes on expenditure which the government pays to itself. Net expenditure should exclude this tax element, but it was not excluded, because the effort would be out of proportion to the small amount of taxation involved (see also Chapter 1).

Certain trading services are included within the public sector because of their financial dependence on government. For the central government, the Post Office is the most important; for local governments, public utilities, such as waterworks and electricity and gas services before nationalization. In accordance with social accounting procedure, current expenditures of these trading services are regarded as self-liquidating and are not included in our figures. On the other hand, capital expenditures are included. Our procedure follows that of the Central Statistical Office, except in one important instance. The C.S.O. regards housing as a trading service, and the deficit on current account is treated as a subsidy. Regarding this as unrealistic, we treated housing as a social service and the deficit as a transfer payment. Total housing expenditure is not affected by this treatment, but the form of expenditure and its division between central and local governments are different. By our method, central government grants for local authority housing disappear on consolidation, and total housing expenditure on current account appears as a transfer item in the local authority account. In the C.S.O. tabulations this expenditure appears partly as a central government subsidy and partly as a local government one.

Further information on definitions of types of government expenditures is given in the discussion of the various classifications employed in later tables.

SOURCES OF INFORMATION ON GOVERNMENT EXPENDITURE

The pioneering work in reclassifying government expenditure according to the requirements of modern economic analysis has been undertaken by the Central Statistical Office. However, the period covered by the

APPENDIX

C.S.O. figures is only from 1938 onward. As the sources and methods used by the C.S.O. for this period are given in considerable detail in *National Income Statistics, Sources and Methods*, Chapters VII, IX, and X, they are not discussed here, but departures from C.S.O. methods of classification are always noted. Our task in this section, therefore, is to list the sources and the methods of compilation for figures before 1938, but we shall have something to say about the adequacy of some of the figures for the period 1938–46.

In general terms, for periods before 1938, the sources used for the official calculations and also for ours are the accounts prepared for the purpose of public control of expenditure. For central government, these accounts are the appropriation accounts and the audited finance accounts published as *Parliamentary Papers*. Local government figures have been compiled from the returns of receipts and expenditure required by Act of Parliament. The sources for the appropriate periods are given below.

Central Government

1890–91—1918–19: These figures are based on a detailed reclassification of the appropriation accounts for selected years. The reliability of the series is probably good, although it was not possible in all cases to be sure that all intra-governmental transactions were removed.

1920–38: Based on information supplied by J. E. G. Utting and Dorothy Cole in "The Income and Expenditure of U.K. Public Authorities, 1920–38" (unpublished). Figures on government expenditure on goods and services from this study have already been published in Jeffreys and Walters, *op. cit.* This information was supplemented, especially in the case of transfer expenditure, from the *Annual Abstracts of Statistics*. The reliability of the series is good.

1939–45: Central Statistical Office, *Statistical Digest of the War*, Table 182. On the question of reliability we quote from the *Digest*, p. 233: "This series has been prepared as far as possible on the same basis as those contained in National Income and Expenditure of the United Kingdom, 1946–49. The correspondence, nevertheless, is not exact. While continuity has been preserved for the war years 1939–45, there remains in certain points of detail an unavoidable break between the figures for this period and the figures for 1938 and for the postwar period."

1946–55: Central Statistical Office, *Blue Book on National Income and Expenditure*, 1957.

Local Government

For local government expenditure, it is more useful to indicate sources by geographical areas rather than by chronological sequence. In any case, the sources for each area are the same throughout the period studied.

For England and Wales the data was compiled from the *Local Taxation Returns*. (The name of the document was changed to *Local Government Financial Statistics* in 1934.) Our information is comparable with that published by the C.S.O. in the annual *Blue Books*. The source is the same in both cases and the C.S.O. have been consulted about their methods of compilation.

For Scotland, local financial returns are collected by the Scottish Home Department. For the years 1935 and after, these are available only in mimeographed form; the figures published before 1935 were published in Local Taxation Returns.

Local financial returns for Ireland until partition in 1920 are available in summary form in British *Parliamentary Papers* and in the *Annual Abstracts of Statistics*. Local financial returns published after 1920 for Northern Ireland were not available, and no attempt was made to calculate figures of local government expenditure for that area. We have written up our estimates for Great Britain by a uniform 1.5 per cent for 1920–38. This is not entirely arbitrary. Summary figures of expenditure of local authorities in Northern Ireland are published in the *Annual Abstracts of Statistics* (see, e.g., Volume No. 84, Table 270, page 227). We have expressed the total expenditure of local authorities in Northern Ireland obtained from this source as a percentage of the uncorrected total expenditure of local authorities for the United Kingdom as contained in the summary tables in the *Annual Abstracts*. The percentage obtained in this way varies very little from the one we have adopted.

NOTES ON INDIVIDUAL APPENDIX TABLES
OF GOVERNMENT EXPENDITURE

Tables A-5 and A-6

These two tables may be considered together. The sources of information which enable us to express government expenditure per head at current and constant prices have already been described.

One result of using a different deflator for GNP and government expenditure at 1900 prices is that there is a divergence between the total government expenditure as a percentage of GNP at current prices and as a percentage of GNP at constant prices. This is illustrated in Table A-6. The divergence is, however, slight; when rounded off to the nearest whole number, it disappears. The last column of Table A-5 is expressed in this form.

TABLE A-5
Total Government Expenditure at Current and 1900 Prices, Selected Years, 1890–1955

YEAR	AT CURRENT PRICES				AT 1900 PRICES				As Percentage of GNP
	Total		Per Head		Total		Per Head		
	£ mn.	Index	£	Index	£ mn.	Index	£	Index	
1890	130.6	47	3.5	51	133.3	47	3.6	53	9
1895	156.8	56	4.0	59	172.3	61	4.4	64	10
1900	280.8	100	6.8	100	280.8	100	6.8	100	14
1905	241.7	86	5.6	82	241.7	86	5.6	82	12
1910	272.0	97	6.1	89	263.6	94	5.9	86	13
1913	305.4	109	6.7	98	284.2	101	6.2	91	12
1915	958.1	341	20.7	303					35
1917	1,515.5	540	32.5	476					39
1918	2,427.0	864	52.1	764					52
1920	1,592.1	567	36.4	533	565.3	201	12.9	189	26
1921	1,429.5	509	32.5	476	552.2	197	12.5	183	29
1922	1,177.3	419	26.6	390	544.5	194	12.3	180	28
1923	1,025.2	365	23.0	337	503.0	179	11.3	166	24
1924	1,027.0	366	22.9	336	504.8	180	11.2	164	24
1925	1,071.9	382	23.8	349	525.4	187	11.7	171	24
1926	1,106.3	394	24.5	359	541.7	193	12.0	176	26
1927	1,105.8	394	24.4	358	557.6	199	12.3	180	24
1928	1,094.7	390	24.0	352	554.8	198	12.2	179	24
1929	1,107.2	394	24.2	355	567.3	202	12.4	182	24

(continued)

TABLE A-5 (concluded)

YEAR	AT CURRENT PRICES				AT 1900 PRICES				As Percentage of GNP
	Total		Per Head		Total		Per Head		
	£ mn.	Index	£	Index	£ mn.	Index	£	Index	
1930	1,144.8	408	25.0	366	601.8	214	13.1	192	26
1931	1,173.5	418	25.5	374	650.3	232	14.1	207	29
1932	1,138.0	405	24.6	361	642.2	229	13.9	204	29
1933	1,066.0	380	22.9	336	615.9	219	13.2	193	26
1934	1,060.9	378	22.7	333	612.0	218	13.1	192	25
1935	1,117.4	398	23.8	349	643.2	229	13.7	201	24
1936	1,186.8	423	25.2	369	672.4	239	14.3	210	25
1937	1,303.5	464	27.6	405	713.7	254	15.1	221	26
1938	1,587.0	565	33.4	490	851.2	303	17.9	262	30
1939	1,960	698	41.0	601					35
1940	3,905	1,391	81.0	1,187					60
1941	5,338	1,901	110.7	1,622					73
1942	5,860	2,087	121.1	1,775					73
1943	6,265	2,231	128.4	1,882					74
1944	6,303	2,245	128.6	1,885					73
1945	5,779	2,058	117.5	1,722					66
1946	4,530	1,613	92.0	1,348	1,474	525	29.9	438	52
1947	4,130	1,471	83.3	1,221	1,243	443	25.1	368	44
1948	4,215	1,501	84.9	1,244	1,169	416	23.6	346	41
1949	4,423	1,575	88.6	1,299	1,199	427	24.0	352	40
1950	4,539	1,616	90.5	1,326	1,195	426	23.8	349	39
1951	5,208	1,855	103.7	1,520	1,255	447	25.0	366	41
1952	5,777	2,057	114.5	1,678	1,311	467	26.0	381	42
1953	6,048	2,154	119.5	1,751	1,346	479	26.6	390	41
1954	5,976	2,128	117.7	1,725	1,315	468	25.9	380	38
1955	6,143	2,188	120.5	1,766	1,309	466	25.7	377	37

TABLE A-6

Total Government Expenditure as Percentage of Gross National Product, at Current and 1900 Prices, Selected Years, 1890–1955
(index, 1900 = 100)

Year	At Current Prices		At 1900 Prices	
	Percentage	Index of Percentage	Percentage	Index of Percentage
1890	8.9	62	8.8	61
1895	10.4	72	10.3	72
1900	14.4	100	14.4	100
1905	12.3	85	12.3	85
1910	12.7	88	12.8	89
1913	12.4	86	12.5	87
1915	35.0	243	35.0	243
1917	39.0	271	38.9	270
1918	51.7	359	51.6	358
1920	26.2	182	26.1	181
1921	29.4	204	29.5	205
1922	27.8	193	28.4	197
1923	24.2	168	24.3	169
1924	23.7	165	23.7	165
1925	24.2	168	24.2	168
1926	25.7	178	25.7	178
1927	24.1	167	24.1	167
1928	24.2	168	24.2	168
1929	23.9	166	24.0	167
1930	26.1	181	26.2	182
1931	28.8	200	29.0	201
1932	28.6	199	28.8	200
1933	25.7	178	25.9	180
1934	24.5	170	24.6	171
1935	24.4	169	24.4	169
1936	24.7	172	24.7	172
1937	25.7	178	25.8	179
1938	30.0	208	30.1	209
1939	35.3	245	34.9	242
1940	60.1	417	59.9	416
1941	72.5	503	72.4	503
1942	72.8	506	72.7	505
1943	73.9	513	73.8	512
1944	72.6	504	72.5	503
1945	66.0	458	65.8	457
1946	51.6	358	52.4	364
1947	44.0	306	44.4	308
1948	40.6	282	41.0	285
1949	40.0	278	40.5	281
1950	39.0	271	39.5	274
1951	40.7	283	41.1	285
1952	41.5	288	41.9	291
1953	40.7	283	41.2	286
1954	37.6	261	38.1	265
1955	36.6	254	37.3	259

Tables A-7, A-8, A-9, and A-10

The distinction between war-related and military and defense expenditure is explained in Chapter 4. It is necessary, however, to describe in more detail the individual components of these forms of expenditure.

INTEREST ON NATIONAL DEBT. These figures represent interest on the debt of central government, after deduction of intergovernmental debt interest payments. They were compiled from Pember and Boyle, *British Government Securities in the Twentieth Century* (privately circulated).

While, as argued in Chapter 4, it is reasonable to regard interest on national debt as purely the consequence of war finance, it is appropriate to do so only in the case of central government debt. We discuss the question of the interest on all public debt in more detail in another context (see notes to Tables A-11 through A-14).

WAR PENSIONS. This figure includes pensions and allowances paid to members of the armed forces and mercantile marine, payments made for medical treatment to pensioners, and expenses of the administration (central and local) of war pensions.

WAR DAMAGE COMPENSATION. This includes payments made to individuals and businesses (but not local authorities) under the War Damage Acts of 1943 and 1949. For further details see C.S.O., *National Income Statistics, Sources and Methods*, pp. 203–204.

RELEASE LEAVE PAY. This represents the payments to demobilized ex-servicemen of the 1939–45 war for paid leave on release.

WAR GRATUITIES. These are the lump-sum payments to service personnel on demobilization from the 1939–45 war.

DEFENSE EXPENDITURE. The definition of military expenditure follows that of the C.S.O., and corresponds to that agreed upon by the North Atlantic Treaty Organization. It thereafter includes, as well as the expenditures of the three main Service departments, the major part of the expenditure of the Ministry of Supply and of the United Kingdom Atomic Energy Authority. To these items must be added civil defense expenditure. For further details, see *National Income Statistics, Sources and Methods*, pp. 249–253.

Statistics for war-related expenditures other than national debt interest payments are not to be found in the sources given above for some parts of the period. Since a random check indicated that these items were almost certainly of negligible importance, they are ignored.

TABLE A-7

Government Expenditure for War-Related and Defense Purposes, at Current Prices, Selected Years, 1890–1955

(millions of pounds)

| | War-Related Expenditure | | | | | | | |
Year	Total	National Debt	War Pensions	War Damage Compensation	Release Leave Pay	War Gratuities	Defense	Total
1890	23.8	23.8					34.9	58.7
1895	22.7	22.7					43.1	65.8
1900	19.6	19.6					134.9	154.5
1905	24.4	24.4					63.1	87.5
1910	20.2	20.2					74.3	94.5
1913	18.7	18.7					91.3	110.0
1920	429.5	324.8	104.7				519.7	949.2
1921	406.1	307.8	98.3				270.0	676.1
1922	383.3	298.8	84.5				168.7	552.0
1923	376.2	301.7	74.5				134.9	511.1
1924	375.7	305.4	70.3				130.9	506.6
1925	372.1	304.5	67.6				133.6	505.7
1926	374.4	310.3	64.1				133.6	508.0
1927	368.9	308.3	60.6				130.0	498.9
1928	362.6	305.1	57.5				125.1	487.7
1929	359.0	304.2	54.8				123.9	482.9

(continued)

TABLE A-7 (concluded)

War-Related Expenditure

Year	Total	National Debt	War Pensions	War Damage Compensation	Release Leave Pay	War Gratuities	Defense	Total
1930	343.3	290.9	52.4				119.2	462.5
1931	339.7	289.7	50.0				115.4	455.1
1932	328.7	281.2	47.5				110.4	439.1
1933	273.9	228.4	45.5				112.4	386.3
1934	251.9	208.2	43.7				118.9	370.8
1935	249.4	206.7	42.7				140.8	390.2
1936	247.4	205.7	41.7				183.0	430.4
1937	249.9	209.4	40.5				254.7	504.6
1938	251.9	212.5	39.4				469.0	720.9
1946	1,091	486	83	124	163	235	1,471	2,562
1947	962	519	89	257	36	61	846	1,808
1948	783	509	90	156	27	1	693	1,476
1949	761	507	89	160	5	—	760	1,521
1950	701	507	86	108	—	—	836	1,537
1951	714	550	84	80	—	—	1,293	2,007
1952	763	609	89	65	—	—	1,641	2,404
1953	794	638	89	67	—	—	1,725	2,519
1954	768	637	91	40	—	—	1,706	2,474
1955	826	707	93	26	—	—	1,606	2,432

TABLE A-8

GOVERNMENT EXPENDITURE FOR WAR-RELATED AND DEFENSE PURPOSES, PER
HEAD OF POPULATION, AT 1900 PRICES, SELECTED YEARS, 1890–1955
(amounts in pounds; index, 1900 = 100)

Year	War-Related Amount	Index	Defense Amount	Index	Total Amount	Index
1890	0.6	120	1.0	30	1.6	42
1895	0.6	120	1.2	36	1.8	47
1900	0.5	100	3.3	100	3.8	100
1905	0.6	120	1.5	45	2.1	55
1910	0.4	80	1.6	48	2.0	53
1913	0.4	80	1.9	58	2.3	61
1920	3.5	700	4.3	130	7.8	205
1921	3.6	720	2.4	73	6.0	158
1922	4.0	800	1.7	52	5.7	150
1923	4.1	820	1.5	45	5.6	147
1924	4.1	820	1.4	42	5.5	145
1925	4.0	800	1.5	45	5.5	145
1926	4.1	820	1.4	42	5.5	145
1927	4.1	820	1.4	42	5.5	145
1928	4.0	800	1.4	42	5.4	142
1929	4.0	800	1.4	42	5.4	142
1930	3.9	780	1.4	42	5.3	139
1931	4.1	820	1.4	42	5.5	145
1932	4.0	800	1.3	39	5.3	139
1933	3.4	680	1.4	42	4.8	126
1934	3.1	620	1.5	45	4.6	121
1935	3.1	620	1.7	52	4.8	126
1936	3.0	600	2.2	67	5.2	137
1937	2.9	580	3.0	91	5.9	155
1938	2.9	580	5.3	161	8.2	216
1946	7.3	1,460	9.9	300	17.2	453
1947	6.0	1,200	5.3	161	11.3	297
1948	4.5	900	4.0	121	8.5	224
1949	4.2	840	4.2	127	8.2	216
1950	3.8	760	4.5	136	8.3	218
1951	3.5	700	6.4	194	9.9	261
1952	3.6	720	7.6	230	11.2	295
1953	3.6	720	7.8	236	11.4	300
1954	3.4	680	7.6	230	11.0	289
1955	3.5	700	6.9	209	10.4	274

TABLE A-9

TOTAL GOVERNMENT EXPENDITURE AND EXPENDITURE FOR WAR-RELATED AND DEFENSE PURPOSES, AT CURRENT PRICES, 1890–1955

(millions of pounds)

Year	Total Government Expenditure (1)	National Debt (2)	(1) Minus (2) (3)	National Debt and Other War-Related (4)	(1) Minus (4) (5)	(4) Plus Defense (6)	(1) Minus (6) (7)
1890	130.6	23.8	106.8	23.8	106.8	58.7	71.9
1895	156.8	22.7	134.1	22.7	134.1	65.8	91.0
1900	280.8	19.6	261.2	19.6	261.2	154.5	126.3
1905	241.7	24.4	217.3	24.4	217.3	87.5	154.2
1910	272.0	20.2	251.8	20.2	251.8	94.5	177.5
1913	305.4	18.7	286.7	18.7	286.7	110.0	195.4
1920	1,592.1	324.8	1,267.3	429.5	1,162.6	949.2	642.9
1921	1,429.5	307.8	1,121.7	406.1	1,023.4	676.1	753.4
1922	1,177.3	298.8	878.5	383.3	794.0	552.0	625.3
1923	1,025.2	301.7	723.5	376.2	649.0	511.1	514.1
1924	1,027.0	305.4	721.6	375.7	651.3	506.6	520.4
1925	1,071.9	304.5	767.4	372.1	699.8	505.7	566.2
1926	1,106.3	310.3	796.0	374.4	731.9	508.0	598.3
1927	1,105.8	308.3	797.5	368.9	736.9	498.9	606.9
1928	1,094.7	305.1	789.6	362.6	732.1	487.7	607.0
1929	1,107.2	304.2	803.0	359.0	748.2	482.9	624.3

(continued)

TABLE A-9 (concluded)

Year	Total Government Expenditure (1)	National Debt (2)	(1) Minus (2) (3)	National Debt and Other War-Related (4)	(1) Minus (4) (5)	(4) Plus Defense (6)	(1) Minus (6) (7)
1930	1,144.8	290.9	853.9	343.3	801.5	462.5	682.3
1931	1,173.5	289.7	883.8	339.7	833.8	455.1	718.4
1932	1,138.0	281.2	856.8	328.7	809.3	439.1	698.9
1933	1,066.0	228.4	837.6	273.9	792.1	386.3	679.7
1934	1,060.9	208.2	852.7	251.9	809.0	370.8	690.1
1935	1,117.4	206.7	910.7	249.4	868.0	390.2	727.2
1936	1,186.8	205.7	981.1	247.4	939.4	430.4	756.4
1937	1,303.5	209.4	1,094.1	249.9	1,053.6	504.6	798.9
1938	1,587.0	212.5	1,374.5	251.9	1,335.1	720.9	866.1
1946	4,530	486	4,044	1,091	3,439	2,562	1,968
1947	4,130	519	3,611	962	3,168	1,808	2,322
1948	4,215	509	3,706	783	3,432	1,476	2,739
1949	4,423	507	3,916	761	3,662	1,521	2,902
1950	4,539	507	4,032	701	3,838	1,537	3,002
1951	5,208	550	4,658	714	4,494	2,007	3,201
1952	5,777	609	5,168	763	5,014	2,404	3,373
1953	6,048	638	5,410	794	5,254	2,519	3,529
1954	5,976	637	5,339	768	5,208	2,474	3,502
1955	6,143	707	5,436	826	5,317	2,432	3,711

TABLE A-10

GOVERNMENT EXPENDITURE OTHER THAN FOR WAR-RELATED PURPOSES,
PER HEAD OF POPULATION, AT 1900 PRICES, SELECTED YEARS, 1890–1955
(amounts in pounds; index, 1900 = 100)

	Total Government Expenditure		*National Debt*		GOVERNMENT EXPENDITURE LESS: *National Debt and Other War-Related*[a]		*War-Related and Defense*	
EAR	Amount	Index	Amount	Index	Amount	Index	Amount	Index
890	3.6	53	3.0	48	3.0	48	2.0	67
895	4.4	65	3.8	60	3.8	60	2.6	87
900	6.8	100	6.3	100	6.3	100	3.0	100
905	5.6	82	5.0	79	5.0	79	3.5	117
910	5.9	87	5.5	87	5.5	87	3.9	130
913	6.2	91	5.8	92	5.8	92	3.9	130
920	12.9	190	10.2	162	9.4	149	5.1	170
921	12.5	184	9.8	156	8.9	141	6.5	217
922	12.3	181	9.2	146	8.3	132	6.6	220
923	11.3	166	8.0	127	7.2	114	5.7	190
924	11.2	165	7.9	125	7.1	113	5.7	190
925	11.7	172	8.4	133	7.7	122	6.2	207
926	12.0	176	8.6	136	7.9	125	6.5	217
927	12.3	181	8.9	141	8.2	130	6.8	227
928	12.2	179	8.8	140	8.2	130	6.8	227
929	12.4	182	9.0	143	8.4	133	7.0	233
930	13.1	193	9.8	156	9.2	146	7.8	260
931	14.1	207	10.6	168	10.0	159	8.6	287
932	13.9	204	10.5	167	9.9	157	8.6	287
933	13.2	194	10.4	165	9.8	156	8.4	280
934	13.1	193	10.5	167	10.0	159	8.5	283
935	13.7	201	11.2	178	10.6	168	8.9	297
936	14.3	210	11.8	187	11.3	179	9.1	303
937	15.1	222	12.7	202	12.2	194	9.2	307
938	17.9	263	15.5	256	15.0	238	9.7	323
946	29.9	440	26.7	424	22.6	359	12.7	423
947	25.1	369	21.9	348	19.1	303	13.8	460
948	23.6	347	20.7	328	19.1	303	15.1	503
949	24.0	353	21.2	336	19.8	314	15.8	527
950	23.8	350	21.1	335	20.0	317	15.5	517
951	25.0	368	22.3	354	21.5	341	15.1	503
952	26.0	382	23.2	368	22.4	356	14.8	493
953	26.6	391	23.7	376	23.0	365	15.2	507
954	25.9	381	23.1	367	22.5	357	14.9	497
955	25.7	378	22.7	360	22.2	352	15.3	510

[a] War pensions, war damage compensation, release leave pay, and war gratuities.

Tables A-11–A-12, A-13, and A-14

These tables give full details of the economic classification of government expenditures as a whole. For a full description of the various components, see *Sources and Methods*, Chapter 8. These definitions are considered briefly below.

TABLE A-11

GOVERNMENT EXPENDITURE ON TRANSFERS AND SUBSIDIES, TOTALS AND PER HEAD, AT CURRENT AND 1900 PRICES, SELECTED YEARS, 1890–1955 (index, 1900 = 100)

YEAR	AT CURRENT PRICES				AT 1900 PRICES			
	Total		Per Head		Total		Per Head	
	£ mn.	Index	£	Index	£ mn.	Index	£	Index
1890	33.7	93	.9	102	34.4	95	.9	105
1895	37.7	104	1.0	109	41.4	114	1.1	120
1900	36.2	100	.9	100	36.2	100	.9	100
1905	43.5	120	1.0	115	43.1	119	1.0	114
1910	55.1	152	1.2	140	52.5	145	1.2	133
1913	58.9	163	1.3	147	54.0	149	1.2	134
1915	90.4	250	2.0	222				
1917	251.1	694	5.4	612				
1918	310.8	859	6.7	759				
1920	602.5	1,664	13.8	1,565	216.7	599	5.0	562
1921	640.4	1,769	14.5	1,652	251.1	694	5.7	648
1922	574.1	1,586	13.0	1,472	263.3	727	5.9	675
1923	517.3	1,429	11.6	1,318	252.3	697	5.7	643
1924	506.6	1,399	11.3	1,282	248.3	686	5.5	628
1925	520.4	1,438	11.6	1,312	255.1	705	5.7	643
1926	534.3	1,476	11.8	1,342	261.9	723	5.8	658
1927	527.7	1,458	11.6	1,322	266.5	736	5.9	667
1928	534.1	1,475	11.7	1,332	269.7	745	5.9	673
1929	541.4	1,496	11.9	1,437	276.2	763	6.1	687

(continued)

TABLE A-11 (concluded)

YEAR	AT CURRENT PRICES Total £ mn.	AT CURRENT PRICES Total Index	AT CURRENT PRICES Per Head £	AT CURRENT PRICES Per Head Index	AT 1900 PRICES Total £ mn.	AT 1900 PRICES Total Index	AT 1900 PRICES Per Head £	AT 1900 PRICES Per Head Index
1930	568.9	1,572	12.4	1,409	297.9	823	6.5	737
1931	593.1	1,638	12.9	1,464	327.7	905	7.1	809
1932	595.2	1,644	12.9	1,460	334.4	924	7.2	820
1933	538.6	1,488	11.6	1,316	309.5	855	6.7	756
1934	519.3	1,435	11.1	1,265	298.4	824	6.4	726
1935	523.5	1,446	11.2	1,269	300.9	831	6.4	730
1936	514.6	1,422	10.9	1,242	292.4	808	6.2	706
1937	516.0	1,425	10.9	1,240	285.1	788	6.0	685
1938	545.6	1,507	11.5	1,306	294.9	815	6.2	706
1939	543	1,500	11.4	1,292				
1940	647	1,787	13.4	1,525				
1941	978	2,702	20.3	2,305				
1942	1,039	2,870	21.5	2,440				
1943	1,117	3,086	22.9	2,601				
1944	1,141	3,152	23.3	2,645				
1945	1,425	3,936	29.0	3,292				
1946	2,181	6,025	44.3	5,035	720	1,989	14.6	1,662
1947	2,092	5,779	42.2	4,795	646	1,785	13.0	1,481
1948	2,009	5,550	40.5	4,601	574	1,586	11.6	1,315
1949	2,005	5,539	40.2	4,564	559	1,544	11.2	1,273
1950	2,031	5,610	40.5	4,599	549	1,517	10.9	1,243
1951	1,970	5,442	39.2	4,457	490	1,354	9.8	1,109
1952	2,088	5,768	41.4	4,703	492	1,359	9.8	1,108
1953	2,157	5,959	42.6	4,843	498	1,376	9.8	1,118
1954	2,211	6,108	43.5	4,948	503	1,390	9.9	1,125
1955	2,333	6,445	45.8	5,201	513	1,417	10.1	1,144

175

TABLE A-12

GOVERNMENT EXPENDITURE ON GOODS AND SERVICES, TOTAL, PER HEAD, AND AS PERCENTAGE OF TOTAL GOVERNMENT EXPENDITURE AND GROSS NATIONAL PRODUCT, AT CURRENT AND 1900 PRICES, SELECTED YEARS, 1890–1955
(index, 1900 = 100)

| | AT CURRENT PRICES | | | | AT 1900 PRICES | | | | AS PERCENTAGE OF: | | | |
| | Total | | Per Head | | Total | | Per Head | | Total Expenditure | | GNP | |
YEAR	£ mn.	Index	£	Index	£ mn.	Index	£	Index	At Current Prices	At 1900 Prices	At Current Prices	At 1900 Prices
1890	96.9	40	2.6	43	98.9	40	2.6	44	74	74	7	7
1895	119.1	49	3.0	51	130.9	54	3.3	56	76	76	8	8
1900	244.6	100	5.9	100	244.6	100	5.9	100	87	87	13	13
1905	198.2	81	4.6	77	198.6	81	4.6	77	82	82	10	10
1910	216.9	89	4.8	81	211.1	86	4.7	79	80	80	10	10
1913	246.5	101	5.4	91	230.2	94	5.0	85	81	81	10	10
1915	867.7	355	18.7	315					91		32	
1917	1,264.4	517	27.1	456					83		33	
1918	2,116.2	865	45.5	765					87		45	
1920	989.6	405	22.6	381	348.6	143	8.0	134	62	62	16	
1921	789.1	323	17.9	302	301.1	123	6.8	115	55	55	16	
1922	603.2	247	13.6	229	281.2	115	6.3	107	51	52	14	
1923	507.9	208	11.4	192	250.7	102	5.6	95	50	50	12	
1924	520.4	213	11.6	195	256.5	105	5.7	96	51	51	12	12
1925	551.5	225	12.2	206	270.3	111	6.0	101	52	51	12	12
1926	572.0	234	12.6	213	279.8	114	6.2	104	52	52	13	13
1927	578.1	236	12.7	214	291.1	119	6.4	108	52	52	13	13
1928	560.6	229	12.3	207	285.1	117	6.3	105	51	51	12	12
1929	565.8	231	12.4	208	291.1	119	6.4	107	51	51	12	12

(continued)

TABLE A-12 (concluded)

| | AT CURRENT PRICES | | | | AT 1900 PRICES | | | | AS PERCENTAGE OF: | | | |
| | Total | | Per Head | | Total | | Per Head | | Total Expenditure | | GNP | |
YEAR	£ mn.	Index	£	Index	£ mn.	Index	£	Index	At Current Prices	At 1900 Prices	At Current Prices	At 1900 Prices
1930	575.9	235	12.6	211	303.9	124	6.6	111	50	50	13	13
1931	580.4	237	12.6	212	322.6	132	7.0	118	50	50	14	14
1932	542.8	222	11.7	197	307.8	126	6.6	112	48	48	14	14
1933	527.4	216	11.3	191	306.4	125	6.6	111	50	50	13	13
1934	541.6	221	11.6	195	313.6	128	6.7	113	51	51	13	13
1935	593.9	243	12.7	213	342.3	140	7.3	123	53	53	13	13
1936	672.2	275	14.3	240	380.0	155	8.1	136	57	57	14	14
1937	787.5	322	16.7	280	428.6	175	9.1	152	60	60	16	15
1938	1,041.4	426	21.9	369	556.3	227	11.7	197	66	65	20	20
1939	1,417.0	579	29.7	499					72		26	
1940	3,258.0	1,332	67.6	1,137					83		50	
1941	4,360.0	1,783	90.4	1,522					82		59	
1942	4,821.0	1,971	99.6	1,676					82		60	
1943	5,148.0	2,105	105.5	1,775					82		61	
1944	5,162.0	2,110	105.3	1,772					82		59	
1945	4,354.0	1,780	88.5	1,490					75		50	
1946	2,349.0	960	47.7	803	754.0	308	15.3	258	52	51	27	27
1947	2,038.0	833	41.1	692	597.0	244	12.0	203	49	48	22	21
1948	2,206.0	902	44.5	748	595.0	243	12.0	202	52	51	21	21
1949	2,418.0	989	48.4	815	640.0	262	12.8	216	55	53	22	22
1950	2,508.0	1,025	50.0	841	646.0	264	12.9	217	55	54	22	21
1951	3,238.0	1,324	64.5	1,085	765.0	313	15.2	256	62	61	25	25
1952	3,689.0	1,508	73.1	1,231	819.0	335	16.2	273	64	63	26	26
1953	3,891.0	1,591	76.9	1,294	848.0	347	16.8	282	64	63	26	26
1954	3,765.0	1,539	74.1	1,247	812.0	332	16.0	269	63	62	24	24
1955	3,810.0	1,558	74.8	1,258	796.0	325	15.6	263	62	61	23	23

TABLE A-13

GOVERNMENT EXPENDITURE ON CAPITAL ACCOUNT, TOTALS AND PER HEAD,
AT CURRENT AND 1900 PRICES, SELECTED YEARS, 1890–1955
(index, 1900 = 100)

| | AT CURRENT PRICES | | | | AT 1900 PRICES | | | |
| | *Total* | | *Per Head* | | *Total* | | *Per Head* | |
YEAR	£ mn.	Index	£	Index	£ mn.	Index	£	Index
1890	10.2	20	0.3	22	10.4	21	0.3	23
1895	21.0	42	0.5	44	23.1	46	0.6	48
1900	50.4	100	1.2	100	50.4	100	1.2	100
1905	38.4	76	0.9	73	40.4	80	0.9	76
1910	45.1	89	1.0	82	47.5	94	1.1	87
1913	39.2	78	0.9	70	40.0	79	0.9	72
1915	43.4	86	0.9	77				
1917	91.6	182	2.0	161				
1918	105.8	210	2.3	186				
1920	101.9	202	2.3	191	29.3	58	0.7	55
1921	150.0	298	3.4	280	50.5	100	1.2	94
1922	109.5	217	2.5	202	54.7	109	1.2	101
1923	72.4	144	1.6	133	38.3	76	0.9	70
1924	81.7	162	1.8	149	41.5	82	0.9	75
1925	104.6	208	2.3	190	51.2	102	1.1	93
1926	121.3	241	2.7	220	58.9	117	1.3	107
1927	128.0	254	2.8	231	63.8	127	1.4	116
1928	108.7	216	2.4	195	56.9	113	1.3	102
1929	112.1	222	2.5	201	59.6	118	1.3	107
1930	119.7	237	2.6	214	65.1	129	1.4	116
1931	126.9	252	2.8	226	72.0	143	1.6	128
1932	103.6	206	2.2	184	61.1	121	1.3	108
1933	88.5	176	1.9	156	54.2	108	1.2	96
1934	87.8	174	1.9	154	52.8	105	1.1	93
1935	103.7	206	2.2	181	60.6	120	1.3	106
1936	132.8	263	2.8	231	73.5	146	1.6	128
1937	175.1	347	3.7	303	90.3	179	1.9	157
1938	218.7	434	4.6	377	111.6	221	2.4	193
1939	177.0	351	3.7	304				
1940	114.0	226	2.4	193				
1941	76.9	151	1.6	130				
1942	61.0	121	1.3	103				
1943	48.0	95	1.0	80				
1944	41.0	81	.8	69				
1945	97.0	192	2.0	161				
1946	58.0	115	1.2	97	−2.0	−4	—	−3
1947	295.0	585	6.0	488	59.0	117	1.2	98
1948	445.0	883	9.0	735	92.0	183	1.9	152
1949	441.0	875	8.8	724	90.0	179	1.8	148
1950	437.0	867	8.7	714	86.0	171	1.7	140
1951	798.0	1,583	15.9	1,302	158.0	313	3.2	258
1952	799.0	1,585	15.8	1,298	137.0	272	2.7	223
1953	841.0	1,669	16.6	1,362	143.0	284	2.8	232
1954	637.0	1,264	12.5	1,028	102.0	202	2.0	165
1955	618.0	1,226	12.1	994	95.0	188	1.9	152

TABLE A-14

GOVERNMENT EXPENDITURE ON CURRENT ACCOUNT, TOTALS, PER HEAD, AND AS PERCENTAGE OF TOTAL GOVERNMENT EXPENDITURE AND GROSS NATIONAL PRODUCT, CURRENT AND 1900 PRICES, SELECTED YEARS, 1890–1955

| | AT CURRENT PRICES | | | | AT 1900 PRICES | | | | AS PERCENTAGE OF: | | | |
| | Total | | Per Head | | Total | | Per Head | | Total Expenditure | | GNP | |
YEAR	£ mn.	Index	£	Index	£ mn.	Index	£	Index	At Current Prices	At 1900 Prices	At Current Prices	At 1900 Prices
1890	120.4	52	3.2	57	122.9	53	3.3	59	92	92	8	8
1895	135.8	59	3.5	62	149.2	65	3.8	68	87	87	9	9
1900	230.4	100	5.6	100	230.4	100	5.6	100	82	82	12	12
1905	203.3	88	4.7	84	201.3	87	4.7	83	84	83	10	10
1910	226.9	98	5.1	90	216.1	94	4.8	86	83	82	11	11
1913	266.2	116	5.8	104	244.2	106	5.3	96	87	86	11	11
1915	914.7	397	19.7	352					95		33	
1917	1,423.9	618	30.5	545					94		37	
1918	2,321.2	1,007	49.9	890					96		49	
1920	1,490.2	647	34.1	608	536.0	233	12.3	219	94	95	25	22
1921	1,279.5	555	29.1	519	501.7	218	11.4	204	90	91	26	22
1922	1,067.8	463	24.1	430	489.8	213	11.1	197	91	90	25	23
1923	952.8	414	21.4	382	464.7	202	10.4	186	93	92	23	21
1924	945.3	410	21.1	376	463.3	201	10.3	184	92	92	22	22
1925	967.3	420	21.5	383	474.2	206	10.5	188	90	90	22	22
1926	985.0	428	21.8	389	482.8	210	10.7	191	89	89	23	23
1927	977.8	424	21.5	385	493.8	214	10.9	194	88	89	21	21
1928	986.0	428	21.6	386	497.9	216	10.9	195	90	90	22	22
1929	995.1	432	21.8	389	507.7	220	11.1	198	90	89	22	21

(continued)

TABLE A-14 (concluded)

YEAR	AT CURRENT PRICES				AT 1900 PRICES				AS PERCENTAGE OF:			
	Total		Per Head		Total		Per Head		Total Expenditure		GNP	
	£ mn.	Index	£	Index	£ mn.	Index	£	Index	At Current Prices	At 1900 Prices	At Current Prices	At 1900 Prices
1930	1,025.1	445	22.4	399	536.7	233	11.7	209	90	89	23	23
1931	1,046.6	454	22.7	406	578.3	251	12.6	224	89	89	26	26
1932	1,034.4	449	22.3	399	581.1	252	12.5	224	91	90	26	26
1933	977.5	424	21.0	375	561.7	244	12.1	216	92	91	24	24
1934	973.1	422	20.9	372	559.2	243	12.0	214	92	91	22	23
1935	1,013.7	440	21.6	386	582.6	253	12.4	222	91	91	22	22
1936	1,054.0	457	22.4	400	598.9	260	12.7	227	89	89	22	22
1937	1,128.4	490	23.9	426	623.4	271	13.2	235	87	87	22	23
1938	1,368.3	594	28.8	514	739.6	321	15.6	278	86	87	26	26
1939	1,783.0	774	37.3	667					91		32	
1940	3,791.0	1,645	78.6	1,404					97		58	
1941	5,262.0	2,284	109.1	1,949					99		71	
1942	5,799.0	2,517	119.8	2,139					99		72	
1943	6,217.0	2,698	127.4	2,276					99		73	
1944	6,262.0	2,718	127.8	2,281					99		72	
1945	5,682.0	2,466	115.5	2,063					98		65	
1946	4,472.0	1,941	90.9	1,622	1,476.0	641	30.0	536	99	100	51	52
1947	3,835.0	1,664	77.4	1,381	1,184.0	514	23.9	426	93	95	41	42
1948	3,770.0	1,636	76.0	1,357	1,077.0	467	21.7	387	89	92	36	38
1949	3,982.0	1,728	79.8	1,424	1,109.0	481	22.2	397	90	92	36	37
1950	4,102.0	1,780	81.8	1,460	1,109.0	481	22.1	395	90	93	35	37
1951	4,410.0	1,914	87.8	1,568	1,097.0	476	21.8	390	85	87	34	36
1952	4,978.0	2,161	98.7	1,762	1,174.0	510	23.3	416	86	90	36	37
1953	5,207.0	2,260	102.9	1,837	1,203.0	522	23.8	424	86	89	35	37
1954	5,339.0	2,317	105.1	1,877	1,213.0	526	23.9	427	89	92	34	35
1955	5,525.0	2,398	108.4	1,936	1,214.0	527	23.8	425	90	93	33	35

Government Expenditure on Current Account

This item includes government current expenditure on goods and services and government transfers to persons and subsidies.

Current expenditure on goods and services comprises payments for services of employees and purchases of goods and services by nontrading branches of government. It will be recalled that certain trading services, notably the Post Office, were included in the government sector, but their current payments were regarded as self-liquidating and are not therefore included in this total. While services rendered between nontrading branches of the government will disappear on consolidation, payments to the Post Office for telephone and postal facilities will not. Generally speaking, allowance is made in the payments to employees for pension payments, but practice depends on the type of scheme. Thus, while payments under noncontributory schemes are simply included in this subtotal, only contributions by the government as employer are included in contributory schemes. There are exceptions to these rules.

Transfers include current grants to persons, or for persons through nonprofit bodies, resident in the United Kingdom, and national debt interest payments. Reasons have been given for regarding the deficit on current account for housing services as a transfer to persons rather than a subsidy, while the C.S.O. regards it as a subsidy. A more important difference arises concerning public debt interest. The C.S.O. includes debt interest paid by local authorities as a transfer payment. It seems to us more reasonable, at least for our purpose, to treat interest paid by local authorities as loan charges. Local authority borrowing has its counterpart in fixed assets—notably houses—and does not represent loans outstanding as a result of war borrowing as central government debt does. Accordingly, local debt interest payments appear as part of current expenditure on goods and services. The main items under this general heading are national insurance benefits, notably pensions, and national assistance payments such as family allowances and poor relief. Certain grants to persons and other bodies, especially grants abroad and war gratuities, are included in this total rather than in capital expenditure. We follow C.S.O. procedure for those grants, except that we include capital transfers abroad as well.

Subsidies represent payments to producers which may reduce selling prices below factor costs of production. Defining a producer raises a number of difficulties. It is to be noted, for example, that universities receiving grants through the University Grants Committee are treated as part of the personal sector, so that these payments represent transfers to persons. The main items under this heading are agriculture and food subsidies.

Government Expenditure on Capital Account

This category can be divided into two sections: gross fixed capital formation, and changes in the value of stocks.

The difficulties of dividing government expenditure on goods and services between current and capital items are well known. It could be claimed, for example, that some welfare services, such as education, represent capital investment in a wide sense, for they may increase national productivity. The main items of gross fixed capital formation included here are expenditures on housing, roads, airports, factories (including factories leased to private industry in development areas), undertaken by government nontrading bodies, and capital expenditure by such trading bodies as the Post Office at the central level.

Changes in the value of stocks have only become an important item since World War II. Stocks now held by the government include strategic reserves of food and raw materials, surplus war stores, and stocks of trading bodies included in the public sector. Increase in stocks is calculated by taking the costs of purchases less receipts from sales. In some years this item has been negative because of the large sales of surplus war stores.

Tables A-15, A-16, and A-17

These tables show the growth of government expenditure by functional categories. The items classified under each heading are listed below. We have already noted certain discrepancies from the C.S.O. classification, but in general our classification follows it closely and, indeed, much of the information summarized below is extracted from *Sources and Methods.* There are eight main categories.

1. GENERAL ADMINISTRATION. This category includes the costs of finance and tax collection and the costs of providing common services such as the heating and lighting of government buildings, stationery, and printing. It includes also the costs of electoral and parliamentary machinery; the costs of maintaining the offices of the Registrar-General, Public Records, and Royal Commissioners; and a host of minor services. In other words, it is rather a hodgepodge, for it does not include the costs of administration (if these could be defined) of individual services, such as education, health, and so on, which are included under the separate categories below. There is no possibility of separating these costs from other costs. Comparability between official estimates for postwar years and our own estimates (for the central government, based on the Cambridge study mentioned above) demands that we accept this rather heterogeneous category.

2. NATIONAL DEBT. This category is simply a record of the interest on

the national debt paid to other sectors of the economy and paid abroad. It excludes intergovernmental payments, such as the interest paid to the Post Office Savings Bank Fund and to the National Insurance Fund.

3. LAW AND ORDER. This category includes expenditure for the police force, and for prisons, law courts, judges' salaries, public prosecutions, and so on.

4. OVERSEAS SERVICES. This category covers expenditures at home and abroad arising from the nation's external relations, such as expenditures of the Foreign Office, colonial administration, the British Council, and overseas broadcasting. It does not include grants to separate colonial territories or to other countries. Expenditure on defense abroad is included under the next heading.

5. MILITARY AND DEFENSE. This category consists of three subcategories:
Expenditure of service departments, undertaken in order to maintain the fighting forces on air, land, and sea.
Other military expenditure, consisting of the costs of maintaining the Ministry of Defence, the research expenditure of the Ministry of Supply, subsidies to colonial defense services, expenditure of the Ministry of Labour and National Service in calling up servicemen.
Civil defense expenditure, being current expenditure by both central and local government on training and organization of civil defense.

6. SOCIAL SERVICES. This category covers education and child care, health services, national insurance (unemployment, sickness benefits, retirement pensions, etc.), national assistance (relief of the poor and family allowances), housing (subsidies and capital expenditure), and food subsidies.

7. ECONOMIC SERVICES. This category can be divided into four parts:
Services to agriculture, forestry, and fishing, covering expenditures of the Ministry of Agriculture, Fisheries and Food and its Scottish counterparts, and other government departments aiding these activities.
Industry and commerce, in large part representing expenditure of the Board of Trade, but after 1946 including expenditure of the Ministry of Power. Some government expenditure on industrial research is also included.
Transport, chiefly the cost of maintaining the Ministry of Transport, which covers also the salaries of coast guards and expenditure on mercantile marine services, and also the expenditures of the Ministry of Civil Aviation and meteorological services provided by the Air Ministry.
Employment, representing the expenditure of the Ministry of Labour on employment exchanges, and on administration of industrial services for the disabled.

8. ENVIRONMENTAL SERVICES. This category includes the provision of basic services, notably, roads and public lighting, fire services, water, sewage and refuse disposal, land drainage and coast protection, town and country planning, and maintenance of parks.

In Table A-17 the figures of functional categories and of GNP are expressed in percentages at current prices (see notes to Table A-6).

TABLE A-15

GOVERNMENT EXPENDITURE BY FUNCTION, AMOUNTS AND PERCENTAGES OF TOTAL GOVERNMENT EXPENDITURE, AT CURRENT PRICES, SELECTED YEARS, 1890–1955

(amounts in millions of pounds)

FUNCTION

Year	Administration and Other	National Debt	Law and Order	Overseas Services	Military Defense	Social Services	Economic Services	Environmental Services	All Services
1890	15.8	23.8	9.0	.4	34.9	27.3	14.4	5.0	130.6
1895	16.3	22.7	8.4	.8	43.1	39.7	18.4	7.4	156.8
1900	16.5	19.6	9.8	1.0	134.9	50.6	36.4	12.0	280.8
1905	19.6	24.4	11.4	1.4	63.1	68.3	39.4	13.8	241.7
1910	22.1	20.2	12.9	1.1	74.3	89.1	37.8	14.5	272.0
1913	21.2	18.7	17.4	1.1	91.3	100.8	39.5	15.4	305.4
1915	26.8	57.7	13.6	1.7	716.6	93.4	35.6	12.7	958.1
1917	27.4	185.2	12.6	2.3	1,123.0	127.8	24.5	12.7	1,515.5
1918	31.2	264.8	15.8	3.2	1,955.8	114.3	27.4	14.5	2,427.0
1920	71.5	324.8	33.3	2.5	519.7	411.8	203.2	25.3	1,592.1
1921	70.1	307.8	37.7	4.3	270.0	490.7	220.0	28.9	1,429.5
1922	59.2	298.8	33.1	2.4	168.7	423.2	163.2	28.7	1,177.3
1923	52.4	301.7	29.5	4.2	134.9	358.7	114.5	29.3	1,025.2
1924	51.3	305.4	29.6	2.6	130.9	365.0	111.8	30.4	1,027.0
1925	49.3	304.5	29.8	1.6	133.6	389.3	131.7	32.1	1,071.9
1926	49.5	310.3	30.4	.9	133.6	424.4	125.3	31.9	1,106.3
1927	47.9	308.3	30.6	1.2	130.0	436.0	119.8	32.0	1,105.8
1928	49.1	305.1	30.8	1.3	125.1	434.3	117.1	31.9	1,094.7
1929	47.7	304.2	31.3	1.9	123.9	438.0	126.5	33.7	1,107.2

(continued)

TABLE A-15 (continued)

Year	Administration and Other	National Debt	Law and Order	Overseas Services	Military Defense	Social Services	Economic Services	Environmental Services	All Services
					FUNCTION				
1930	46.4	290.9	31.9	1.4	119.2	484.7	132.4	37.9	1,144.8
1931	46.3	289.7	31.8	1.2	115.4	516.8	130.7	41.6	1,173.5
1932	45.1	281.2	30.8	1.3	110.4	511.1	116.6	41.5	1,138.0
1933	44.3	228.4	30.9	1.7	112.4	497.2	111.8	39.3	1,066.0
1934	45.5	208.2	31.9	1.2	118.9	498.3	117.1	39.8	1,060.9
1935	48.2	206.7	34.0	1.2	140.8	519.2	125.5	41.8	1,117.4
1936	50.2	205.7	35.9	1.5	183.0	532.7	132.5	45.3	1,186.8
1937	54.8	209.4	37.2	1.6	254.7	554.4	141.6	49.7	1,303.5
1938	60.6	212.5	38.7	3.0	473.2	596.3	151.4	51.3	1,587.0
1950	175	507	79	179	836	2,094	572	97	4,539
1951	168	550	87	85	1,293	2,234	681	110	5,208
1952	167	609	96	77	1,641	2,438	629	120	5,777
1953	173	638	105	73	1,725	2,588	609	137	6,048
1954	179	637	110	72	1,706	2,611	518	143	5,976
1955	182	707	115	80	1,606	2,739	531	183	6,143

(continued)

TABLE A-15 (continued)

PERCENTAGE OF TOTAL GOVERNMENT EXPENDITURE

Year	Admini- stration and Other	National Debt	Law and Order	Overseas Services	Military Defense	Social Services	Economic Services	Environ- mental Services
1890	12.1	18.2	6.9	.3	26.7	20.9	11.0	3.8
1895	10.4	14.5	5.4	.5	27.5	25.3	11.7	4.7
1900	5.9	7.0	3.5	.4	48.0	18.0	13.0	4.3
1905	8.1	10.1	4.8	.6	26.1	28.3	16.3	5.7
1910	8.1	7.4	4.7	.4	27.3	32.8	13.9	5.3
1913	6.9	6.1	5.7	.4	29.9	33.0	12.9	5.0
1915	2.8	6.0	1.4	.2	74.8	9.7	3.7	1.3
1917	1.8	12.2	.8	.2	74.1	8.4	1.6	.8
1918	1.3	10.9	.7	.1	80.6	4.7	1.1	.6
1920	4.5	20.4	2.1	.2	32.6	25.9	12.8	1.6
1921	4.9	21.5	2.6	.3	18.9	34.3	15.4	2.0
1922	5.0	25.4	2.8	.2	14.3	35.9	13.9	2.4
1923	5.1	29.4	2.9	.4	13.2	35.0	11.2	2.9
1924	5.0	29.7	2.9	.3	12.7	35.5	10.9	3.0
1925	4.6	28.4	2.8	.1	12.5	36.3	12.3	3.0
1926	4.5	28.0	2.7	.1	12.1	38.4	11.3	2.9
1927	4.3	27.9	2.8	.1	11.8	39.4	10.8	2.9
1928	4.5	27.9	2.8	.1	11.4	39.7	10.7	2.9
1929	4.3	27.5	2.8	.2	11.2	39.6	11.4	3.0

(continued)

TABLE A-15 (concluded)

Year	Administration and Other	National Debt	Law and Order	Overseas Services	Military Defense	Social Services	Economic Services	Environmental Services
			PER CENT OF TOTAL GOVERNMENT EXPENDITURE					
1930	4.1	25.4	2.8	.1	10.4	42.3	11.6	3.3
1931	3.9	24.7	2.7	.1	9.8	44.0	11.1	3.5
1932	4.0	24.7	2.7	.1	9.7	44.9	10.2	3.6
1933	4.2	21.4	2.9	.2	10.5	46.6	10.5	3.7
1934	4.3	19.6	3.0	.1	11.2	47.0	11.0	3.8
1935	4.3	18.5	3.0	.1	12.6	46.5	11.2	3.7
1936	4.2	17.3	3.0	.1	15.4	44.9	11.2	3.8
1937	4.2	16.1	2.9	.1	19.5	42.5	10.9	3.8
1938	3.8	13.4	2.4	.2	29.8	37.6	9.5	3.2
1950	3.9	11.2	1.7	3.9	18.5	46.1	12.6	2.1
1951	3.2	10.6	1.7	1.6	24.8	42.9	13.1	2.1
1952	2.9	10.5	1.7	1.3	28.4	42.2	10.9	2.1
1953	2.9	10.5	1.7	1.2	28.5	42.8	10.1	2.3
1954	3.0	10.7	1.8	1.2	28.5	43.7	8.7	2.4
1955	3.0	11.5	1.9	1.3	26.1	44.6	8.6	3.0

187

TABLE A-16

TOTAL GOVERNMENT EXPENDITURE BY FUNCTION, PER HEAD OF POPULATION, AT CURRENT PRICES, SELECTED YEARS, 1890–1955

(pounds per head)

Year	Administration	National Debt	Law and Order	Overseas Services	Military	Social Services	Economic Services	Environmental Services	All Services
1890	0.4	0.6	0.2	—	1.0	0.8	0.4	0.1	3.5
1895	0.4	0.6	0.2	—	1.1	1.0	0.5	0.2	4.0
1900	0.4	0.5	0.2	—	3.3	1.2	0.9	0.3	6.8
1905	0.4	0.6	0.3	—	1.5	1.6	0.9	0.3	5.6
1910	0.5	0.5	0.3	—	1.7	2.0	0.8	0.3	6.1
1913	0.5	0.4	0.4	—	2.0	2.2	0.9	0.3	6.7
1915	0.6	1.2	0.3	—	15.5	2.0	0.8	0.3	20.7
1917	0.6	4.0	0.3	—	24.1	2.7	0.5	0.3	32.5
1918	0.7	5.7	0.3	0.1	42.0	2.4	0.6	0.3	52.1
1920	1.6	7.4	0.8	0.1	11.9	9.4	4.6	0.6	36.4
1921	1.6	7.0	0.9	0.1	6.1	11.1	5.0	0.7	32.5
1922	1.3	6.7	0.8	0.1	3.8	9.5	3.7	0.7	26.6
1923	1.2	6.7	0.7	0.1	3.0	8.0	2.6	0.7	23.0
1924	1.1	6.8	0.7	0.1	2.9	8.1	2.5	0.7	22.9
1925	1.1	6.8	0.7	—	3.0	8.6	2.9	0.7	23.8
1926	1.1	6.9	0.7	—	2.9	9.4	2.8	0.7	24.5
1927	1.1	6.8	0.7	—	2.9	9.6	2.6	0.7	24.4
1928	1.1	6.7	0.7	—	2.7	9.5	2.6	0.7	24.0
1929	1.0	6.7	0.7	—	2.7	9.6	2.8	0.7	24.2

(continued)

TABLE A-16 (concluded)

Year	Administration	National Debt	Law and Order	Overseas Services	Military	Social Services	Economic Services	Environmental Services	All Services
1930	1.1	6.3	0.7	—	2.6	10.6	2.9	0.8	25.0
1931	1.0	6.3	0.7	—	2.5	11.2	2.9	0.9	25.5
1932	1.0	6.1	0.7	—	2.4	11.0	2.5	0.9	24.6
1933	1.0	4.9	0.7	—	2.4	10.7	2.4	0.8	22.9
1934	1.0	4.5	0.7	—	2.5	10.7	2.5	0.8	22.7
1935	1.0	4.4	0.7	—	3.0	11.1	2.7	0.9	23.8
1936	1.1	4.4	0.7	—	3.9	11.3	2.8	1.0	25.2
1937	1.2	4.4	0.8	—	5.4	11.7	3.0	1.1	27.6
1938	1.3	4.5	0.8	0.1	9.9	12.5	3.2	1.1	33.4
1950	3.5	10.1	1.6	3.6	16.7	41.7	11.4	1.9	90.5
1951	3.3	11.0	1.7	1.7	25.7	44.5	13.6	2.2	103.7
1952	3.3	12.1	1.9	1.5	32.5	48.3	12.5	2.4	114.5
1953	3.4	12.6	2.1	1.5	34.1	51.1	12.0	2.7	119.5
1954	3.5	12.6	2.2	1.4	33.6	51.4	10.2	2.8	117.7
1955	3.6	13.9	2.2	1.6	31.5	53.4	10.4	3.6	120.5

TABLE A-17

TOTAL GOVERNMENT EXPENDITURE BY FUNCTION, AT CURRENT PRICES, AS PERCENTAGE OF GROSS NATIONAL PRODUCT, SELECTED YEARS, 1890–1955

Year	Administration	National Debt	Law and Order	Overseas Services	Military	Social Services	Economic Services	Environmental Services	All Services
1890	1.1	1.6	0.6	—	2.4	1.9	1.0	0.3	8.9
1895	1.1	1.5	0.6	0.1	2.9	2.6	1.2	0.5	10.4
1900	0.8	1.0	0.5	0.1	6.9	2.6	1.9	0.6	14.4
1905	1.0	1.2	0.6	0.1	3.2	3.5	2.0	0.7	12.3
1910	1.0	0.9	0.6	0.1	3.5	4.2	1.8	0.7	12.7
1913	0.9	0.8	0.7	—	3.7	4.1	1.6	0.6	12.4
1915	1.0	2.1	0.5	0.1	26.2	3.4	1.3	0.5	35.0
1917	0.7	4.8	0.3	0.1	28.9	3.3	0.6	0.3	39.1
1918	0.7	5.6	0.3	0.1	41.7	2.4	0.6	0.3	51.7
1920	1.2	5.4	0.5	—	8.6	6.8	3.3	0.4	26.2
1921	1.4	6.3	0.8	0.1	5.6	10.1	4.5	0.6	29.4
1922	1.4	7.1	0.8	0.1	4.0	10.0	3.9	0.7	27.8
1923	1.2	7.1	0.7	0.1	3.2	8.5	2.7	0.7	24.2
1924	1.2	7.0	0.7	0.1	3.0	8.4	2.6	0.7	23.7
1925	1.1	6.9	0.7	—	3.0	8.8	3.0	0.7	24.2
1926	1.2	7.2	0.7	—	3.1	9.9	2.9	0.7	25.7
1927	1.0	6.7	0.7	—	2.8	9.5	2.6	0.7	24.1
1928	1.1	6.7	0.7	—	2.8	9.6	2.6	0.7	24.2
1929	1.0	6.6	0.7	—	2.7	9.5	2.7	0.7	23.9

(continued)

190

TABLE A-17 (concluded)

Year	Administration	National Debt	Law and Order	Overseas Services	Military	Social Services	Economic Services	Environmental Services	All Services
1930	1.1	6.6	0.7	—	2.7	11.1	3.0	0.9	26.1
1931	1.1	7.1	0.8	—	2.8	12.7	3.2	1.0	28.8
1932	1.1	7.1	0.8	—	2.8	12.9	2.9	1.0	28.6
1933	1.1	5.5	0.7	—	2.7	12.0	2.7	0.9	25.7
1934	1.1	4.8	0.7	—	2.7	11.5	2.7	0.9	24.5
1935	1.1	4.5	0.7	—	3.1	11.3	2.7	0.9	24.4
1936	1.0	4.3	0.7	—	3.8	11.1	2.8	0.9	24.7
1937	1.1	4.1	0.7	—	5.0	10.9	2.8	1.0	25.7
1938	1.1	4.0	0.7	0.1	8.9	11.3	2.9	1.0	30.0
1950	1.5	4.4	0.7	1.5	7.2	18.0	4.9	0.8	39.0
1951	1.3	4.3	0.7	0.7	10.1	17.5	5.3	0.9	40.7
1952	1.2	4.4	0.7	0.6	11.8	17.5	4.5	0.9	41.5
1953	1.2	4.3	0.7	0.5	11.6	17.4	4.1	0.9	40.7
1954	1.1	4.0	0.7	0.5	10.7	16.4	3.3	0.9	37.6
1955	1.1	4.2	0.7	0.5	9.6	16.3	3.2	1.1	36.6

Tables A-18, A-19, A-20, A-21, A-22, A-23, and A-24

The sources of these tables were described in the general notes on government expenditure. The revenue figures in Table A-16 are from the same sources.

The general method of classification is that found in *Sources and Methods*. There are, however, two exceptions. The first, housing expenditure, was discussed above. The second is that we include the Metropolitan Police Force in the local government figures, while this category appears in the central government figures in the C.S.O. classification. We regard it as more appropriate to treat it as local expenditure, although the Metropolitan Police Force is financed entirely by the central government.

In view of our treatment of local debt interest as part of expenditure on goods and services, loan charges are allocated to specific services according to the treatment in *Local Government Financial Statistics*.

The statistics of social services transfer payments by type (Table A-24) use the sources given in *Sources and Methods* for education transfers, and the returns on poor relief in *British Parliamentary Papers* for expenditures on poor relief.

TABLE A-18

LOCAL GOVERNMENT CURRENT EXPENDITURE BY FUNCTION AND REVENUE
SOURCE, CURRENT PRICES, SELECTED YEARS, 1890–1955
(millions of pounds)

| YEAR | ADMINISTRATION AND OTHER *Met by:* | | | LAW AND ORDER *Met by:* | | |
	Total	Allocated Grants	Other Sources	Total	Allocated Grants	Other Sources
1890						
1895						
1900						
1905						
1910						
1913						
1915						
1917						
1918						
1920	19.0	1.0	18.0	21.6	10.3	11.3
1921	17.7	0.6	17.1	23.1	10.6	12.5
1922	16.3	0.5	15.8	21.2	10.2	11.0
1923	15.5	0.7	14.8	20.3	9.8	10.5
1924	15.7	0.7	15.0	20.9	10.1	10.8
1925	15.9	0.7	15.2	22.0	10.7	11.3
1926	16.3	0.6	15.7	23.1	11.3	11.8
1927	16.9	0.5	16.4	23.5	11.4	12.1
1928	17.7	0.5	17.2	23.8	11.5	12.3
1929	15.2	0.5	14.7	24.1	11.7	12.4
1930	14.7	0.5	14.2	24.7	11.9	12.8
1931	14.3	0.5	13.8	24.9	12.0	12.9
1932	13.7	0.5	13.2	24.3	11.5	12.8
1933	13.9	0.5	13.4	24.2	11.5	12.7
1934	14.4	0.5	13.9	24.9	11.9	13.0
1935	15.6	0.5	15.1	26.5	12.7	13.8
1936	15.5	0.5	15.0	27.7	13.3	14.4
1937	17.0	0.4	16.6	28.6	13.8	14.8
1938	18.6	0.4	18.2	29.5	14.3	15.2
1939	19.6	0.9	18.7	33.8	17.1	16.7
1940	25.1	5.0	20.1	37.5	20.0	17.5
1941	33.6	11.9	21.7	41.1	22.5	18.6
1942	36.1	13.6	22.5	42.1	23.7	18.4
1943	35.5	13.3	22.2	41.3	23.1	18.2
1944	36.8	14.7	22.1	40.2	22.1	18.1
1945	38.7	15.8	22.9	40.0	20.6	19.4
1946	35.0	5.0	30.0	39.0	20.0	19.0
1947	41.0	7.0	34.0	44.0	22.0	22.0
1948	47.0	7.0	40.0	48.0	24.0	24.0
1949	48.0	6.0	42.0	52.0	25.0	27.0
1950	48.0	4.0	44.0	57.0	27.0	30.0
1951	49.0	3.0	46.0	63.0	30.0	33.0
1952	47.0	3.0	44.0	69.0	34.0	35.0
1953	49.0	3.0	46.0	75.0	36.0	39.0
1954	46.0	3.0	43.0	79.0	38.0	41.0
1955	51.0	3.0	48.0	83.0	41.0	42.0

YEAR	CIVIL DEFENSE[a] Met by:			SOCIAL SERVICES Met by:		
	Total	Allocated Grants	Other Sources	Total	Allocated Grants	Other Sources
1890						
1895						
1900						
1905						
1910						
1913						
1915						
1917						
1918						
1920	—	—	—	124.3	48.2	76.1
1921	—	—	—	145.3	56.0	89.3
1922	—	—	—	145.7	54.2	91.5
1923	—	—	—	139.3	52.3	87.0
1924	—	—	—	138.3	51.6	86.5
1925	—	—	—	143.6	52.3	91.3
1926	—	—	—	155.0	53.4	101.6
1927	—	—	—	152.1	53.9	98.2
1928	—	—	—	153.0	56.0	97.0
1929	—	—	—	156.1	57.0	99.1
1930	—	—	—	159.3	53.3	106.0
1931	—	—	—	159.4	50.4	109.0
1932	—	—	—	159.9	47.1	112.8
1933	—	—	—	163.3	45.7	117.6
1934	—	—	—	171.1	47.5	123.6
1935	—	—	—	181.1	54.6	126.5
1936	—	—	—	187.5	58.0	129.5
1937	—	—	—	191.0	56.0	135.0
1938	3.5	2.2	1.3	196.9	55.4	141.5
1939	32.9	26.7	6.2	200.0	57.7	142.3
1940	63.0	55.7	7.3	200.1	62.4	137.7
1941	89.1	83.5	5.6	204.5	68.3	136.2
1942	80.1	75.5	4.6	211.5	72.9	138.6
1943	62.2	58.3	3.9	222.2	76.7	145.5
1944	50.6	47.8	2.8	237.4	84.4	153.0
1945	24.3	24.3	—	272.4	105.1	167.3
1946	13.0	14.0	(−1.0)	315.0	123.0	192.0
1947	8.0	8.0	(—)	359.0	142.0	217.0
1948	3.0	4.0	(−1.0)	344.0	166.0	176.0
1949	2.0	1.0	(1.0)	339.0	185.0	154.0
1950	2.0	1.0	(1.0)	355.0	198.0	157.0
1951	3.0	2.0	(1.0)	403.0	224.0	179.0
1952	3.0	3.0	(—)	449.0	250.0	199.0
1953	3.0	3.0	(—)	478.0	269.0	209.0
1954	3.0	3.0	(—)	523.0	288.0	235.0
1955	3.0	3.0	(—)	576.0	325.0	251.0

| | HOUSING | | | ECONOMIC SERVICES | | |
| | | Met by: | | | Met by: | |
YEAR	Total	Allocated Grants	Other Sources	Total	Allocated Grants	Other Sources
1890						
1895						
1900						
1905						
1910						
1913						
1915						
1917						
1918						
1920	1.9	0.6	1.3	42.7	5.1	37.6
1921	5.5	4.1	1.4	49.5	9.3	40.2
1922	8.4	7.1	1.3	49.6	11.4	38.2
1923	9.5	8.2	1.3	50.2	12.9	37.3
1924	10.0	8.5	1.5	54.9	15.2	39.7
1925	11.0	8.8	2.2	59.1	17.0	42.1
1926	12.3	9.5	2.8	60.6	17.4	43.2
1927	13.8	10.9	2.9	62.7	18.3	44.4
1928	15.0	12.2	2.8	63.2	18.1	45.1
1929	16.0	13.1	2.9	63.0	17.9	45.1
1930	17.1	13.8	3.3	64.2	16.6	47.6
1931	17.7	14.2	3.5	64.5	15.8	48.7
1932	18.0	14.6	3.4	60.4	13.3	47.1
1933	18.5	15.1	3.4	58.3	11.9	46.4
1934	19.4	15.6	3.8	59.0	12.0	47.0
1935	20.2	16.2	4.0	60.2	12.2	48.0
1936	20.8	16.6	4.2	61.8	12.6	49.2
1937	21.6	17.0	4.6	62.6	12.7	49.9
1938	22.9	17.7	5.2	63.5	12.7	50.8
1939	24.2	18.5	5.7	64.5	17.2	47.3
1940	24.5	18.8	5.7	66.0	23.0	43.0
1941	24.9	18.7	6.2	71.8	31.2	40.6
1942	24.4	18.3	6.1	62.2	22.6	39.6
1943	23.9	18.1	5.8	52.2	13.6	38.6
1944	24.6	18.4	6.2	50.1	10.9	39.2
1945	25.1	18.5	6.6	54.2	9.7	44.5
1946	28.0	19.0	9.0	66.0	16.0	50.0
1947	32.0	20.0	12.0	74.0	19.0	55.0
1948	37.0	23.0	14.0	81.0	20.0	61.0
1949	39.0	25.0	14.0	88.0	21.0	67.0
1950	40.0	27.0	13.0	91.0	21.0	70.0
1951	45.0	30.0	15.0	98.0	24.0	74.0
1952	54.0	36.0	18.0	107.0	26.0	81.0
1953	62.0	43.0	19.0	112.0	28.0	84.0
1954	70.0	50.0	20.0	120.0	30.0	90.0
1955	77.0	56.0	21.0	127.0	32.0	95.0

YEAR	Total	ENVIRONMENTAL SERVICES Met by: Allocated Grants	Other Sources
1890			
1895			
1900			
1905			
1910			
1913			
1915			
1917			
1918			
1920	21.5	0.1	21.4
1921	22.9	0.5	22.4
1922	21.3	0.4	20.9
1923	20.8	0.4	20.4
1924	21.3	0.6	20.7
1925	21.9	0.7	21.2
1926	22.5	0.8	21.7
1927	23.2	0.9	22.3
1928	23.6	1.0	22.6
1929	24.3	1.1	23.2
1930	25.5	1.3	24.2
1931	26.2	1.5	24.7
1932	26.5	1.7	24.8
1933	27.2	1.9	25.3
1934	28.0	1.9	26.1
1935	28.9	2.0	26.9
1936	30.3	2.0	28.3
1937	31.8	2.0	29.8
1938	33.3	1.9	31.4
1939	33.9	1.8	32.1
1940	34.1	1.8	32.3
1941	34.9	1.8	33.1
1942	35.2	1.8	33.4
1943	36.2	1.9	34.3
1944	37.6	1.8	35.8
1945	39.9	1.8	38.1
1946	45.0	2.0	43.0
1947	50.0	2.0	48.0
1948	55.0	2.0	53.0
1949	60.0	2.0	58.0
1950	63.0	2.0	61.0
1951	66.0	1.0	65.0
1952	74.0	1.0	73.0
1953	83.0	6.0	77.0
1954	87.0	3.0	84.0
1955	89.0	2.0	87.0

EXPENDITURES, ALL SERVICES

YEAR	Total	Met by Central Government Grants			Met by Rates and Other
		Allocated	Unallocated	Total	
1890	41.7			10.4	31.3
1895	51.5			14.0	37.5
1900	65.4			19.9	45.5
1905	91.5			29.4	62.1
1910	102.6			31.7	70.9
1913	112.3			33.6	78.7
1915	114.2			34.8	79.4
1917	116.3			38.2	78.1
1918	133.3			42.1	91.2
1920	231.0	65.3	3.0	68.3	162.7
1921	264.0	81.1	3.0	84.1	179.9
1922	262.5	83.8	3.3	87.1	175.4
1923	255.6	84.3	5.0	89.3	166.3
1924	261.1	86.9	6.0	92.9	168.2
1925	273.5	90.2	6.5	96.7	176.8
1926	289.8	93.0	6.8	99.8	190.0
1927	292.2	95.9	7.3	103.2	189.0
1928	296.3	99.3	7.4	106.7	189.6
1929	298.7	101.3	19.3	120.6	178.1
1930	305.5	97.4	46.9	144.3	161.2
1931	307.0	94.4	54.0	148.4	158.6
1932	302.8	88.7	53.6	142.3	160.5
1933	305.4	86.6	54.2	140.8	164.6
1934	316.8	89.4	54.5	143.9	172.9
1935	332.5	98.2	54.1	152.3	180.2
1936	343.6	103.0	54.3	157.3	186.3
1937	352.6	101.9	56.5	158.4	194.2
1938	368.2	104.6	57.4	162.0	206.2
1939	408.9	139.9	57.1	197.0	211.9
1940	450.3	186.7	56.9	243.6	206.7
1941	499.9	237.9	59.3	297.2	202.7
1942	491.6	228.4	59.0	287.4	204.2
1943	473.5	205.0	58.3	263.3	210.2
1944	477.3	200.1	58.2	258.3	219.0
1945	494.6	195.8	69.3	265.1	229.5
1946	541.0	199.0	73.0	272.0	269.0
1947	608.0	220.0	73.0	293.0	315.0
1948	615.0	246.0	69.0	315.0	300.0
1949	628.0	265.0	59.0	324.0	304.0
1950	656.0	280.0	57.0	337.0	319.0
1951	727.0	314.0	63.0	377.0	350.0
1952	803.0	353.0	69.0	422.0	381.0
1953	862.0	388.0	72.0	460.0	402.0
1954	928.0	415.0	81.0	496.0	432.0
1955	1,006.0	462.0	83.0	545.0	461.0

a Official sources show grants for civil defense as larger than total expenditure for that function in some years. This is an accounting problem. The figures for income from other sources (obtained by difference) are given in parentheses to avoid confusion.

TABLE A-19

Year	Administration and Other		Law and Order		Civil Defense[a]	
	Allocated Grants	Other Revenues	Allocated Grants	Other Revenues	Allocated Grants	Other Revenues
1890						
1895						
1900						
1905						
1910						
1913						
1915						
1917						
1918						
1920	5	95	47	53		
1921	4	96	46	54		
1922	3	97	48	52		
1923	4	96	48	52		
1924	4	96	49	51		
1925	4	96	49	51		
1926	4	96	49	51		
1927	3	97	48	52		
1928	3	97	48	52		
1929	4	96	49	51		
1930	4	96	48	52		
1931	3	97	48	52		
1932	3	97	47	59		
1933	3	97	48	52		
1934	3	97	48	52		
1935	3	97	48	52		
1936	3	97	48	52		
1937	3	97	48	52		
1938	3	97	48	52		
1939	4	96	51	49	63	37
					81	19
1940	20	80	53	47	88	12
1941	36	64	55	45	94	6
1942	38	62	56	44	94	6
1943	37	63	56	44	94	6
1944	40	60	55	45	95	5
1945	40	60	51	49	100	
1946	14	86	51	49	(100)	—
1947	17	83	50	50	(100)	—
1948	15	85	50	50	(100)	—
1949	13	87	48	52	(100)	—
1950	8	92	47	53	(100)	—
1951	6	94	48	52	(100)	—
1952	6	94	49	51	(100)	—
1953	6	94	48	52	(100)	—
1954	7	93	48	52	(100)	—
1955	6	94	49	51	(100)	—

Year	Social Services		Housing		Economic Services	
	Allocated Grants	Other Revenues	Allocated Grants	Other Revenues	Allocated Grants	Other Revenues
1890						
1895						
1900						
1905						
1910						
1913						
1915						
1917						
1918						
1920	39	61	34	66	12	88
1921	39	61	74	26	19	81
1922	37	63	84	16	23	77
1923	38	62	86	14	26	74
1924	37	63	85	15	28	72
1925	36	64	81	19	29	71
1926	34	66	77	23	29	71
1927	35	65	79	21	29	71
1928	37	63	81	19	29	71
1929	37	63	82	18	28	72
1930	33	67	81	19	26	74
1931	32	68	80	20	25	75
1932	29	71	81	19	22	78
1933	28	72	82	18	20	80
1934	28	72	80	20	20	80
1935	30	70	80	20	20	80
1936	31	69	80	20	20	80
1937	29	71	79	21	20	80
1938	28	72	77	23	20	80
1939	29	71	76	24	27	73
1940	31	69	77	23	35	65
1941	33	67	75	25	43	57
1942	34	66	75	25	36	64
1943	35	65	76	24	26	74
1944	36	64	75	25	22	78
1945	39	61	74	26	18	82
1946	39	61	68	32	24	76
1947	40	60	62	38	26	74
1948	48	52	62	38	25	75
1949	55	45	64	36	24	76
1950	56	44	68	32	23	77
1951	56	44	67	33	24	76
1952	56	44	67	33	24	76
1953	56	44	69	31	25	75
1954	55	45	71	29	25	75
1955	56	44	73	27	25	75

Year	Environmental Services		All Services		
	Allocated Grants	Other Revenues	Allocated Grants	Unallocated Grants	Other Revenues
1890			25		75
1895			27		73
1900			30		70
1905			32		68
1910			31		69
1913			30		70
1915			30		70
1917			33		67
1918			32		68
1920	1	99	29	1	70
1921	2	98	31	1	68
1922	2	98	32	1	67
1923	2	98	33	2	65
1924	3	97	34	2	64
1925	3	97	33	2	65
1926	3	97	32	2	66
1927	4	96	33	2	65
1928	4	96	34	2	64
1929	4	96	34	6	60
1930	5	95	32	15	53
1931	6	94	30	18	52
1932	6	94	29	18	53
1933	7	93	28	18	54
1934	7	93	28	17	55
1935	7	93	30	16	54
1936	7	93	30	16	54
1937	6	94	29	16	55
1938	6	94	28	16	56
1939	5	95	34	14	52
1940	5	95	41	13	46
1941	5	95	47	12	41
1942	5	95	46	12	42
1943	5	95	44	12	44
1944	5	95	42	12	46
1945	5	95	40	14	46
1946	4	96	37	13	50
1947	4	96	36	12	52
1948	4	96	40	11	49
1949	3	97	42	9	49
1950	3	97	43	9	48
1951	2	98	43	9	48
1952	1	99	44	9	47
1953	7	93	45	8	47
1954	3	97	45	9	46
1955	2	98	46	8	46

[a] Official sources show grants for civil defense as larger than total expenditure for that function in some years. This is an accounting problem. The figures for income from other sources (obtained by difference) are given in parentheses to avoid confusion.

TABLE A-20

EXPENDITURES OF CENTRAL AND LOCAL GOVERNMENTS, TOTALS, INDEXES, AND PERCENTAGES, AT CURRENT AND 1900 PRICES, SELECTED YEARS, 1890–1955

(amounts in millions of pounds; index, 1900 = 100)

| | EXPENDITURE AT CURRENT PRICES | | | |
| | Central Government | | Local Government | |
YEAR	Amount	Index	Amount	Index
1890	80.5	44	50.1	51
1895	89.4	49	67.4	68
1900	181.9	100	98.9	100
1905	118.1	65	123.6	125
1910	141.8	78	130.2	132
1913	168.7	93	136.7	138
1915	826.5	454	131.6	133
1917	1,393.6	766	121.9	123
1918	2,287.6	1,258	139.4	141
1920	1,274.8	701	317.3	321
1921	1,029.0	566	400.5	405
1922	813.2	447	364.1	368
1923	702.9	386	322.3	326
1924	690.1	379	336.9	341
1925	701.3	386	370.6	375
1926	702.6	386	403.7	408
1927	692.2	381	413.6	418
1928	695.4	382	399.3	404
1929	702.0	386	405.2	410
1930	725.2	399	419.6	424
1931	744.6	409	428.9	434
1932	736.1	405	401.9	406
1933	676.3	372	389.7	394
1934	661.6	364	399.3	404
1935	689.6	379	427.8	433
1936	725.9	399	460.9	466
1937	805.4	433	498.1	504
1938	1,055.8	580	531.2	537
1939	1,408.9	775	551.1	557
1940	3,367.1	1,851	537.9	544
1941	4,779.8	2,628	558.2	564
1942	5,323.2	2,926	536.8	543
1943	5,758.9	3,166	506.1	512
1944	5,797.6	3,187	505.4	511
1945	5,235.5	2,878	543.5	550
1946	3,837.0	2,109	693.0	701
1947	3,223.0	1,772	907.0	917
1948	3,228.0	1,775	987.0	998
1949	3,413.0	1,876	1,010.0	1,021
1950	3,479.0	1,913	1,060.0	1,072
1951	4,022.0	2,211	1,186.0	1,199
1952	4,433.0	2,437	1,344.0	1,359
1953	4,581.0	2,518	1,467.0	1,483
1954	4,473.0	2,459	1,503.0	1,520
1955	4,607.0	2,533	1,536.0	1,553

(continued)

| YEAR | EXPENDITURE AT 1900 PRICES | | | | Total Local Government Expenditure at Current Prices as Percentage of | |
| | Central Government | | Local Government | | | Total Government Expenditure |
	Amount	Index	Amount	Index	GNP	
1890	82.2	45	51.1	52	3.4	38.4
1895	98.2	54	74.1	75	4.5	43.0
1900	181.9	100	98.9	100	5.1	35.2
1905	113.6	62	128.1	130	6.3	51.1
1910	129.3	71	134.3	136	6.1	47.9
1913	147.2	81	137.0	139	5.5	44.8
1915					4.8	13.7
1917					3.1	8.0
1918					3.0	5.7
1920	457.6	252	107.7	109	5.2	19.9
1921	403.1	222	149.1	151	8.2	28.0
1922	373.1	205	171.4	173	8.6	30.9
1923	343.1	189	159.9	162	7.6	31.4
1924	338.2	186	166.6	168	7.8	32.8
1925	344.0	189	181.4	183	8.4	34.6
1926	354.5	195	187.2	189	9.4	36.5
1927	349.5	192	208.1	210	9.0	37.4
1928	351.2	199	203.6	206	8.8	36.5
1929	358.2	197	209.1	211	8.8	36.6
1930	379.7	209	222.1	225	9.6	36.7
1931	411.5	226	238.8	241	10.5	36.5
1932	413.7	227	228.5	231	10.1	35.3
1933	388.8	214	227.1	230	9.4	36.6
1934	380.3	209	231.7	234	9.2	37.6
1935	396.3	218	246.9	250	9.3	38.3
1936	411.9	226	260.5	263	9.6	38.8
1937	443.5	244	270.2	273	9.8	38.2
1938	567.8	312	283.4	287	10.0	33.5
1939					9.9	28.1
1940					8.3	13.8
1941					7.6	10.5
1942					6.7	9.2
1943					6.0	8.1
1944					5.8	8.0
1945					6.2	9.4
1946	1,257.9	692	216.1	219	7.9	15.3
1947	987.7	543	255.3	258	9.7	22.0
1948	914.3	503	254.7	258	9.5	23.4
1949	943.3	519	255.7	259	9.1	22.8
1950	933.3	513	261.7	265	9.1	23.4
1951	990.2	544	264.8	268	9.3	22.8
1952	1,031.8	567	279.2	282	9.6	23.3
1953	1,045.4	575	300.6	304	9.9	24.3
1954	1,006.5	553	308.5	312	9.4	25.2
1955	1,001.9	551	307.1	311	9.2	25.0

LOCAL GOVERNMENT EXPENDITURE BY ECONOMIC CATEGORY,
AT CURRENT PRICES, SELECTED YEARS, 1890–1955
(amounts in millions of pounds)

| | | DISTRIBUTION BY ECONOMIC CATEGORY | | |
| | | Goods and Services | | Transfers |
YEAR	Total	Current	Capital	
1890	50.1	38.5	8.4	3.2
1895	67.4	48.0	15.9	3.5
1900	98.9	61.7	33.5	3.7
1905	123.6	87.2	32.1	4.3
1910	130.2	98.2	27.6	4.4
1913	136.7	108.6	24.4	3.7
1915	131.6	110.3	17.4	3.9
1917	121.9	112.3	5.6	4.0
1918	139.4	128.9	6.1	4.4
1920	317.3	221.1	86.3	9.9
1921	400.5	241.0	136.5	23.0
1922	364.1	231.5	101.6	31.0
1923	322.3	225.0	66.7	30.6
1924	336.9	232.4	75.8	28.7
1925	370.6	242.1	97.1	31.4
1926	403.7	248.9	113.9	40.9
1927	413.6	254.9	121.4	37.3
1928	399.3	261.8	103.0	34.5
1929	405.2	263.9	106.5	34.8
1930	419.6	270.7	114.1	34.8
1931	428.9	270.5	121.9	36.5
1932	401.9	262.7	99.1	40.1
1933	389.7	262.4	84.3	43.0
1934	399.3	270.6	82.5	46.2
1935	427.8	283.3	95.3	49.2
1936	460.9	293.6	117.3	50.0
1937	498.1	305.2	145.5	47.4
1938	531.2	320.0	163.0	48.2
1939	551.1	358.7	142.2	50.2
1940	537.9	403.6	87.6	46.7
1941	558.2	456.4	58.3	43.5
1942	536.8	448.1	45.2	43.5
1943	506.1	427.4	32.6	46.1
1944	505.4	427.3	28.1	50.0
1945	543.5	440.2	48.9	54.4
1946	693.0	478.0	152.0	63.0
1947	907.0	534.0	299.0	74.0
1948	987.0	540.0	372.0	75.0
1949	1,010.0	553.0	382.0	75.0
1950	1,060.0	577.0	404.0	79.0
1951	1,186.0	640.0	459.0	87.0
1952	1,344.0	701.0	541.0	102.0
1953	1,467.0	751.0	605.0	111.0
1954	1,503.0	803.0	575.0	125.0
1955	1,536.0	858.0	530.0	148.0

(continued)

PERCENTAGE DISTRIBUTION BY ECONOMIC CATEGORY

	Goods and Services				Transfers	
	Current		Capital			
YEAR	All Local	All Government	All Local	All Government	All Local	All Government
1890	76.8	32.0	16.8	82.4	6.4	9.5
1895	71.2	35.3	23.6	75.7	5.2	9.3
1900	62.4	26.8	33.9	66.5	3.7	10.2
1905	70.6	42.9	26.0	83.6	3.5	9.9
1910	75.4	43.3	21.2	61.2	3.4	8.0
1913	79.4	40.8	17.9	62.2	2.7	6.3
1915	83.8	12.1	13.2	40.1	3.0	4.3
1917	92.1	7.9	4.6	6.1	3.3	1.6
1918	92.5	5.6	4.4	5.8	3.1	1.4
1920	69.7	14.8	27.2	84.7	3.1	1.6
1921	60.2	18.8	34.1	91.0	5.7	3.6
1922	63.6	21.7	27.9	92.8	8.5	5.4
1923	69.8	23.6	20.7	92.1	9.5	5.9
1924	69.0	24.6	22.5	92.8	8.5	5.7
1925	65.3	25.0	26.2	92.8	8.5	6.0
1926	61.7	25.3	28.2	93.9	10.1	7.7
1927	61.6	26.1	29.4	94.8	9.0	7.1
1928	65.6	26.6	25.8	94.8	8.6	6.5
1929	65.1	26.5	26.3	95.0	8.6	6.4
1930	64.5	26.4	27.2	95.3	8.3	6.1
1931	63.1	25.8	28.4	96.1	8.5	6.2
1932	65.4	25.4	24.6	95.7	10.0	6.7
1933	67.3	26.8	21.7	95.3	11.0	8.0
1934	67.8	27.8	20.7	94.0	11.5	8.9
1935	66.2	27.9	22.3	91.9	11.5	9.4
1936	63.7	27.9	25.5	88.3	10.8	9.7
1937	61.3	27.0	29.2	83.1	9.5	9.2
1938	60.2	23.4	30.7	74.5	9.1	8.8
1939	65.1	20.1	25.8	80.3	9.1	9.2
1940	75.0	10.6	16.3	76.8	8.7	7.2
1941	81.8	8.7	10.4	76.7	7.8	4.4
1942	83.5	7.7	8.4	74.1	8.1	4.2
1943	84.5	6.9	6.4	67.9	9.1	4.1
1944	84.5	6.8	5.6	68.5	9.9	4.4
1945	81.0	7.7	9.0	50.4[a]	10.0	3.8
1946	69.0	10.7	21.9	(100.0)[a]	9.1	2.9
1947	58.9	13.9	33.0	(100.0)[a]	8.1	3.5
1948	54.7	14.3	37.7	83.6	7.6	3.7
1949	54.8	13.9	37.8	86.6	7.4	3.7
1950	54.4	14.1	38.1	92.4	7.5	3.9
1951	54.0	14.5	38.7	57.5	7.3	4.4
1952	52.1	14.1	40.3	67.7	7.6	4.9
1953	51.2	14.4	41.2	71.9	7.6	5.1
1954	53.4	15.0	38.3	90.3	8.3	5.7
1955	55.9	15.5	34.5	85.8	9.6	6.3

[a] In these years, local government capital expenditures exceeded total government capital formation. This was the result of changes in the value of stocks held by the central government (see Appendix notes under government expenditures on capital account).

TABLE A-22

LOCAL GOVERNMENT TRANSFER PAYMENTS BY TYPE OF SOCIAL SERVICE,
ON CURRENT ACCOUNT, SELECTED YEARS, 1890–1955

Year	Education	Housing	Poor Relief[a]	Total Social Services
1890	—	—	3.2	3.2
1895	—	—	3.5	3.5
1900	—	—	3.7	3.7
1905	—	—	4.3	4.3
1910	—	—	4.4	4.4
1913	—	—	3.7	3.7
1915	—	—	3.9	3.9
1917	—	—	4.0	4.0
1918	—	—	4.4	4.4
1920	1.6	1.9	6.4	9.9
1921	2.7	5.5	14.8	23.0
1922	2.7	8.4	19.9	31.0
1923	2.5	9.5	18.6	30.6
1924	2.5	10.0	16.2	28.7
1925	2.7	11.0	17.7	31.4
1926	3.2	12.3	25.4	40.9
1927	3.0	13.8	20.5	37.3
1928	3.0	15.0	16.5	34.5
1929	3.2	16.0	15.6	34.8
1930	3.4	17.1	14.3	34.8
1931	3.7	17.7	15.1	36.5
1932	3.8	18.0	18.3	40.1
1933	3.7	18.5	20.8	43.0
1934	3.2	19.4	23.6	46.2
1935	3.1	20.2	25.9	49.2
1936	3.2	20.8	26.0	50.0
1937	3.4	21.6	22.4	47.4
1938	3.5	22.9	21.8	48.2
1939	3.5	24.2	22.5	50.2
1940	3.8	24.5	18.4	46.7
1941	5.0	24.9	13.6	43.5
1942	7.5	24.4	11.6	43.5
1943	10.9	23.9	11.3	46.1
1944	13.2	24.6	12.2	50.0
1945	16.0	25.1	13.3	54.4
1946	20.0	28.0	15.0	63.0
1947	26.0	32.0	16.0	74.0
1948	30.0	37.0	8.0	75.0
1949	36.0	39.0	—	75.0
1950	39.0	40.0	—	79.0
1951	42.0	45.0	—	87.0
1952	48.0	54.0	—	102.0
1953	49.0	62.0	—	111.0
1954	55.0	70.0	—	125.0
1955	71.0	77.0	—	148.0

[a] Outdoor relief.

LOCAL GOVERNMENT EXPENDITURE BY FUNCTION, AT CURRENT
PRICES, SELECTED YEARS, 1890–1955
(amounts in millions of pounds)

	Function							
Year	Administration and Other	Law and Order	Civil Defense	Social Services	Hou-sing	Economic Services	Environmental Services	All Services
1890	7.2	5.1		19.4		13.5	4.9	50.1
1895	8.4	5.7		28.3		17.7	7.3	67.4
1900	8.7	6.1		37.1		35.2	11.8	98.9
1905	10.2	8.0		53.7		38.1	13.6	123.6
1910	10.7	8.8		60.2		36.2	14.3	130.2
1913	10.1	9.6		64.3		37.8	14.9	136.7
1915	10.2	9.8		66.2		32.9	12.5	131.6
1917	10.7	9.9		66.8		21.9	12.6	121.9
1918	14.4	11.3		75.6		23.9	14.2	139.4
1920	21.0	21.8		127.9	45.7	76.3	24.6	317.3
1921	19.9	23.2		149.7	88.1	91.5	23.1	400.5
1922	18.1	21.3		148.9	58.9	88.8	28.1	364.1
1923	16.6	20.3		142.0	29.7	85.1	28.6	322.3
1924	16.8	21.0		142.0	34.6	93.1	29.4	336.9
1925	17.5	22.1		149.4	49.1	101.6	30.9	370.6
1926	18.0	23.3		162.7	66.9	102.3	30.5	403.7
1927	18.4	23.8		161.3	75.6	103.9	30.6	413.6
1928	19.4	24.1		162.8	59.2	103.4	30.4	399.3
1929	17.8	24.6		166.8	53.0	110.9	32.1	405.2
1930	17.7	25.1		172.9	51.2	116.6	36.1	419.6
1931	17.4	25.3		175.1	53.7	117.7	39.7	428.9
1932	16.8	24.6		172.6	47.2	101.2	39.5	401.9
1933	16.7	24.5		172.9	45.5	92.9	37.2	389.7
1934	17.2	25.3		180.6	44.9	93.9	37.4	399.3
1935	18.7	27.0		193.0	50.4	99.6	39.1	427.8
1936	19.5	28.7		203.0	59.0	108.9	41.8	460.9
1937	21.8	30.0		211.5	70.2	119.0	45.6	498.1
1938	24.3	31.2	4.2	225.1	80.0	120.8	45.6	531.2
1939	24.0	35.5	41.9	226.4	63.8	114.4	45.1	551.1
1940	27.5	38.7	77.7	215.8	40.4	97.4	40.4	537.9
1941	34.9	41.7	105.4	211.9	31.0	95.1	38.2	558.2
1942	37.5	42.5	89.4	215.4	29.2	84.9	37.9	536.8
1943	36.5	41.6	65.4	225.2	29.4	69.5	38.7	506.1
1944	37.7	40.4	51.5	240.2	31.3	64.8	39.5	505.4
1945	40.3	40.2	24.5	275.8	46.9	73.7	42.1	543.5
1946	37.0	40.0	13.0	323.0	127.0	104.0	49.0	693.0
1947	44.0	45.0	8.0	375.0	240.0	134.0	61.0	907.0
1948	51.0	50.0	3.0	372.0	304.0	136.0	71.0	987.0
1949	52.0	55.0	2.0	382.0	302.0	136.0	81.0	1,010.0
1950	53.0	62.0	2.0	411.0	304.0	138.0	90.0	1,060.0
1951	56.0	70.0	3.0	471.0	333.0	152.0	101.0	1,186.0
1952	52.0	78.0	3.0	526.0	406.0	168.0	111.0	1,344.0
1953	54.0	85.0	3.0	555.0	461.0	180.0	129.0	1,467.0
1954	52.0	88.0	3.0	601.0	436.0	188.0	135.0	1,503.0
1955	58.0	92.0	3.0	658.0	395.0	195.0	135.0	1,536.0

(continued)

			Percentage Distribution of Total				
Year	Administration and Other	Law and Order	Civil Defense	Social Services	Housing	Economic Services	Environmental Services
1890	14.4	10.2		38.7		26.9	9.8
1895	12.4	8.5		42.0		26.3	10.8
1900	8.8	6.2		37.5		35.6	11.9
1905	8.3	6.5		43.4		30.8	11.0
1910	8.2	6.8		46.2		27.8	11.0
1913	7.4	7.0		47.0		27.7	10.9
1915	7.8	7.4		50.3		25.0	9.5
1917	8.8	8.1		54.8		18.0	10.3
1918	10.3	8.1		54.2		17.1	10.2
1920	6.6	6.9		40.3	14.4	24.0	7.8
1921	5.0	5.8		37.4	22.0	22.8	7.0
1922	5.0	5.8		40.9	16.2	24.4	7.7
1923	5.2	6.3		44.0	9.2	26.4	8.9
1924	5.0	6.2		42.2	10.3	27.6	8.7
1925	4.7	6.0		40.3	13.2	27.4	8.4
1926	4.5	5.8		40.3	16.6	25.3	7.5
1927	4.4	5.8		39.0	18.3	25.1	7.4
1928	4.9	6.0		40.8	14.8	25.9	7.6
1929	4.4	6.1		41.2	13.1	27.3	7.9
1930	4.2	6.0		41.2	12.2	27.8	8.6
1931	4.1	5.9		40.8	12.5	27.4	9.3
1932	4.2	6.1		42.9	11.7	25.2	9.8
1933	4.3	6.3		44.4	11.7	23.8	9.5
1934	4.3	6.3		45.2	11.2	23.5	9.4
1935	4.4	6.3		45.1	11.8	23.3	9.1
1936	4.2	6.2		44.0	12.8	23.6	9.1
1937	4.4	6.0		42.5	14.1	23.9	9.1
1938	4.6	5.9	0.8	42.4	15.1	22.7	8.6
1939	4.3	6.4	7.6	41.1	11.6	20.8	8.2
1940	5.1	7.2	14.4	40.1	7.5	18.1	7.5
1941	6.2	7.5	18.9	38.0	5.6	17.0	6.8
1942	7.0	7.9	16.7	40.1	5.4	15.8	7.1
1943	7.2	8.2	12.9	44.5	5.8	13.7	7.6
1944	7.5	8.0	10.2	47.5	6.2	12.8	7.8
1945	7.4	7.4	4.5	50.8	8.6	13.6	7.7
1946	5.3	5.8	1.9	46.6	18.3	15.0	7.1
1947	4.9	5.0	0.9	41.3	26.4	14.8	6.7
1948	5.2	5.1	0.3	37.7	30.8	13.8	7.2
1949	5.1	5.4	0.2	37.8	29.9	13.5	8.0
1950	5.0	5.8	0.2	38.8	28.7	13.0	8.5
1951	4.7	5.9	0.3	39.7	28.1	12.8	8.5
1952	3.9	5.8	0.2	39.1	30.2	12.5	8.3
1953	3.7	5.8	0.2	37.8	31.4	12.3	8.8
1954	3.5	5.9	0.2	40.0	29.0	12.5	9.0
1955	3.8	6.0	0.2	42.8	25.7	12.7	8.8

TABLE A-24

LOCAL GOVERNMENT EXPENDITURE BY FUNCTION, AS PERCENTAGE OF TOTAL GOVERNMENT
EXPENDITURE ON EACH FUNCTION, SELECTED YEARS, 1890–1955

Year	Administration and Other	Law and Order	Military and Defense	Social Services	Housing	Economic Services	Environmental Services	All Services
1890	46	57		71		94	98	38
1895	52	68		71		96	99	43
1900	53	62		73		97	98	35
1905	52	70		79		97	99	51
1910	48	68		68		96	99	48
1913	48	55		64		96	97	45
1915	38	72		71		92	98	14
1917	39	79		52		89	99	8
1918	46	72		59		87	98	6
1920	29	65		35	100	38	97	20
1921	28	62		37	100	42	97	28
1922	31	64		41	100	54	98	31
1923	32	69		43	100	74	98	31
1924	33	71		43	100	83	97	33
1925	35	74		44	100	77	96	35
1926	36	77		46	100	82	96	36
1927	38	78		45	100	87	96	37
1928	40	78		43	100	88	95	36
1929	37	79		43	100	88	95	37
1930	38	79		40	100	88	95	37
1931	38	80		38	100	90	95	37
1932	37	80		37	100	87	95	35
1933	38	79		38	100	83	95	37
1934	38	79		40	100	80	94	38
1935	39	79		41	100	79	94	38
1936	39	80		43	100	82	92	39
1937	40	81		44	100	84	92	38
1938	40	81	1	44	100	80	89	33
1950	30	78	—	23	89	24	93	23
1951	33	80	—	25	90	22	92	23
1952	31	81	—	26	92	27	93	23
1953	31	81	—	27	93	30	94	24
1954	29	80	—	28	92	36	94	25
1955	32	80	—	28	94	37	74	25

Table 1

These figures are tentative estimates compiled by Jindrich Veverka for a separate study of this period, now in preparation. They are not strictly comparable with the series from 1890 to 1955. Sources for the figures follow.

GROSS NATIONAL PRODUCT. *1800–50:* Based on Phyllis Deane, "National Income in the 19th Century," *Economic History Review*, second series, Volume 8, 1955–56, and also on unpublished material supplied by the same author.

1851–69: Estimates based upon A. L. Bowley, *Wages and Income in the United Kingdom since 1860*, London, 1937, and J. C. Stamp, *British Incomes and Property*, London, 1927.

1870–99: Extracted from Jeffreys and Walters, *op. cit.*

GOVERNMENT EXPENDITURE: Figures are based on the finance and appropriation accounts for the central government and local taxation returns. The local statistics for the first half of the century are deficient.

PRICE INDEX. The same index is used to deflate both magnitudes. For the first half of the century, the index of wholesale prices of domestic and imported commodities is to be found in A. D. Gayer, W. W. Rostow, and A. J. Schwartz, *The Growth and Fluctuations of the British Economy, 1790–1850*, Oxford, 1953. For the second half of the century, we have used Bowley's index of retail prices.

Tables 7 and 8

These are computed from the information given in Appendix tables, so that no further explanation of sources is necessary.

Table 10

For 1920–38 statistics are from Utting and Cole, *op. cit.* For later years, *Blue Book on National Income and Expenditure.*

Tables 17–22 (Nationalized Industries)

All these tables are based on information supplied by the Central Statistical Office. Most of it is published in the annual *Blue Books*, but some more detailed unpublished information was supplied by the Central Statistical Office.

Table 23

The full list of assumptions is given in Chapter 8, together with the main sources.

Index

Abel-Smith, Brian, 10 n.
Abramovitz, Moses, xxi n., 4 n., 70 n., 93, 97 n., 99, 124 n.
Adams, A. A., 157
Adams, H. C., 17 n.
Annual Abstract of Statistics, 146, 152, 158, 162-163

Baldwin, Stanley, 69
Bastable, C. F., xxvii n., 53 n.
Benham, F., 13 n.
Beveridge, W. H., 136 n., 158
Beveridge Plan, 94
Bland, Hubert, 65 n.
Blue Book on National Income and Expenditure, 101, 123, 152, 157, 160, 162-163, 209
Boer War, 36, 38, 41, 59 n., 147 n.
Booth, Charles, 93
Bowley, A. L., 156, 209
Bridges, Sir Edward, 70 n.
British Parliamentary Papers, 192
Brougham, Lord, 93
Buchanan, J. M., 13 n.
Bullock, A., 40 n.,

Cairncross, A. K., 154, 157
Capital account expenditures, 77-85, 110-112, 178, 182, 203-205
Central government expenditures, 96-97, 104-109, 160-162, 201-202
Central Office of Information, 103 n.
Central Statistical Office, 6 n., 10, 11 n., 124 n., 152, 157, 158, 160-163, 167, 181-182, 192, 209
Chamberlain, Joseph, 40
Chancellor of the Exchequer, 36, 68-70, 148
Chester, D. N., 103 n., 121 n.
Churchill, Sir Winston, 40 n., 64 n., 69 n.
Coase, Ronald, 4 n.
Cole, Dorothy, 10, 162, 209
Colm, G., xxx, xxxi n.
Colwyn Committee, 53, 66
Committee on National Expenditures, 65
Concentration process, xxiv-xxv, xxx, 29-30, 96-97, 104, 114, 118-119, 134; *see also* Displacement effect
Corn Laws, 65
Corry, B. A., 64
Crimean War, 36, 38
Culbertson, J. M., xxx, xxx n.

Current account expenditures, 77-85, 110-112, 137-138, 179-181, 203-205

Dalton, Hugh, xxii n., 94 n.
Deane, Phyllis, 209
Defense expenditures, *see* War-related expenditures
Depression, xxvi, 50, 91, 122
Displacement effect: and bunched investment, 80; and concentration process, 29-30, 107-108; and expenditure on current and capital account, 77; and expenditure by economic and functional categories, 81-89; explanation of, xxiv-xxxi, 27-28; and the future of government expenditure, 134, 149; and local government expenditures, 107-110, 114; and nationalized industries, 121-122, 131-133; and parliamentary control of expenditure, 34, 68-70; and resource-using expenditures, 70-73; and secular change, 31-33, 47-50, 63; and social services expenditures, 90-95; and statistical procedure, 34; and war-related and defense expenditures, 41, 52, 60-63, 90-97, 110, 133
Domar, E., 14-15
Drees, W., Jr., 19 n., 68 n.

Eckstein, Otto, 143 n.
Economic growth, expenditures and, 14-16
Education expenditures, 39, 93, 104, 112, 116-117, 119, 139; *see also* Social service expenditures
Electricity Act, 1947, 121 n.
Eliasberg, Vera F., xxi n., 4 n., 70 n., 93, 97 n., 99, 124 n.
Employment level, effect on expenditures, xxvi, 24, 31-33, 49-51
England, 163; local government of, 98
Enke, S., 13 n.
Exchequer Equalization Grant, 102-103

Fabian Socialists, 65, 131
Fabricant, Solomon, xxx n., 22 n.
Functional distribution of expenditures: local government, 100-104, 111-117, 193-200, 206-208; total, 80-95, 103-105, 182-191; *see also* Education expenditures; Health expenditures; Housing expenditures; Social services expenditures; War-related expenditures

211